D0117533

Reading Matters 4

As part of Houghton Mifflin's ongoing
commitment to the environment, this text
has been printed on recycled paper.

Reading Matters 4

An Interactive Approach to Reading

Nadia Henein
Mary Lee Wholey

Continuing Education Language Institute
Concordia University

HOUGHTON MIFFLIN COMPANY   Boston   New York

Editor in Chief: Patricia A. Coryell
Director of ESL Publishing: Susan Maguire
Senior Development Editor: Kathy Sands Boehmer
Editorial Associate: Manuel Muñoz
Senior Project Editor: Kathryn Dinovo
Senior Manufacturing Coordinator: Priscilla J. Bailey
Marketing Manager: Annamarie Rice
Marketing Associate: Claudia Martínez

Cover image: Harold Burch

Photo credits: p. 1: Tom McCarthy/PhotoEdit; p. 13: AP/Wide World Photos; p. 19: AFP/Corbis;
p. 23: Tony Freeman/PhotoEdit; p. 39: Raoul Minsart/Corbis; p. 44: Copyright, May 13, 1996,
U.S. News & World Report. Visit us at our Web site at www.usnews.com for additional information;
p. 64: C. J. Gunther; p. 70: Tony Freeman/PhotoEdit; p. 79: Scott Campbell/International Stock;
p. 83: Alan Oddie/PhotoEdit; p. 139: Sally Wiener Grotta/The Stock Market; p. 145:
J. Apelseth/Photonet; p. 150: Philip Greenberg/NYT Pictures; p. 165: Darren Winter/Corbis;
p. 166: Jeff Greenberg/The Image Works; p. 185: Esbin Anderson/The Image Works; p. 188: Liane
Enkelis/Stock Boston; p. 209: Bruce Ayres/Stone; p. 215: Jim McDonald/Corbis; p. 224: Richard
Hutchings/PhotoEdit; p. 231: Terry Vine/Stone; p. 233: Jeff Greenberg/Stone; p. 237: Amy C.
Etra/PhotoEdit; p. 247: Rhoda Sidney/PhotoEdit; p. 257: Robert Brenner/PhotoEdit; p. 261:
Mark Richards/PhotoEdit

college.hmco.com

Copyright © 2002 by Houghton Mifflin Company. All rights reserved.

No part of this work may be reproduced or transmitted in any form or by any means, electronic
or mechanical, including photocopying and recording, or by any information storage or retrieval
system without the prior written permission of the copyright owner unless such copying is
expressly permitted by federal copyright law. With the exception of nonprofit transcription in
Braille, Houghton Mifflin is not authorized to grant permission for further uses of copyrighted
selections reprinted in this text without the permission of their owners. Permission must be
obtained from the individual copyright owners as identified herein. Address requests for
permission to make copies of Houghton Mifflin material to College Permissions, Houghton
Mifflin Company, 222 Berkeley Street, Boston, MA 02116-3764.

Printed in the U.S.A.

Library of Congress Control Number: 2001087560

ISBN: 0-395-90429-3

123456789-CRS-05 04 03 02 01

Contents

Introduction

The *Reading Matters* series is a four-level reading program comprised of texts at the high beginning/low intermediate, intermediate, high intermediate, and advanced levels. This series combines stimulating readings with well-designed tasks that develop both fluency and accuracy at each level.

Extensive Reading

To develop fluency in reading, students need a significant amount of exposure to text, that is, extensive reading. Extensive reading provides the opportunity to develop automatic text-processing skills. *Reading Matters* offers reading selections of sufficient length so that readers get the chance to increase the amount of time spent in silent reading. Variety in text styles is an important component of extensive reading. The series features a variety of styles and genres so that readers develop an awareness of not only the scope of reading but also the various purposes for which texts are written. Authentic texts or adapted authentic texts are used at appropriate levels.

Intensive Reading

Reading Matters features activities that help students to develop fluency and accuracy in reading by activating two complementary text processing methods: top-down and bottom-up.

TOP-DOWN

Top-down processes are those that the reader applies to understand reading globally. Readers use their background knowledge of the topic and make predictions about what they expect to find out from reading. Readers confirm their predictions and begin to build a mental framework of the information in the reading selection. Awareness of rhetorical patterns, such as chronological ordering, cause and effect, and other discourse features, aids in the comprehension of information from reading. In addition, the activities in *Reading*

Matters help to develop an awareness of a range of reading strategies, such as skimming, scanning, or previewing, that readers have at their disposal. The ability to apply these strategies appropriately is an important component of reading competency.

BOTTOM-UP

Knowledge of grammar and vocabulary has an effect on reading ability. Although readers can predict content from their knowledge of text structure or their background knowledge, a certain level of vocabulary recognition is required for processing text. *Reading Matters* introduces and develops vocabulary-building skills through such activities as guessing from context, recognizing meaning, grouping words, and identifying the use of special terms. In addition to a solid vocabulary, fluent readers have a good knowledge of syntactic structure. Actively examining the important grammatical features of a text provides a meaningful context for this kind of learning. To build reading competency, both the amount of exposure to reading and the identification of and practice in the use of learning strategies for both vocabulary and grammar are tremendously important. *Reading Matters* provides direction to readers through activities in the "Vocabulary Building," "Expanding Your Language," and "Read On" sections.

Skills Integration and Interaction

Reading is an active process. Interaction between and among students helps facilitate this process. In exchanging ideas about the information in a text, readers confirm what they have understood. This confirmation process helps them develop accuracy in reading. It also provides a motivation for reading, as well as a clear purpose in reading. Interaction with other students can be best accomplished when speaking tasks are an integral part of a reading activity and/or the activity leads to the undertaking of writing tasks.

The interrelationship of skills integration and interaction requires a holistic approach to task design. The activities in *Reading Matters* are sequenced, and the recycling of tasks in various combinations allows the progressive development of reading competency in ways that are fresh and effective. The tasks are structured so that the learner builds skills and strategies progressively but in ways that offer challenge as well as variety. In *Reading Matters,* the reader uses and reuses the language of the selection both implicitly to bolster an answer and explicitly in retelling the reading. Paired reading selections provide complementary or contrasting information on a topic. The readers orally explain the information from the reading they chose to readers who chose a different selection. Then, together, they apply that information to carry out a new activity.

Text Organization

Reading Matters 4 contains six thematic units with two chapters in each unit covering topics related to the themes. Between one and four reading selections are featured in each chapter. The unit themes feature topics of high interest to both academically oriented and general audiences. Most important, the selections are long enough for students to progressively develop fluency in reading. Through the chapter readings, students are able to build a rich semantic network without sacrificing variety so that interest in the topic is not exhausted. Within the unit, reading selections are structured so that the information from one selection can be compared with another.

You can choose among the chapters of a unit selectively to suit the needs of different program types and teaching approaches. Complexity in both text type and length and difficulty in task type is structured so that it builds gradually from chapter to chapter and unit to unit. Some overlap in level of language and task is built into each of the texts in the *Reading Matters* series so that you can accommodate the different reading levels of students within a class.

UNIT ORGANIZATION

Each unit in *Reading Matters 4* features the following sections:

- *Introducing the Topics.* This introductory section features the chapter opener photo and quote, and activities designed to stimulate the readers' curiosity about, prior experience with, or personal relevance of the theme. The tasks are interactive and draw on a variety of media: text, visual, and graphic.

- The two chapters in each unit present different topics loosely related to the theme.

CHAPTER ORGANIZATION

For each of the reading selections, the following tasks are presented:

- *Chapter Openers* include prereading reflection and discussion questions, graphs, questionnaires, surveys, illustrations. The purpose of this section is to stimulate discussion of key ideas and concepts presented in the reading and to introduce key vocabulary. Encourage students to explain their ideas as completely as possible. Teach students strategies for maximizing their interaction, such as turn taking, eliciting responses from all group members, naming a group leader and reporter. Whenever possible, re-form groups to give students a chance to talk more until they feel comfortable with the topic. Elicit key ideas and language from the students.

- *Exploring and Understanding Reading* contains content questions of varying levels of complexity, questions that guide students in the development of their reading strategies for improving general comprehension, for developing an awareness of text structure, and for evaluating the content of a text in detail. Emphasize the purpose of the activity and how it is tied to the development of a particular strategy. It is important to help students build tolerance for uncertainty. Point out that the purpose of comparing and checking their answers with the information in the reading is to give them the opportunity to verify as well as to become familiar with the information. Act as a resource to help students find the accurate information. An answer key is provided to be used when needed.

- *Paired Readings: Recapping, Retelling, and Reacting to the Reading* are interactive activities that involve oral presentation of information from the readings, oral exchanges of information, and discussion that involves critical evaluation of ideas including comparison/contrast and debate. Emphasize the importance of explaining the information in as natural and conversational a style as possible. To help students develop their skill at extracting important information from a text, point out the purpose of note taking, highlighting, and underlining key information. Emphasize the importance of practicing at home for in-class presentations.

- *Vocabulary Building* comprises tasks that introduce vocabulary-building strategies such as the understanding of the interrelationship of grammatical structure and meaning, using context cues, and other aids to the fluent processing of reading selections.

- *Expanding Your Language* presents activities that offer students the opportunity to use the material and strategies presented in each selection for the purposes of their own speaking and writing. Encourage students to use these activities to further their own comprehension of the readings. Through these activities students can improve their speaking and writing fluency.

- *Read On. Taking It Further* presents opportunities for personal reading and related activities, including suggestions for further reading as well as reading and writing journal entries, vocabulary logs, and word play. While this work is done outside of class, time can be found in the class schedule to report on some of the activities. This gives students a purpose for the work and practice in developing their reading skills and strategies.

Acknowledgments

We are grateful to Susan Maguire, who first suggested the idea for the series. A special thanks goes to Kathy Sands Boehmer, who has been an invaluable help throughout the lengthy process of bringing this manuscript into its present form. Thanks also to the production and editorial staff at Houghton Mifflin.

Our gratitude to the people who read the manuscript and offered useful suggestions and critical comments: Donna Duchow, Mesa College; Terese K. Francis, Doane College; Duffy Galda, Pima Community College; and Anne-Marie Schlender, California State University, Hayward.

We would like to acknowledge the support and inspiring work of colleagues and students at the Continuing Education Language Institute (CELI) of Concordia University in Montreal. A special thanks goes to Adrianne Sklar for her advice and suggestions after reading drafts of the material. The continuing support of Lili Ullmann and Phyllis Vogel has been invaluable to us. Thanks to Devorah Ritter who helped in the preparation of the answer key.

Finally, thanks to our families, Jerry, Jonah, and Yael, and Sherif, Ghada, and Dina.

This volume is dedicated to Shung Mi Kook and to the many students we have been privileged to teach.

Mary Lee Wholey and Nadia Henein

Reading Matters 4: Overview

UNIT	SKILLS	ACTIVITIES	VOCABULARY	EXPANSION
UNIT 1 Birthrights	▪ predicting (1 & 2) ▪ previewing (1) ▪ skimming (1) ▪ scanning (1) ▪ highlighting (1) ▪ surveying (2) ▪ finding the main points of an argument (2) ▪ distinguishing between fact and opinion (2) ▪ note-taking for presenting arguments (2)	▪ agree or disagree (1) ▪ giving your opinion (1) ▪ applying the information (1) ▪ retelling the information (2) ▪ analyzing a short story (2)	▪ figuring out the referent (1) ▪ guessing from context (1) ▪ recognizing the use of emotional language (2) ▪ using signal words or markers (2)	▪ topic writing (1) ▪ reaction writing (2) ▪ debating (1) ▪ oral presentation (1)
UNIT 2 Health	▪ predicting information from a diagram (3) ▪ predicting; agree and disagree (4) ▪ chunking paragraphs; finding main ideas (3) ▪ analyzing chunks (3) ▪ finding the thesis (3) ▪ understanding details in reports (3) ▪ skimming (4) ▪ scanning for specific information (4)	▪ interviewing (3) ▪ becoming an expert (3) ▪ giving an opinion (4 & 6) ▪ recapping, reacting to and retelling a story (4) ▪ comparing stories (4)	▪ looking for definitions in the body of a text (3) ▪ recognizing descriptive language (3) ▪ vocabulary in context; inferring meaning (4) ▪ word forms; nouns, adjectives and adverbs (4)	▪ discussion questions (3) ▪ speaking from reading (4) ▪ two-minute taped talk (4) ▪ topic writing (3 & 4) ▪ reaction writing (4)

Reading Matters 4: Overview *(continued)*

UNIT	SKILLS	ACTIVITIES	VOCABULARY	EXPANSION
UNIT 3 Memory	▪ analyzing introductions (5) ▪ skimming for specific terms (5) ▪ note-taking (5 & 6) ▪ understanding conclusions (5) ▪ previewing (6) ▪ reporting on a study (6)	▪ using analogies (5) ▪ taking a Memory Quiz (5) ▪ interviewing (6) ▪ comparing and contrasting (6)	▪ using quotes (5) ▪ paraphrasing (5) ▪ word forms (6) ▪ guessing from context (6)	▪ reporting (5) ▪ point of view (5) ▪ comparing and contrasting (5) ▪ stating opinion (6) ▪ making an oral presentation (6) ▪ reaction writing (6)
UNIT 4 The Age of Communica-tions	▪ getting information from a graph (7) ▪ categorizing information in the news (7) ▪ highlighting (7) ▪ note-taking from chunking (7) ▪ note-taking; categorizing (7) ▪ scanning (8) ▪ examining the introduction to a longer reading (8) ▪ identifying audience and purpose (8) ▪ note-taking to report factual information (8) ▪ answering questions from notes (8)	▪ applying the information; categorizing (7) ▪ recapping, retelling, reacting to a story (7) ▪ analyzing quotes (8) ▪ giving an opinion (8) ▪ applying the information; problem and solutions (8)	▪ vocabulary in context (7) ▪ jigsaw sentences (7) ▪ word forms (8) ▪ word choice (8)	▪ giving and getting advice (7) ▪ role play (7) ▪ interviewing (7) ▪ topic writing (7) ▪ reaction writing (7) ▪ speaking from reading (8) ▪ taking a position (8)

Reading Matters 4: Overview *(continued)*

UNIT	SKILLS	ACTIVITIES	VOCABULARY	EXPANSION
UNIT 5 Creativity	• understanding and paraphrasing suggestions (9) • summarizing information from a text (9) • understanding the uses of imagery and example (9) • applying the information to analyze a situation (9) • predicting information (10) • skimming for details (10) • scanning for research results (10) • note-taking for retelling (10)	• exploring points of view (9) • recapping, retelling, reacting to the story (10) • giving your opinion (10) • arguing your point of view (10) • summary writing (9)	• figuring out the referent (9) • word forms; adjectives (9) • jigsaw sentences (9) • comparisons (10) • definitions (10)	• reaction writing (9) • oral presentation (9) • two-minute taped talk (10) • topic writing (10)
UNIT 6 Work	• predicting (11) • surveying (11) • scanning for the development of point of view (11) • summarizing an argument (11) • previewing (12) • inferring information (12)	• identifying markers (11) • defining terms (11) • getting information from tables and charts (12) • personalizing (12)	• understanding loaded language (11) • guessing from context (11) • figuring out the referent (11) • jigsaw sentences (12) • expressions (12)	• role play (11) • reaction writing (11) • selecting from different options (12) • interviewing (12) • letter writing (12)

UNIT 1

Birthrights

As the family is, so is the offspring.

– Russian Proverb

1

Introducing the Topics

Today, as in the past, families are the most important social units in society. What choices do we face in having a family? In this unit we will find out about some of the recent issues that affect today's families. Chapter 1 explores the new directions in the North American family, examining the different responsibilities of fathers and mothers and the effects these have on the lives of children. In Chapter 2, we discover how families are affected by advances in reproductive technology. How do families cope with multiple births?

Points of Interest

DIFFERENCES OF OPINION

In this unit you will be reading about ideas and positions on which people differ. How do you decide if you agree or disagree with information you read?

Check the things that help you decide if you agree with information in a reading.

a. _____ You have read or heard about these ideas before.

b. _____ You have personal experience with these ideas.

c. _____ A friend thinks the information is true.

d. _____ A person who is knowledgeable on the subject agrees with the information.

e. _____ The information is based on facts that can be verified.

f. _____ The information is based on opinions.

Compare your list with a partner or with a small group. Explain your answers.

Think about these questions. Share your ideas with a partner or with a small group.

1. How have families changed in the last twenty years? How would you characterize these changes?
2. What do parents expect of their children? What are these expectations based on?
3. What do children expect of their parents? What are these expectations based on?
4. What should society do to help families? How much or how little does it do today?

CHAPTER 1

The Family: Moving in Many Directions

Chapter Openers

AGREE OR DISAGREE: CHANGES IN THE FAMILY

Read each of these statements. Write *A* if you agree or *D* if you disagree with the statement.

1. _____ Families today are under more pressure than they were in the past.

2. _____ Family members need to have time to help one another cope in their daily lives.

3. _____ Couples are usually prepared for the difficulties they may face in marriage.

4. _____ Today's generation is more interested in work than in family.

5. _____ Men play as important a role in raising children as women do.

6. _____ It is possible to "have it all"—marriage, a family, and a successful career.

Work with a partner or in a small group. Explain the reasons for your opinions as completely as possible.

Exploring and Understanding Reading

PREDICTING

Read the following statements that describe some characteristics of family life. Write *T* for the ones that are true today and *TW* for those that were true twenty years ago.

a. _____ Very few women are "working mothers."

b. _____ "Mommy and Me" classes are very popular.

c. _____ Families are busy and small.

d. _____ Women in their 60s can have children.

e. _____ There are very few support services for families.

f. _____ Men are involved with child rearing.

g. _____ Women have maternity leave with no job security.

Compare your answers and explain your reasoning with a partner. Based on these statements, predict the ideas you expect the reading to contain.

SKIMMING

Read the article quickly to find out the following information:

■ **READING TIP:**
When you skim a reading selection, you read quickly to find out some of the important ideas in the reading. Skimming helps you focus on what you can understand in the reading and makes rereading easier and more productive.

1. Are today's families considered more traditional or less traditional than in the past?
2. What are three important differences between family life today and what it was twenty years ago?
3. What are the reasons for the changes in today's society?

Discuss your answers with a partner.

NEW YORK TIMES—WESTCHESTER WEEKLY

Families Grow Less Traditional

By Kate Stone Lombardi

1. Twenty years ago, the term working mother was still new. Phrases like latch-key children and having it all were also popular. There were few offerings like Mommy and Me classes because few parents wanted to pay for scheduled play time with their toddler. Parking was no problem for Metro-North commuters since a system known as "kiss and ride" predominated, in which a wife dropped off her husband at the station, then left with the family station wagon.

2. Today, the vast majority of women with children under 6 work outside the home. Affordable, safe child care has become a major concern for parents. "Having it all" has meant for many families having very little time, as busy parents and their tightly scheduled children must now set aside family time in order to be together.

3. Families are not only busier but also smaller. In 1990, the most recent figures available, the average household size was 2.64 in Westchester, down from 3.08 in 1970. The Norman Rockwell scenario of a traditional family as mother and father and several children is an even less accurate picture than it was two decades ago. One in every five mothers with children younger than 18 in the country is raising her offspring alone.

4. Artificial insemination and other assisted fertility treatments have become routine, leading to a six-fold increase in multiple births. West Patent Elementary School in Bedford has 7 sets of twins in its 75-member second grade. Another 7 sets of twins have entered the 200-pupil second-grade class of Primrose Elementary School in Somers.

5. Fertility technology has also pushed the laws of nature concerning what constitutes a natural family. New techniques have allowed sperm to be collected from dead men and a 63-year-old woman to give birth. Computer technology has also evolved sharply, enabling parents to monitor their children at camp and in day-care centers through cyber visits, and allowing far-flung family members to send e-mail to one another on the Internet.

6. All of these factors continue to change the shape of the family in the county and nationwide. Interviews with family court judges, doctors, psychologists, teachers, government and community leaders and families portray a picture of family life that is much more complex, with far greater stress but with more support services, than was the case in past decades. "The typical family certainly isn't Mom and Dad, Dick and Jane and Spot anymore," said Dr. Jody Shachnow, associate director of social work at New York Hospital-Cornell Medical Center in White Plains. "It's not even 'The Brady Bunch.' It's a very different, extraordinarily varied family picture. There is a lot more of a challenge to the traditional roles and the traditional family, and within families, everyone is busier, parents and the kids."

7. Gay parents are more common. Twenty years ago, Nan Bailey, a financial planner, could not imagine herself as a suburban parent. Today, she and her companion of 12 years, Dr. Barbara Berger, are raising their two children in Larchmont. Each conceived a child through artificial insemination. Billy, 5, and Julia, 6 months, share the same anonymous sperm donor. Ms. Bailey and Dr. Berger are formally adopting each other's child.

8. "Sometimes when I'm talking with gay parents in the city, they say, 'Oh, how brave of you to have moved to the suburbs,'" Ms. Bailey said. "But the support has been wonderful from the school, the church and the block. We feel very blessed to be living in this day and age."

9. Dr. Shachnow said that in the course of her family practice she sees older couples struggling with fertility problems, parents coping with adoptions of children from foreign countries, young couples adjusting to the birth of a new baby, adolescents having difficulties establishing their identity and, of course, spouses trying to work out marital problems.

10. She said that in her experience, working women still bear the brunt of housework and child care, though among younger couples she sees men tend to be more involved in child rearing and housework than those of earlier generations.

11. "Today when the child arrives, I don't see one postpartum depression, I see two," Dr. Shachnow said. "They've both gotten used to this life style with two paychecks and having what they want and doing what they want."

As women have delayed starting their families, infertility rates have soared. Conceiving a child has evolved into an expensive and stressful ordeal, but treatments developed over the last two decades have made parents out of couples who once had little hope.

12. "Up until 1978, there really wasn't anything to be done for a large segment of the population if surgical techniques failed," said Dr. Hugh Melnick, director of Advanced Fertility Services of Westchester. "Nothing could be done for women who had tubular problems or men who had sperm problems. Now with in vitro we can bypass the fallopian tubes, and we have the capacity of picking up a single sperm and injecting it into the egg. All these people, if they were trying 20 years ago, would have been childless."

13. Two decades ago, a woman who became pregnant and took a maternity leave had no guarantee that her job would be waiting for her when she returned. At that time an employer could refuse to pay disability costs of pregnant workers, even if they paid for elective surgery for male employees. Concepts like job sharing, telecommuting and even part-time work for new parents were novel.

14. Only 10 years ago, when Sallie Fraenkel, vice president of program enterprises and distribution at Showtime, proposed a part-time work schedule after the birth of her daughter, Emily, she was flatly refused. "The company had no policy, and it was not looked kindly upon," she said. "You either worked full time or you didn't work at all." Ms. Fraenkel was eventually rehired as a consultant and now is on staff working four days a week. Today flexible work schedules are common.

15. If a woman retained her job, she faced an even more formidable job of finding child care than she does today. "What happened in the 1970s and particularly in the early 1980s was that there was a tremendous migration of middle-class women into the work force," said Sally Ziegler, former director of the Child Care Council of Westchester. "There was a huge growth in day care, though there's still not enough infant care and probably not enough after-school care."

16. In the 1970s, the focus on day-care centers was to maintain cleanliness and safety, Mrs. Ziegler said. Today there is a recognition of the importance of emotional and intellectual growth during the early years of childhood, and child-care centers now emphasize developmentally appropriate practices.

17. The Child Care Council handles more than 4,000 child-care referrals a year, and Lottie Harris, the current director, said that number is rising, particularly as more families are removed from public assistance. There are a total of 14,572 registered slots of day care in the county. That includes child-care centers, group family day care and school-age programs.

18. In the county's 40 school districts, 19 offer programs to care for children either before or after school hours. The Avon Corporation in Rye has the only corporate on-site child care center, but several corporations have formed consortiums to finance child-care centers where priority slots are allocated to employees. Several hospitals have on-site day care for staff members, and three colleges—Sarah Lawrence, Purchase College and Westchester Community College—provide on-site day care for the children of students and faculty members.

19. Nannies have also become a visible presence in the county. Nanny networks have evolved and organize social outings and discussion groups. Some towns even offer Nanny and Me classes for baby sitters and their charges.

20. In addition to the child-care industry, which has burgeoned with the advent of dual-career families, a number of service businesses have formed to fill the gaps for families with two busy commuters. Catering concerns have thrived in and around train stations. Dry-cleaning trucks have set up shop in parking spots at train stations. Businesses like Cleaner Options, which provides door-to-door pickup and delivery of dry cleaning, are thriving.

21. Children also lead busier lives. "We were already talking about 'the hurried child' 20 years ago, and if that was hurried then, I don't know what we'd call it now." Dr. Shachnow said.

22. Many children are in programs throughout the day, with little time for daydreaming or imaginary play. In several towns, clergy members have been meeting recently with soccer and Little League officials concerning scheduling conflicts, so that busy children would not be forced to choose between athletics and worship.

23. The stress that families are under is highly visible in the Family Court system, said Chief Justice Adrienne Hofmann Scancarelli, supervising judge for the Family Court of the Ninth Judicial District, which covers Westchester. Judge Scancarelli said she sees more children on medication and increased drug abuse, poverty, homelessness and violence.

24. "There is so much social change," Dr. Shachnow said. "The boundaries of the family are becoming much more porous. Children are constantly bombarded with good and bad. They can learn about serial killers and then watch the Sojourner up on Mars. It's mind boggling how much there is to assimilate."

UNDERSTANDING DETAILS

Scanning for Information

■ *READING TIP:*
Scanning is a useful strategy for finding information to answer specific questions.

Read quickly through the entire reading selection to find the answers for these questions. Note the question number in the margin where the information is located for future reference.

1. a. How many mothers with children under the age of six are working outside the home?

    _____

    b. How has this affected the pace of family life?

    _____

2. How many mothers in Westchester county were single parents in 1990?

    _____

3. What reproductive techniques are available today that weren't in the past?

    a. _____

    b. _____

    c. _____

4. a. How common are gay parents as compared with the past?

    _____

b. How are they accepted by their community?

_____

5. How possible is it for today's working mothers to return to work as compared with the past?

_____

6. What kind of services are there more of today?

   a. _____

   b. _____

7. What is happening to the lives of children today?

_____

Compare answers with a partner. Verify the information in the reading that supports your answer.

Looking Back: Highlighting

From what you remember of the information in the reading, list in note form five important characteristics of family life today that have changed over the past twenty years.

   a. _____

   b. _____

   c. _____

   d. _____

   e. _____

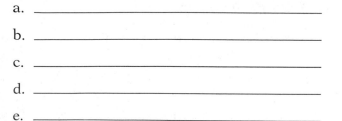

■ **READING TIP:**
Highlighting is a useful strategy for finding and remembering important facts and ideas you read. To highlight, use a colored highlighting pen to mark information. Be careful to mark only the words and phrases that you want to stand out—not the whole sentence.

1. Reread the article and highlight the parts of the reading that contain information about each of these five main ideas. Write the main ideas in the margin of the reading.

2. Based on the highlighting, which two main ideas are explained in the most detail?

   a. _____

   b. _____

After Reading

A. Decide whether or not the following statements from the reading are positive developments. Be prepared to give reasons for your opinions.

1. Couples have gotten used to this lifestyle with two paychecks and having what they want and doing what they want.
2. Children lead busier lives. Many children are in programs throughout the day.
3. Computer technology enables parents to monitor their children at camp and in day-care centers through cyber visits and allowing far-flung family members to send e-mail to one another on the Internet.

B. Choose one or more statements that surprised or interested you. Discuss them with others in your group.

Work with a partner or in a small group. Compare your ideas. Try to persuade your partner to change his or her position. Report your opinions, reasons and examples to the class.

Childhood in a changing world: What should parents allow their children to do?

In "Families Grow Less Traditional," the writer stated that family life today has put a lot of pressure on everyone, especially children. What responsibilities do parents have toward their children? How can society make sure that parents aren't encouraging their children to do things that are dangerous for them to do? The following is an essay about the tragedy of Jessica Dubroff and the question of what parents should and shouldn't allow their children to do.

Read the following essay and discuss whether or not you think this tragedy is the result of the changes in family life today.

THE MONTREAL GAZETTE

Stolen Childhood

Children are not miniature adults, but many parents seem to think so

By Jeffrey I. Derevensky

1. The headlines around the world echo with the tragic death of Jessica Dubroff, a 7-year-old aspiring pilot from Pescadero, Calif. This 4-foot-2-inch, 55-pound child who required cushions and aluminum extensions for her feet to reach the rudder pedals, was on the second leg of her attempt to be the youngest individual to complete a flight across the United States. While other little girls might have been playing with their Barbies and preoccupied with school and homework, Jessica, supported by her parents and flight instructor, was bent on setting a flying record.

2. A significant controversy will likely ensue for months to come. Questions concerning the flight instructor's decision to take off in such poor weather and her parents' willingness to allow this expedition will continue. In light of this tragic accident, the U.S. Federal Aviation Administration announced that it will reassess its policy permitting young children to take the controls of an aircraft.

3. This tragedy underscores a more important issue concerning our child-rearing practices. While it is likely safe to assume that most parents would not let their 7-year-old take control of their automobile on a cross-country trip, let alone an aircraft, we as a society appear to be removing the childhood in our children's development.

4. We want our children to walk and talk earlier, we enter them into preschool programs at 2 years of age, sometimes even earlier. We want them to dress like adults, behave like adults and think like adults. Unfortunately, or fortunately, children are not miniature adults. Their thinking processes remain remarkably different from those of adults.

5. As parents, we painstakingly try to impart our ideas, values and expectations n our children often with disregard for their ability to understand, empathize or care about our concerns. I observed a teacher reprimanding a child in a Grade 3 classroom about his lack of scholastic effort, task commitment and academic achievement.

She explained to the child, and the entire class, that if he did not significantly improve he would not be promoted to Grade 4 at the end of the year. She further went on indicating that if he did not go to Grade 4 how would he get to Grade 5, 6, junior high school, university and graduate school. She had discussed 15 years of his life. No doubt, he was more interested in when recess was coming and whether his mom would let him play outside after school today.

6. While this may appear an isolated incident, the truth remains that we are slowly removing our children's childhood. We have little respect for their opinions and feelings and expect them to behave, think and respond as adults

7. Walk into a shopping center and observe children and adult interactions. Complaining that she is hot, a young girl proceeds to remove her jacket. Her mother responds, "It's not hot in here, don't take off your jacket." Another child is told to go to the washroom and responds, "I don't need to." His parent responds, "Yes, you do." A child indicates he is thirsty and the parent responds "No, you're not." This explicit message is that parents know what's best and that it is permissible to be hot, thirsty, hungry, tired and require the washroom when we say so.

8. While tying a little girl's running shoes—Thomas Gordon in Parent Effectiveness Training so aptly terms this "the battle of the shoestrings"—in a class of 4-year-olds, I noticed a little boy in the corner who had his shoes on the wrong feet. While his parents had purchased running shoes with "velcro," thereby eliminating the need to tie them, he nevertheless had inadvertently put the left shoe on the right foot and the

right shoe on his left foot. I pointed this out to him and he said, "No problem" and proceeded to cross his legs so it appeared that the shoes were now on the correct foot.

9. While this is so naive, for Peter, the problem was solved. As parents, we believe wearing one's shoes on the wrong feet causes pain and is uncomfortable for the child. In all my years as a child psychologist, I have never heard one child complain. In fact, most indicate, "What's the difference?"

10. Parenting is not easy. While many children are adept, at a very early age, in the use of video recorders, computers and the Internet, their level of thinking and understanding is often very limited. Depending upon one's age and developmental level, they can not think, reason, perform or understand as adults. Flying across the United States in a single-engine Cessna appears like an arduous task for an adult, let alone a 7-year old.

11. Jean Piaget, one of the most noted child psychologists and epistemologists of the 20th century delineated different stages of children's thought processes. Yet when asked by parents and educators how to move children through these stages more quickly, he responded, "Why would you want to do that?"

12. Why are we rushing our children to become adults? Why do we expect them to think like adults? They have a whole lifetime ahead of them to deal with the multitude of joys, problems, adventures, goals and records to break. We must begin to listen to our children, understand and be sensitive to their abilities, strengths and limitations.

13. We need to allow them to be children, because they're only young once.

DISCUSSION QUESTIONS. WHAT IS YOUR OPINION?

Think about these questions. Share your ideas with a partner or in a small group.

1. Who was Jessica Dubroff and what happened to her?
2. What does the writer feel is the issue at the heart of the tragedy of Jessica Dubroff?
3. What examples does the writer use to show that parents some times fail to recognize what their children are capable of understanding? What is the consequence of this failure?
4. What mistake does the writer feel that adults make in their expectations for children?
5. Do you agree or disagree with the writer's point of view?
6. Can parents in today's family give their children the time they need to be children?
7. Do you agree with the author's conclusions or not?

Vocabulary Building

FIGURING OUT THE REFERENT

In English an important way to understand the meaning of information in a sentence is by asking if these ideas are referred to in a sentence or sentences that precede or come before. Writers in English commonly use pronouns and synonyms to refer to preceding ideas. In this exercise you will try to identify the referent (preceding idea) for the information given in the following sentences.

A. The following statements are taken from "Stolen Childhood." Use your understanding of key words to find and write the referents for each of the words in bold.

1. In light of **this** tragic accident . . . (paragraph 2)

   _____

2. **We** want our children to walk and talk earlier . . . (paragraph 4)

   _____

3. **She** had discussed 15 years of **his** life. (paragraph 5)

   _____

4. While **this** may appear an isolated incident . . . (paragraph 6)

_____

5. **This explicit message** is that parents know what's best . . .
(paragraph 7)

_____

6. While **this** is so naive . . . (paragraph 9)

_____

Compare your answers with a partner. Refer to the reading.

**B. Scan the reading and find two other sentences with words that
have referents. Underline the sentences and what they refer to.**

Compare your answers with a partner.

VOCABULARY IN CONTEXT

**A. Complete each sentence with one of the words in the list. Use
your understanding of the context to help you guess.**

a. accurate	b. affordable	c. bombarded
d. bypass	e. capacity	f. conceiving
g. constitutes	h. monitor	

1. We decided to _____ the crowd so we took a different
route to reach our appointment.

2. We don't have a lot of money to spend on lunch so we'll look for

a restaurant that is _____.

3. The music hall was filled to _____ and it was impossible to get into the concert.

4. _____ a baby sometimes takes older women a
long time.

5. What _____ a crime depends on what the country's
law allows.

6. The radio station was _____ with a record number of requests to play the latest hit record.

7. The teacher came over every ten minutes to _____ the students' progress.

8. She needed _____ information in order to carry out her work.

B. Decide which form of the word in boldface to use in each of the following sentences.

evolved

1. The _____ of the family from a large extended number of people to a smaller number has happened only in the last

   two or three generations. The family _____ gradually at first but now the changes have taken place more quickly.

consultant

2. Sally _____ with her boss but the _____

   was very brief. He asked her to invite the other _____ to join them the next day to continue the meeting.

migration

3. A number of people _____ into the area thirty years

   ago. These _____ were important for the economic

   growth in the area, proving that _____ can be positive for society.

establishing

4. The restaurant had a new _____ that brought in a lot

   of changes. The _____ practice of opening early was

   changed. _____ these changes was not easy but it was effective.

Check your answers. Work with a partner and take turns reading the sentences.

Expanding Your Language

SPEAKING

A. *Debate:* Are parents asking or expecting too much of their children today? What is your position on this question? Brainstorm a list of ideas in support of your position. Work with a partner to add to the list. Think of as many reasons and examples as you can to defend your position. Prepare to talk for one minute for each point you want to make. Debate your position with two students who chose another position. Take turns presenting your points. Listen carefully to your partners and ask questions about the information. Share your conclusions with your classmates.

B. *Oral Presentation:* What are the relationships and responsibilities that people share in your family or in your culture? Prepare some information for a short (three-minute) talk on this subject. Note your ideas. Practice once or twice so that you are comfortable explaining the information to others. Present your information with others in a small group.

WRITING

Topic Writing: From the ideas that you have gathered in this chapter and your own experience, write about the important changes in the family that you think have occurred and the changes that you think will occur in the future. To carry out this writing, follow these steps:

1. Write a list of ideas. For each idea, think of some facts, examples, stories, explanations or other information of your own.
2. Make an outline for these ideas, grouping ideas that are related.
3. Using your outline as a guide, write a paragraph about each of the main ideas.
4. Reread the first draft and check to see that the topic of each paragraph is clearly stated in the first sentence. Make any changes needed.
5. Reread and change the order of—or add information to—this draft.

Submit this writing to your teacher.

CHAPTER 2

Cheaper by the Dozen?

■ **Chapter Openers**

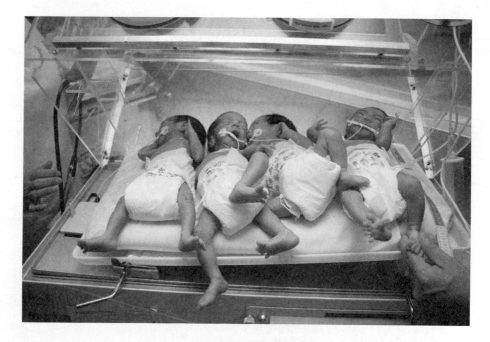

AGREE OR DISAGREE: MULTIPLE BIRTHS

Circle *A* if you agree or *D* if you disagree with the statement. Be prepared to give reasons for your choice.

1. A   D   Doctors today can help many infertile couples to conceive children.

19

2. A D   Infertile couples should use any method that works to be able to have children.

3. A D   Babies born prematurely have very few medical problems.

4. A D   Today, raising a large family is no more difficult than raising a small one.

5. A D   Eight babies (octuplets) is too many to carry in one pregnancy.

Work with a partner or in a small group. Explain the choices you make and the beliefs on which they are based.

GETTING INFORMATION FROM DIAGRAMS TO COMPLETE A CHART

When Fertility Drugs Work Too Well

Women's hormonal rhythms normally ensure production of just one viable egg every month. By forcing the release of numerous eggs at once, fertility drugs raise the chance of multiple birth.

The Normal Ovary

Under ordinary circumstances, an ovary is the size of a grape. Inside there are fluid-filled sacs 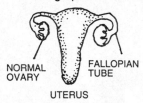 called follicles, each housing an egg, or ovum. During normal ovulation, one follicle matures, releasing its egg for fertilization in the fallopian tube.

NORMAL OVARY   FALLOPIAN TUBE   UTERUS

The Ovary on Drugs

Fertility drugs jump-start follicle development, increasing the likelihood that more than one 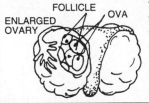 follicle will release a fertile egg. Drug treatment can make the ovaries swell up to 10 times their normal volume—roughly the size of a grapefruit.

FOLLICLE   OVA   ENLARGED OVARY

Multiple Birth

The human uterus isn't designed to hold numerous fetuses. When it is forced to, the crowding causes early delivery. The consequences for babies can range from brain damage to death.

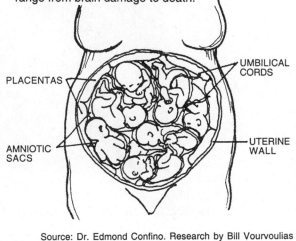

PLACENTAS   UMBILICAL CORDS   AMNIOTIC SACS   UTERINE WALL

Source: Dr. Edmond Confino. Research by Bill Vourvoulias

Based on the information in these diagrams, complete the following charts.

1. Compare the size and production of a normal ovary and one of a woman taking fertility drugs.

	Normal Ovary	*Ovary on Drugs*
Size of ovary		
Number of eggs developing in follicles		
Chance of fertilization		

2. List the dangers associated with multiple births for mother and babies.

Mother	*Babies*

Compare your answers with a partner. Use the information to discuss your opinions about the following question:

What are the risks of taking fertility drugs and how can they be managed?

Exploring and Understanding Reading

PREDICTING FROM TITLES

The next reading selection expresses the viewpoints of the writer on the topic of multiple births made possible by today's fertility drugs. Read the title. Before reading the article, read the following statements and check (✓) those that you would expect to find. (Use the title to predict the author's position. Think of the reasons why he holds that opinion.)

I expect to find

1. _____ many ideas that I agree with.

2. _____ some ideas that I agree with.

3. _____ some ideas that I disagree with.

4. _____ many ideas that I disagree with.

5. _____ ideas that are the author's point of view or opinion.

6. _____ factual information that is true.

7. _____ factual information that may not be true.

Work with a partner or in a small group. Explain your choices as completely as possible.

SURVEYING

Read the introduction (all of the first two paragraphs). Then read the beginning of each of the following paragraphs and all of the last two paragraphs.

■ *READING TIP:*
Surveying is a useful reading skill. To survey, you (a) read the introduction, and (b) read the first sentence of every paragraph after that. An introduction can contain information that will interest the reader in the topic of the article. The first sentence often expresses the main idea of a paragraph.

Eight Is Too Many

By Ezekiel J. Emanuel

1. Just like the McCaughey septuplets of Iowa, whose first birthday recently made headlines in *People* magazine, the Chukwu octuplets of Texas have become a media spectacle. Daily bulletins detailing each child's respiratory status, ultrasound results, and other developments fill the papers—not just the tabloids, but respectable outlets like the *New York Times* and the *Washington Post,* as well. Inevitably, writers describe the eight live births in glowing terms—amazing, wonderful, even a miracle; they describe the mother as the brave survivor of adversity; they portray the hard-battling physicians as heroes and champions.

2. But what are we all celebrating? Modern reproductive technologies have brought the miracle of children to many infertile couples, thereby producing enormous good. The McCaughey septuplets and Chukwu octuplets, however, represent too much of that good thing. They are the product of fertility technology misused—an error, not a wonder, and one that even the few public voices of skepticism seem not fully to appreciate.

3. First and most obvious, large multiple births lead to all sorts of medical problems, for mothers and children alike. Nkem Chukwu had to stay in the hospital for months prior to delivery, on a bed that tilted her nearly upside down. It's too early to know how well her surviving children will fare (one died seven days after birth), but the odds do not favor

them. Among children born prematurely and weighing just two pounds or less—the largest of the Chukwu infants weighed one pound, eleven ounces at birth—breathing difficulties, brain damage and fluid imbalances are not rare.

4. The result is a comparatively high level of infant mortality and, in the survivors, long-term complications. Studies of low-birth-weight children (not from multifetal pregnancies but from premature births) have shown that approximately 20 percent have severe disabilities; among those weighing less than 750 grams (1.7 pounds) at birth, 50 percent have functional impairments. A recent study that followed these very small infants to school showed that up to 50 percent of them scored low on standardized intelligence tests, including 21 percent who were mentally retarded. In addition, nine percent had cerebral palsy, and 25 percent had severe vision problems. As a result, 45 percent ended up enrolling in special-education programs.

5. Equally important, but rarely articulated, are the emotional health risks children in multiple births face. Loving and raising children through the normal development milestones is enormously wonderful and rewarding. But it is also hard work. Raising children is not a sprint to a healthy birth but a marathon through variable terrain until the goal of independent adulthood. The real way to assess these miraculous pregnancies—indeed, any pregnancy—is whether they are ultimately good for children. Quite clearly, they are not.

6. Attending to the physical, emotional, intellectual, and social needs of children for 18 years is hard and demanding. For infants and toddlers there are the simple physical demands—feeding, changing diapers, bathing, chasing after them to prevent injuries. Then there are the emotional and intellectual demands—cuddling them, talking to them, responding meaningfully to their smiles and first words, reading books to them, playing with them and their toys, handling the tantrums, and so on. And, while the physical demands may lessen once children grow (although parents who often feel like chefs, maids, chauffeurs, and all-around gofers may disagree with that), the emotional and intellectual demands become more complex with time. Older children need help with homework, mediation of sibling rivalry, constructive discipline, support in the trials and tribulations of friendships, encouragement in their participation in sports and other activities, help in coping with losses and defeats, and guidance through the many pitfalls of adolescence.

7. It is challenging enough to balance the demands of one or two children of different ages and attend to their needs; it is simply not physically possible for two parents to do this successfully for seven children of the same age, even if one of the parents is a full-time caregiver. Regardless of the motivation, dedication, love or stamina of these parents, the sheer limitations of time make it impossible for each of seven identically aged children to receive appropriate parental attention and affection.

8. Just ask yourself: Would you trade being born a healthy single or twin for being born one of the "miraculous" septuplets,

even a healthy one? Most of us would probably say "no" because of parental attention we would have lost. And we would be right to think that way.

9. The McCaugheys' experience proves the point. They have been able to raise their septuplets for one year only because they can fall back on a veritable army of volunteers—scores of people with tightly coordinated schedules who assist in the food preparation, feeding, diapering, and care of the seven babies. Few families with quintuplets or more children can expect or rely on such community effort. (Indeed, a Washington, D.C. couple who recently bore quintuplets, had hardly any community help at all until some belated publicity highlighted the family's plight.) And, while the McCaughey's community-wide effort appears to have worked for the first year of life, it's hardly a sure thing that the assistance will always be there. The first is the year when, despite the demands on time, parents are more interchangeable and caregiving has the greatest, most unmitigated emotional rewards. The terrible twos and threes will try the patience and dedication of volunteers.

10. What's more, having multiple caregivers cannot fully subsitute for parental time. While it's true that many children do just fine spending large amounts of time in paid day care, where multiple providers care for them, these children at least have the chance to go home and have one-on-one parental time spread among just a few siblings, of different ages. (Having multiple caregivers also becomes more problematic as the children grow, because of child-rearing styles that may differ from those of the parents, particularly on issues

like discipline.) This is not possible in the McCaughey or Chukwu families, and it never will be. Spending just 20 minutes a day focusing on each individual child—hardly a lavish amount—will take nearly two and a half hours each day. When competing with sleep, meals, shopping, and all the other demands of basic existence for a family with septuplets, this focused time is likely to disappear.

11. Remember, too, that, while the McCaughey septuplets seem to have brought together a community to support their care, such children also impose significant costs on the community. It is now estimated that the hospital costs from birth to discharge (or death) for the Chukwu infants will exceed $2 million. And the health care costs don't stop after birth. Any complications—neurological, vision, or other problems—can drive the medical care costs sky-high. Plus, no one knows how much will be required for permanent problems that require ongoing special-education and other accommodations. Yes, there's health insurance. But health insurance exists to cover ill health and problems such as cancer, genetic defects, and accidents that are the result of random chance. The birth of octuplets, by contrast, is not a chance event; it is the result of deliberate actions (or inactions) by physicians, patients, and society. Remember, too, that financial resources are limited; money spent on octuplets is money not spent on other children with special health care and educational needs.

12. For these reasons, the standard of medical care is not to proceed with such large multiple births. But this raises legitimate ethical problems for many couples. The most common method for interrupting multiple pregnancies is "selective reduction"—that is, doctors abort some of the fetuses for the sake of the mother's health. Many people believe couples who agree to infertility treatments must not only be informed about—but should consent to—the potential need for selective reduction even before beginning the treatments. Yet this is clearly not an option for families like the McCaugheys and the Chukwus, who oppose abortion on religious grounds.

13. Fortunately, this issue doesn't have to be so morally knotty. In the usual treatment for problems with egg maturation and release (this is what both the McCaughey and Chukwu families were treated for), doctors prescribe drugs such as human menopausal gonadotrophin (hMG) or Clomiphene (commonly known as Clomid) to stimulate egg development. Then they administer an additional drug, human chorionic gonadatrophin (hcG), to induce ovulation. Using measurement of estrogen and ultrasound monitoring, physicians can assess the number of egg follicles developing in the ovaries. If they observe too many developing follicles, making the likelihood of multiple fertilizations high, physicians can withhold the drugs necessary to stimulate ovulation and advise against intercourse or withhold sperm injection until the next cycle, when they can go through the process again. To be sure, that treatment process can be a little more frustrating for aspiring parents. And many couples are reluctant to skip a cycle because it wastes thousands of dollars on the drugs and treatments, usually out of their own pockets. But carrying septuplets to term has costs, too.

14. In the end, new laws or regulations won't fix this problem. The real solution is leadership by the medical profession and by the media. Reproductive specialists who care for infertile couples are not simply passive technicians following the orders of the parents. They are engaged professionals guiding important technology that can create great joy—but also great pain. Professionalism requires deliberating with the parents about the goals and purposes of the treatments: doctors should draw upon their experience to advise and strongly recommend the best course to the parents, which is to avoid large multiple pregnancies.

15. And the media must stop glorifying the septuplets and octuplets. We live in an era that measures success in terms of quantity, that thinks bigger is necessarily better, where the best is defined by size. The best movie is the one that makes the most money; the best law firm is the one with the highest billings; the best painting is auctioned for the highest price; and the best book is the best-selling book. But, in this case, bigger may not be better—indeed, it may actually be worse. The true miracle of birth is the mysterious process by which the fusing of an egg and a sperm can create in just nine months the complex organism that is an infant with the potential to become an independent, thinking, feeling, socially responsible adult. In this way, the millions of babies born each year are miraculous whether born of singleton, twin, triplet, or octuplet pregnancies. It is the wonder of each infant that we should celebrate.

–The New Republic

Based on your survey, check the statement that you think best expresses the author's point of view and purpose in writing the article.

1. _____ Use of fertility drugs raises ethical issues that can be easily resolved.

2. _____ Multiple births made possible because of fertility drugs are problematic and undesirable.

3. _____ Multiple births are problematic and undesirable and therefore steps should be taken to discourage them.

4. _____ Despite the difficulties of multiple births, people are greatly interested in them.

Compare your answer with a partner.

FINDING THE MAIN POINTS OF THE ARGUMENT

In making his argument the author presents a number of important points. Read the points that are listed below. Scan the article and write a letter (a, b, c, etc.) that shows their order of appearance in the article. Write the letter for each point in the margin where you find the idea first appears. Bracket ([ ]) the part(s) of the reading that develop each idea.

1. _____ The case of the McCaugheys as an example of the difficulties families face in raising multiples

2. _____ The ethical problems parents facing multiple births could have

3. _____ The medical problems that large multiple births can present

4. _____ The solutions proposed by the author

5. _____ The costs of multiple births on the community

6. _____ The ways that multiple births affect the children's emotional health

7. _____ The options doctors have in preventing multiple births

Compare your answers with a partner. Verify that you have bracketed the same paragraphs. Check your answers with your teacher.

UNDERSTANDING DETAILS

Fact and Opinion

■ **READING TIP:** *Look at the wording of the sentence. Is the information objective (dates, statistics, results of expert work) or subjective (qualified information, or information that appeals to emotion)?*

A. Decide if the following statements are facts (information that can be independently verified) or opinion (information that represents an individual's point of view). Write *F* for fact or *O* for opinion. Be prepared to discuss the reasons for your choices.

1. _____ They [the McCaughey septuplets and Chukwu octuplets] are the product of fertility technology misused—an error, not a wonder, and one that even the few public voices of skepticism seem not fully to appreciate.

2. _____ Among children born prematurely and weighing just two pounds or less—the largest of the Chukwu infants weighed one pound, eleven ounces at birth—breathing difficulties, brain damage, and fluid imbalances are not rare.

3. _____ Loving and raising children through the normal developmental milestones is enormously wonderful and rewarding.

4. _____ Attending to the physical, emotional, intellectual, and social needs of children for 18 years is hard and demanding.

5. _____ Spending just 20 minutes a day focusing on each individual child—hardly a lavish amount—will take nearly two and a half hours each day.

6. _____ Remember, too, that financial resources are limited; money spent on octuplets is money not spent on other children with special health care and educational needs.

7. _____ Many people believe couples who agree to infertility treatments must not only be informed about—but should consent to—the potential need for selective reduction even before beginning the treatments.

Work with a partner. Compare your answers and give reasons for the choices you made. Locate and underline the information in the reading.

NOTE-TAKING: MAKING STRONG ARGUMENTS

The writer makes certain points and uses facts and examples to support these points. He provides this information to strengthen his point of view. Making notes of this information helps you to develop your critical reading skills.

B. Find two other statements of fact and two of opinion. Highlight these and be prepared to discuss them. Work with a partner and together choose one or two of the points from the list of main points of the argument. Working alone, prepare notes that show the main ideas, supporting points and important details. Use the divided-page system of organization shown in the following example to make your notes.

■ *NOTE-TAKING TIP:*
Some important note-taking skills to notice in this example are: writing only the key words; using abbreviation and using your own words; and using spacing, numbering, and other symbols to show the logical connections among ideas.

Example

MAIN IDEAS	SUPPORTING IDEAS AND DETAILS
A. Types of medical problems from large multiple births	

1. Problems for Mother
   • stay in bed for months
     tilted nearly upside down

2. Problems for Babies
   a. common for babies less than 2 lb:
      breathing difficulties
      brain damage
      fluid imbalance
      • as a result: infant mortality high
   b. long term health problems in survivors
      Studies of premies show:
      • 20% severe disabilities
      • 50% functional impairments (deafness, etc.)
   c. learning problems
      50% low scores on stand. IQ tests
      21% mentally retarded
      9% cerebral palsy
      25% severe vision problems
      • as a result: 45% in special ed. prog.

Work with a partner who prepared notes on the same main ideas. To compare notes, take turns explaining the information for each point to your partner.

After Reading

RETELLING THE INFORMATION

Work with a partner who prepared notes for different points. Use your notes to explain the information to your partner.

REACTING TO THE READING

Use the information in your notes to answer the following questions. Be prepared to give the reasons for your answers.

1. Of all the points the author makes in this reading, which do you think has

   a. the most factual information?

   b. the least factual information?

2. Which point has

   a. the most convincing information?

   b. the least convincing information?

   Why?

3. What other points could be made either in favor of or opposed to the author's point of view on this topic?

4. What is your opinion of the author's point of view on this topic?

APPLYING THE INFORMATION: ANALYZING A SHORT STORY

In the next reading selection, which is a short story, the author expresses his opinion about the quality of relationships between parents and children. He believes that parents need to have time to attend to the moral and emotional issues that their children are bound to face.

As you read, think about the type of relationship that exists between this father and son. How does the father react to his son's actions? What does this show about their relationship?

A Small Crime

By Jerry Woxlor

When he was nine years old he was brought to the door by a policeman who kept one hand on his arm as if to stop him from running away. He had been caught writing with a crayon on a wall of the subway station and his parents were expected to discipline him. The entire rest of the day he stayed in his room waiting for his father to come home from the shirt factory. A slap in the face, he thought, perhaps that's all I'll get. And maybe no allowance for the coming week. Still, he could not help but be apprehensive.

At five thirty he heard the front door open. His mother was talking to his father. They talked for a long time, much longer than he felt was necessary. Then the family ate supper. He was not invited and he felt that his punishment had already started. This saddened him greatly because he enjoyed eating supper with his father and telling him about the day's adventure. He tried to pass the time by reading through his comic books, but he was anxious and could not follow through from beginning to end. At seven o'clock he heard the television come on as the family sat down in the living room. Every so often someone changed a channel. By eight thirty night had fallen and he felt more alone than he had ever been

at any time in his life. He looked out into the garden behind his room. He could see the outline of the young tree his grandfather had planted a month before. It was beginning to sprout leaves and he tried to decide how many it would have that summer. He decided on fifteen. That knowledge made him feel better. By nine o'clock he was feeling drowsy and had lain out on his bed.

Shortly afterwards his father came into the room and sat down on the bed. The boy sat up putting his feet over the side of the bed. His father looked at him then turned away clasping his hands together. They were sitting side by side. The boy looked down at the floor the whole time.

"I remember when I left Romania," his father said. "I went to the train station in my town and had to sit in a special section for people who were emigrating from the country. There were many other people sitting there, and I remember how funny it was that we all looked the same with our best clothes and old suitcases almost bursting with clothes. But what I remember most of all were the walls. It seemed that every person who had ever sat in that part of the railway station had written on the wall his name, his home town and the new place to which he was going. I spent a long time reading all the names on the wall. Many towns were represented and I even recognized the names of many people with whom I had once been friends. And do you know what I did. I took out my pen, found a clear space on the wall and wrote my own name, my home town, and the date. But you see I did not write on the wall out of mischief, it was my own way of saying *this is who I am—now I am ending an old life and starting a new one.* Perhaps one day you will have the same reason. But as long as times are good and we are welcome here there are other and better ways of letting the world know who you are."

He put his hand on the boy's shoulder as if to say, "don't worry, everything is all right." Then he rose slowly and said: "Be good to your mother and me and leave the walls alone." Then he left the room.

The boy lay back on his bed. Ordinarily it took him only two or three minutes to fall asleep. That night he lay awake for almost half an hour.

How would you describe the parent-child relationship depicted in this story? In your opinion, would this relationship be possible in a family with multiple births? Be prepared to support your answer.

Vocabulary Building

RECOGNIZING THE USE OF EMOTIONAL LANGUAGE

In arguing their point of view, writers often choose words that will persuade us to agree with their opinion. These words carry negative, positive, or neutral meanings. Examine these statements and write *N* if the words in bold carry a negative meaning, *P* for positive, and *NE* for neutral.

1. _____ The McCaughey septuplets and the Chukwu octuplets, however, **represent too much of a good thing**.

2. _____ Raising children is **not a sprint to a healthy birth but a marathon** through variable terrain until the goal of adulthood.

3. _____ **It is challenging enough** to balance the demands of one or two children of different ages and attend to their needs.

4. _____ They have been able to raise their septuplets for one year only because they can **fall back on a veritable army of volunteers**.

5. _____ Such children also **impose significant** costs on the community.

6. _____ Many couples **are reluctant** to skip a cycle because it **wastes** thousands of dollars.

Work with a partner. Compare your answers.

Together, find three statements: one example that conveys a positive meaning, one that is negative, and one that is neutral. Be prepared to present your examples to the class.

SIGNAL WORDS/MARKERS

The author uses words and phrases that signal or mark the beginning of a new idea or a transition from one idea to another. The most common types of signals show that there is a series of ideas in an order of importance or sequencing (listing markers), a contrast between one idea and another (contrasting markers), a causal relation (cause and effect markers), and that the writer is coming to the end or finalizing ideas (concluding markers). Scan the reading "Eight Is Too Many" and find two different examples of the following types of signal markers. Circle the examples and write the markers.

1. Listing markers (e.g., *first, second, . . .*)

    a.  _____

    b. _____

2. Contrasting markers (e.g., *however, on the other hand, . . .*)

   a. _____

   b. _____

3. Causal markers (e.g., *as a result, therefore, . . .*)

   a. _____

   b. _____

4. Concluding markers (e.g., *finally, in the end, . . .*)

   a. _____

   b. _____

Expanding Your Language

SPEAKING

Oral Presentation: **What happens to families who have multiple births? Look for information on the life of one of the families that has had this experience. Research your subject in the library or via the Internet. Prepare some information for a short (three-minute) talk on this subject. Note your ideas. Practice once or twice so that you are comfortable explaining the information to others. Present your information with others in a small group.**

WRITING

Reaction Writing: **Give your opinion about the issue of whether families should have multiple births. What are the options? Is this solely a personal choice? What are the societal costs? Support your opinions with as many reasons and examples as possible.**

Read On: Taking It Further

Researchers have found that the more you read, the more your vocabulary will increase and the more you will understand. A good knowledge of vocabulary will help you to do well in school and in business. To find out more about making reading a habit for yourself, answer the following questionnaire.

READING QUESTIONNAIRE

Rank the activities that you think help you to increase the language you understand. Mark (1) beside the one(s) that help you the most to learn new language. Mark (2) beside the second most helpful activity(ies), continuing with (3), (4), and so on. Mark the same number if you find two activities that help you equally.

( ) Memorizing word lists

( ) Reading texts that are assigned for class

( ) Reading texts that I choose for myself

( ) Talking about the texts that we read for class

( ) Talking about the texts that I choose for myself

( ) Learning how to guess the meaning of words that are new

( ) Doing vocabulary exercises for reading that we study in class

( ) Doing extra vocabulary exercises for homework

( ) Studying the dictionary to find out the parts of words

( ) Using the dictionary to look up new words I don't understand

Discuss your questionnaire with a partner. Do not change your answers. Give reasons for your ranking and explain your experiences with reading. Are there other activities you find help you to increase your vocabulary? Explain what these are and how they help you.

A READING JOURNAL

■ *Tip: Keep a notebook to write your reading journal and vocabulary log entries.*

An important way to improve your reading skills and increase your vocabulary is to find material that you choose to read. This activity is called "Reading for Pleasure." Here are some ideas to start you out.

Reading

Find some readings on the topics in this unit that you are interested in and that are at your level. Your teacher can help you find some stories to read for your pleasure. For example, you could choose a novel about families such as *Cheaper by the Dozen* by

Frank Gilbreth and Ernestine Gilbreth Carey or *American Daughter: Discovering My Mother* by Elizabeth Kendall.

Another source of reading material is your bookstore or library's magazine and newspaper section. Discuss what you would like to read with others in a small group. Your group members could recommend something good for you to read. Try to work with a reading partner. Select a reading that your partner or partners will read as well. Make a schedule for the times when you plan to do your personal reading and a time when you would like to finish.

Speaking

Be ready to talk about what you read with a partner or with others in a small group. You can use your reading journal to help you remember what is important for the others to know.

Reading Journal

Include the following information in your journal entry:

Title of the reading: _____

Author: _____

Subject of the reading:

_____

_____

_____

Who are the important people in the story?

1. _____

2. _____

3. _____

4. _____

5. _____

What are some of the important ideas?

1. _____

2. _____

3. _____

4. _____

5. _____

Recommendation

This selection is (is not) good to read because:

1. _____

2. _____

3. _____

4. _____

5. _____

Vocabulary Log

Choose five important words that you learned from each chapter. Write the words and a definition in your notebook. Check your definition with the teacher.

Chapter 1	*Word*	*Definition*
1.	artifical	man-made
2.		
3.		
4.		
5.		

On a separate page write five sentences using one of the words you choose in each sentence.

UNIT 2

Health: Moving in New Directions

Health is better than wealth.
– English Proverb

Introducing the Topics

Today, North Americans have a broader understanding of what contributes to good health. The fairly new idea of holistic health, the approach to health that recognizes the connection between our body and our mind, is more understood than it was in the past. Chapter 3 takes us into the issue of alternative healing. What nontraditional methods are available today? What should we trust? What is reliable? Chapter 4 explores the elements of a healthy lifestyle. What role does exercise play in maintaining health? How does exercise affect our outlook on life?

Points of Interest

DISCUSSION QUESTIONS: A HEALTHY LIFE

Look at the following graph. Then discuss these questions with others in a small group.

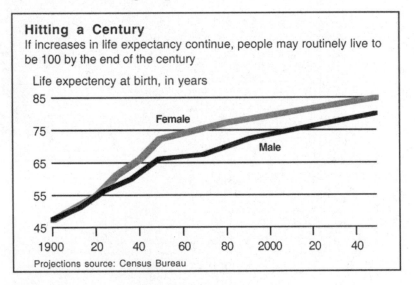

Hitting a Century
If increases in life expectancy continue, people may routinely live to be 100 by the end of the century

Life expectency at birth, in years

Female

Male

Projections source: Census Bureau

1. What is your idea of a healthy lifestyle?
2. Is it easier or more difficult to live in a healthy way? Explain.
3. Is a healthy lifestyle more important today than in the past?
4. What do you do to keep healthy?

CHAPTER 3

Alternative Healing

▮ Chapter Openers

A. WHAT'S THE REPORT ABOUT ALTERNATIVE MEDICINE?

We hear a lot about alternative medicine in the news, but it can mean so many things.

1. Read the following list and check the types of alternative medicine that you know about. Add any you have heard about to the list. Discuss what you know about each.

———— Acupuncture
———— Hypnosis
———— Massage
———— Herbal Medicine

————————————

————————————

————————————

2. Read each of the short reports about alternative medicine quickly and underline or highlight the following information:

- Description of the technique
- Effective uses
- Level of acceptance by doctors or researchers

Acupuncture

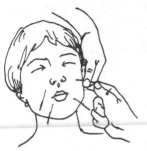

What is it? One of the oldest healing methods known, acupuncture is based on the ancient Chinese belief that there are patterns of energy (Qi) flowing throughout the body. Disease occurs if this flow is blocked or disrupted. When thin needles are inserted into the body at specific points, each linked to a particular organ network, the energy flow supposedly can be restored.

Is it effective? A 1997 National Institutes of Health (NIH) consensus-development conference reported evidence that acupuncture is effective for nausea after surgery or chemotherapy and probably during pregnancy. It may also be helpful as an adjunct treatment for other conditions, including headaches, asthma, stroke rehabilitation and fibromyalgia.

A comparison of detoxification programs in Boston found that people who chose to enter outpatient acupuncture programs were less likely to re-enter than those in residential programs. In a trial of acupuncture as a treatment for chronic pain completed by Finland's National Health Service, 65 percent of patients either stopped taking painkilling drugs or reduced their dosage.

Western doctors, as a rule, dismiss the concept of Qi. Instead, researchers surmise the needles prompt the release of natural painkillers called endorphins, or hormones that stimulate the immune system. Today many experts regard acupuncture as practically mainstream. The NIH panel declared, "There's sufficient evidence of acupuncture's value to expand its use into conventional medicine."

Hypnosis

What is it? Using one of many techniques—like inducing relaxation by asking the subject to count backward—a practitioner brings on a trancelike state. While in it, a patient might focus on healing thoughts or on letting go of negative habits. About one person in ten cannot be hypnotized.

Is it effective? No one knows why, but hypnosis does seem to work for certain conditions. Scientists speculate that it acts by touching the unconscious mind, and putting things generally not within our control, such as pain perception, under our power.

Hypnotism may help alleviate some forms of chronic pain as well as offer relief from stress-related conditions such as asthma. "With almost every medical problem people have, whether it's migraine headaches or irritable-bowel syndrome, there is a significant overlay of anxiety and tension," explains Dr. Dabney M. Ewin, clinical professor of psychiatry at Louisiana State University and Tulane. "If you remove that part, which you can do with hypnosis, they get a whole lot better."

Scientists are studying hypnotism's consistency as a method of anesthesia or pain relief, and its ability to speed healing.

Massage

What is it? This treatment uses touch to apply pressure to the body's skin, muscles, tendons and ligaments. The idea is to ease disorders by relieving tension, promoting blood flow, calming the nervous system and loosening muscles. Massage therapy now encompasses countless techniques, including Swedish, shiatsu and Rolfing.

Is it effective? Yes, according to researcher Maria Hernandez-Reif of the University of Miami's Touch Research Institute. "There is a relationship between stress and our immune systems," she says. The institute has found evidence that massage may reduce the amount of the stress hormone cortisol. Researchers speculate that a reduction in cortisol allows the immune system to spring back.

Researchers are also trying to determine if massage can have specific benefits for children with asthma and cystic fibrosis.

B. DISCUSSION QUESTIONS

Based on what you underlined and your own knowledge, discuss the following questions with a partner or in a small group.

1. How does alternative medicine differ from traditional medicine?
2. What kind of medical problems can alternative medicine be used for?
3. Is alternative medicine safe?
4. Would North American doctors prescribe alternative medicines? Why or why not?
5. Would you ever use alternative medicine? Why or why not?

Exploring and Understanding Reading

PREDICTING: GETTING INFORMATION FROM A DIAGRAM

The article "Acupuncture: Medicine's Latest Miracle" is from a health magazine written for a general audience. Before reading, look at the diagram on page 44 and get information to complete the following paragraph:

According to Chinese traditional medicine acupuncture uses

_____ that are placed along _____ or

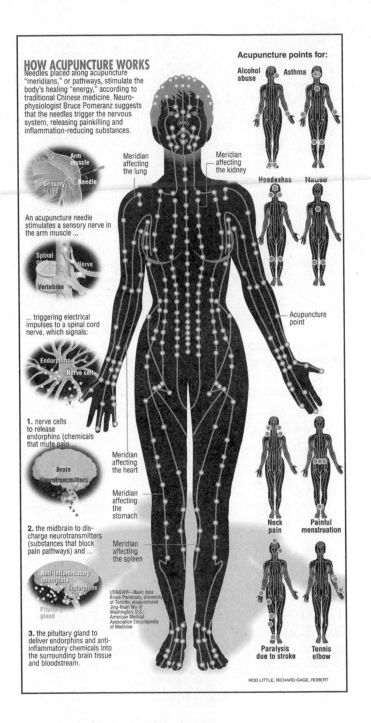

HOW ACUPUNCTURE WORKS

Needles placed along acupuncture "meridians," or pathways, stimulate the body's healing "energy," according to traditional Chinese medicine. Neuro-physiologist Bruce Pomeranz suggests that the needles trigger the nervous system, releasing painkilling and inflammation-reducing substances.

Arm muscle
Sensory nerve   Needle

An acupuncture needle stimulates a sensory nerve in the arm muscle ...

Spinal cord   Nerve
Vertebrae

... triggering electrical impulses to a spinal cord nerve, which signals:

Endorphins
Nerve cell

1. nerve cells to release endorphins (chemicals that mute pain)

Brain
Neurotransmitters

2. the midbrain to discharge neurotransmitters (substances that block pain pathways) and ...

Anti-inflammatory chemicals
Endorphins
Pituitary gland

3. the pituitary gland to deliver endorphins and anti-inflammatory chemicals into the surrounding brain tissue and bloodstream.

Meridian affecting the lung

Meridian affecting the kidney

Meridian affecting the heart

Meridian affecting the stomach

Meridian affecting the spleen

Acupuncture point

Acupuncture points for:

Alcohol abuse   Asthma

Headache   Nausea

Neck pain   Painful menstruation

Paralysis due to stroke   Tennis elbow

USN&WR—Basic data: Bruce Pomeranz, University of Toronto; acupuncturist Jing-Nuan Wu of Washington, D.C.; American Medical Association Encyclopedia of Medicine

ROD LITTLE, RICHARD GAGE, ROBERT

pathways that stimulate the body's own healing energy. Western

doctors think that the _____ trigger the nervous system

to release the body's natural _____. In this process,

the spinal cord sends signals to three areas of the body, the

_____, the _____ and the _____.

Acupuncture can be used to treat people with a variety of medical

problems, including _____, _____,

_____ and nausea. It can even be used to help relieve

_____, _____, _____ and

_____.

Based on the information in the diagram on the facing page and on your own ideas, check those items that you expect to find in an article on this topic and add two ideas of your own.

_____ treatment for different types of health problems

_____ descriptions of personal experiences with acupuncture

_____ doubts about acupuncture

_____ reports about research into acupuncture

_____ reports about conventional treatments for medical problems

_____

_____

Work with a partner to compare your answers. Return to these predictions after you have finished reading and verify your answers.

SURVEYING

Survey the reading. Read the introduction (paragraphs 1–6) and the first sentence of every paragraph after that. After surveying, complete the following:

1. Verify your preview predictions. If you think you were wrong, change them and add any new predictions you have.

2. Write three to five important ideas in the order that they appeared in the reading.

a. _____

b. _____

c. _____

d. _____

e. _____

Compare your ideas with those of a partner. Try to agree on the important ideas you think will be discussed in the article.

Acupuncture: Medicine's Latest Miracle

By Rick Weiss

1. Nancy Rosenstadt sailed through surgery, chemotherapy, and radiation after she was diagnosed with adrenal cancer in 1986. Only afterward, when her cancer was finally obliterated, did she start to go downhill. The treatment, it seems, made her muscles start to shrink and her nerves wither, and no one knew how to stop it.

2. "Nobody could understand it," says the 38-year-old computer programmer. "I tried every kind of doctor—chiropractors, neurologists. The pain was so intense I couldn't lift my body or walk without a cane."

3. Then three years ago, after being featured at a medical conference where doctors called her condition hopeless, Rosenstadt got referred to the National Institutes of Health Clinical Center, the nation's Last Chance Cafe for desperate medical cases. It is here, in the world's largest hospital devoted solely to experimental therapies, that terminally ill patients are granted access to unproved new treatments hot off laboratory benches: custom-designed radioactive antibodies, genetically engineered immune stimulants, human gene therapy.

4. And it is here, on this sprawling federal campus in Bethesda, Maryland, that Rosenstadt has, during the past three years, experienced a recovery she feels is nothing short of miraculous—not as a result of any high-tech drug but at the hands of acupuncturist Xiao-Ming Tian.

5. "He promised me, 'You'll give me this cane someday,'" she says, looking a little cross-eyed as she glances at the wagging needle Ming has jabbed between her eyes. "Well, last year I did give it to him."

6. Ming gave the cane back, she says—it was a ceremonial sort of thing. "But I can walk now. I can drive. I can exercise. It's amazing. You can't understand acupuncture until you try it."

7. Perhaps no other alternative therapy has received more attention in this country or gained acceptance more quickly than acupuncture. Most Americans had never even heard of it until 1971, when *New York Times* foreign correspondent James Reston wrote a startling first person account of the painkilling effects of acupuncture following his emergency appendectomy in China. Today the needling of America is in full swing. Last year alone, Americans made some 9 to 12 million visits to acupuncturists for ailments as diverse as arthritis, bladder infections, back pain, and morning sickness.

8. In a culture that is overwhelmingly shy of needles, what could account for such popularity?

9. Safety, for one thing. There is something to be said for a medical practice that's been around for 5,000 years, with billions of satisfied patients. If acupuncture were dangerous, even its stodgiest critics concede, somebody would have noticed by now.

10. Many people are also encouraged by doctors' growing willingness to refer patients for acupuncture—or to learn the ancient art themselves—despite its unconventional claims. Acupuncturists say that health is simply a matter of tweaking into balance a mysterious life force called *qi*

(pronounced chee), which is said to move through invisible meridians in the body. That's hardly a mainstream view, yet of the 9,000 practicing acupuncturists in this country, fully a third are M.D.s.

11. Most important, there's mounting evidence that acupuncture has something important to offer, especially when it comes to pain. In one big study, acupuncture offered short-term relief to 50 to 80 percent of patients with acute or chronic pain. And in the only controlled trial that followed patients for six months or more, nearly six out of ten patients with low back pain continued to show improvement, compared to a control group that showed no improvement. Other studies have shown that acupuncture may be useful in treating nausea, asthma, and a host of other common ills. . . .

12. Ming pulls aside a curtain and strides into the cubicle where Rosenstadt is resting. A former champion discus thrower, he's a big man with a wide, kind face and balding head. With his twinkling eyes, which look inexplicably wise, and the "M.D." embroidered after his name on his white coat, he appears an almost cartoonishly perfect embodiment of Eastern and Western medicine. In many ways, he is just that. Ming is as likely as the next M.D. to prescribe antibiotics to fight a raging infection. But having studied under China's greatest masters, it is acupuncture that he relies on most. He is the first and only acupuncturist employed by the federal government, a position created for him on the recommendation of Western medical colleagues who had referred some of their patients to him as a last resort and were impressed by his results.

13. "How are you doing?" Ming asks, leaning over Rosenstadt to check on the needles he popped into her skin a few minutes ago. In addition to the one just above the bridge of her nose, there is a needle stuck in the rim of her ear, one in each temple, and five running the length of her left leg.

14. Most are not inserted very deep—perhaps a quarter of an inch—and they do not hurt. Like most patients, Rosenstadt describes the sensation as a tingling or mild buzz, especially noticeable when Ming begins to twirl the needles clockwise and counterclockwise in her skin, a technique that is said to help the needles do their job of moving qi through the body.

15. There are nearly 400 acupuncture points along the body's 14 major meridians, or energy-carrying channels, Ming says, and each has a Chinese name that describes the kind of energy or organ it affects. But to know if he is in exactly the right spot, he must twirl the needle after inserting it and be sure that he gets a response from the patient—a report of feeling a deep heaviness or numbness in the area or, more commonly, a simple "yes."

16. "That is called the *ashi* point," Ming says. "*Ashi* is Chinese for 'Oh, yes,'" he explains. "Every point, when you do it right, is an ashi point."

17. Can a simple twist of a needle really put an ailing body on the path to recovery? Consider the evidence:

Pain Control

18. Bruce Pomeranz, a tall, thin, birdlike physiologist at the University of Toronto, had heard the early stories touting acupuncture as a powerful painkiller and didn't believe a word of it. He was certain it was a trick of the mind, that it worked only because people believed it would work. "I thought it must be placebo," he says. "So I said, 'Okay I'll prove it's placebo.'"

19. Working in his lab in the early 1970s, he and a colleague performed some animal experiments on their own. "We did it at the end of the day," he says, "after the real experiments were done." Taking aim with Chinese charts showing the locations of acupuncture points in animals, they needled some cats and used electrodes to measure the pain responses in individual nerve cells. "To my chagrin," he says, "it worked." Pain-transmitting nerves just didn't fire in the animals given acupuncture.

20. The finding remained an enigma until a few years later, when scientists discovered endorphins, the now famous opiates that are made in the brain in response to pain and that cause "runner's high." "I thought, Wow, now these results make sense," Pomeranz says. In a series of groundbreaking experiments that followed, he and others showed that acupuncture's pain-reducing effects are largely due to its ability to stimulate the release of endorphins. "That gave acupuncture some respectability," he says. Before long, experiments were being done on people, and with astonishing results.

21. In one of the best studies, published in 1987, Joseph Helms, a physician and acupuncturist in Berkeley, California, gave weekly acupuncture treatments to a group of women with a long history of painful menstrual cramps. After three months of treatment, ten out of 11 women reported at least 50 percent less pain, as measured by a package of subjective tests; only two of 11 untreated women, and one of ten women who received weekly counseling (included to see if the benefits of acupuncture were simply from regular contact with a doctor), improved as much. What's more, the acupuncture group ended up using 41 percent less painkilling medication, while the others saw no decrease in drug use. They also had fewer headaches, backaches, and complaints of water retention and breast tenderness.

22. More recent studies suggest that acupuncture is good for just about anything that hurts: tennis elbow, muscle strain, kidney stones. In a small pilot study at the University of Maryland last spring, researchers showed that in adults with osteoarthritis of the knee—a painful degeneration of the joint lining—twice-weekly acupuncture treatments reduced pain and increased mobility in eight out of 12 patients over a period of two months. The same researchers also recently showed that in dental patients undergoing molar extractions, acupuncture reduced the intensity of pain afterward and increased the amount of time that patients could go without painkilling drugs.

Addiction

23. For a nation of addicts—to cigarettes, to alcohol, to drugs—acupuncturists propose a simple antidote: a few needles in the ear, every day, for half an hour.

24. Acupuncture's habit-breaking benefits have been well documented in people hooked on heroin and crack cocaine through a program called Drug Court, in which felony drug offenders are given the chance to enter an intensive program of counseling and daily acupuncture treatments as an alternative to prison. Acupuncture stimulation of four points on the ear has a powerful calming effect, counselors and addicts say. It not only reduces the craving for a fix—perhaps by substituting the brain's own endorphins for the street-drug equivalent—but it also helps addicts relax enough to think clearly about their predicament and to resolve to change their lives.

25. The program has its roots in work by Michael Smith, a psychiatrist and acupuncturist who directs the substance abuse division of Lincoln Hospital in the rough-and-tumble South Bronx, where some 30,000 addicts have been treated with the help of acupuncture in the past 20 years.

26. All told, about half of Drug Court addicts make it through the year-long program, a graduation rate far higher than anything seen in standard residential treatment programs. And an analysis in Miami recently found that more than three quarters of the program's graduates went at least two years without another arrest, compared to the 15 to 20 percent seen with standard drug diversion programs.

27. The needle has had success against other addictions, as well. In a two-month study published in 1989, more than half the alcoholics who got acupuncture stayed sober, compared to 3 percent of those who received "sham" acupuncture treatments, in which needles were inserted in phony acupuncture points. And for a testimonial on acupuncture as an aid to quitting cigarettes, just ask the judge who administers the Drug Court program in Miami's Dade County. He smoked several packs a day for 35 years until five years ago, when he served the same sentence on himself that he had just begun serving on convicted felons: daily appointments with an acupuncturist. After ten days, he kicked the habit for good.

Asthma

28. Among the less well documented but tantalizing reports are those suggesting acupuncture can help ease the shortness of breath that comes with asthma and other respiratory problems. The best study to date, led by Kim A. Jobst at Oxford University, showed improvements as measured by "quality of life" scores and breathlessness measures. Other studies have turned up mixed results. Nine showed reduced dependence on medicine, Jobst says, while three showed no benefit and three concluded that people getting acupuncture actually did worse.

29. If acupuncture does help, the explanation could lie in its apparent ability to work directly on nerves to reduce the spasmodic tendency in asthmatic lungs, keeping them from contracting at the least little irritant in the air. Alternately, it may open narrowed blood vessels in the lungs. Or it may simply prompt patients to relax and breathe more fully. Whatever the mechanism, with asthma incidence and death rates skyrocketing in recent years—and growing evidence that long-term use of standard asthma drugs may be exacerbating rather than easing peoples' symptoms— it would be foolish, Jobst says, to ignore acupuncture's potential.

Other Uses

30. There are scores of other ailments for which there is at least anecdotal evidence that acupuncture is useful, although without proper studies it is impossible for now to say for sure. Skin conditions unresponsive to prescription medications have been reported to clear up within days. Facial paralysis thought to be due to irreparable nerve damage has disappeared after just three or four treatments. Sleeplessness, restlessness, vision and hearing problems, and impotence all have yielded in one report or another to the power of the needle. Some research even suggests that stimulation of a point near the small toe may help turn a breech-position fetus around in the womb before delivery.

31. To critics of acupuncture, this bounty of riches is precisely what constitutes grounds for suspicion: How could one kind of treatment, one simple needle, treat such a wide variety of ailments?

32. "We look at acupuncture and we've got to say, 'Wait a minute. Can one device do all those things?'" says David Lytle, an FDA research biophysicist. "There's a credibility thing that has to be dealt with."

33. Others are equally skeptical. Many mainstream doctors still shake their heads— some even snicker—when asked about acupuncture. After all, there is no objective evidence that qi exists, and there is nothing resembling Chinese meridians in

Western physiology or anatomy books. "No way," they say. "It's just a needle. How in the world *could* it work?"

34. In fact, endorphins could account for quite a lot. These compounds are powerful painkillers and mood enhancers. And they are typically served up by the brain along with a splash of cortisol, an anti-inflammatory hormone that can reduce many kinds of muscle and joint pain, including arthritis.

35. There is also evidence, Pomeranz and others note, that stimulation of sensory nerves that run from the skin to the spinal cord can trigger a burst of activity in so-called sympathetic nerves, which link the spinal cord to various organs. Among the benefits: increased blood flow to those distant organs.

36. Ming just smiles. "It's too complicated to understand," he says. Besides, he points out, it's not as if Western medicine makes so much more sense: Nobody understands how anesthesia works, he says, but nobody says we should stop using it.

Finding a Good Acupuncturist

Your knee shudders with a jolt of electricity every time you go down stairs, or your shoulder is tied up in knots again, and you're thinking about seeing an acupuncturist. Before you do, let your doctor know what you're up to. Most physicians will want to first rule out conditions that can't be helped by the needle, such as acute infections, cancer, and heart disease. After that, here are a few things to keep in mind when choosing an acupuncturist:

Check credentials. A state license doesn't guarantee competency, but it helps, a particularly if you live in one of the 25 states that set rigorous training standards (Alaska, California, Colorado, Florida, Hawaii, Iowa, Louisiana, Maine, Maryland, Massachusetts, Montana, Nevada, New Jersey, New Mexico, New York, North Carolina, Oregon, Pennsylvania, Rhode Island, Texas, Utah, Vermont, Virginia, Washington, Wisconsin, as well as the District of Columbia). In states that don't require a license, choose an acupuncturist certified by the National Commission for the Certification of Acupuncturists. Its 3,100 members have a minimum two years of training at an accredited acupuncture school—or have worked as an apprentice acupuncturist for at least four years—and have passed both a written and practical exam. (For details about the licensing laws in your state or to find out whether a particular acupuncturist is certified, call the NCCA at 202/232-1404.)

Acupuncture licensing requirements for doctors are generally more lenient than for non-M.D.s. For any acupuncture treatments beyond the most rudimentary, it's best to choose a physician who is a member of the American Academy of Medical Acupuncture; it requires a minimum 200 hours of training for membership. (Call the AAMA at 800/521-2262 to find out if your physician is a member.)

Insist on disposable needles. (Most acupuncturists now use them.) Although proper sterilization should kill bacteria and the viruses that cause hepatitis or AIDS, reusable needles always carry a small risk of infection.

Ask about treatment styles. Acupuncture encompasses several distinctive styles. Japanese acupuncture, for example, calls for fewer and finer needles inserted at shallower depths, requiring more precision in needle placement. There's no evidence that one particular style is more effective than another, but you should know what you're getting into.

Check out the cost. A first visit to a non-physician acupuncturist can cost as little as $40 or as much as $100. Follow-up visits usually range from $30 to $70. Physician acupuncturists generally charge a little more. Only a handful of insurance companies cover acupuncture for now, so be sure to check your policy ahead of time.

Be realistic. Decide in advance what your goals are and disclose them with your acupuncturist. If you're not happy with your progress after a few weeks, think about changing acupuncturists or check back with your doctor for advice about other options.

–Health

CHUNKING: GETTING THE MAIN IDEAS

■ READING TIP:
Chunking paragraphs in a reading involves deciding which sections of a reading develop a main idea that links the information. This analysis allows you to identify relationships among ideas.

Write the main idea for each of the following groups of paragraphs. Express those ideas in words or phrases of your own. (The first one has been done as an example.)

Paragraph Groups	Main Ideas
1. 7–11	*some reasons for the popularity of acupuncture*
2. 12–16	
3. 17–22	
4. 23–27	
5. 28–30	
6. 31–35	

Compare your ideas with those of a partner. Your wording may be different but your ideas should be the same.

ANALYZING CHUNKS OF TEXT: IDEA TREES

Each major chunk contains a number of related subordinate ideas. Identify the paragraphs that contain the following subordinate ideas.

1. Reasons for the popularity of acupuncture (paragraphs 7–11)

   _____ Some results of treatment with acupuncture

   _____ Introduction of acupuncture to North America

   _____ Popularity of acupuncture

   _____ Safety of acupuncture

2. Check the paragraphs you chose with a partner.

3. Choose another section and identify the subordinate ideas that are contained within it. Write your own idea tree for this section.

4. Compare your idea trees with a partner. Your wording may be different but the paragraphs you chose should be the same.

LOOKING BACK: THESIS STATEMENT

A. The thesis statement is one or two sentences that express the important ideas of the article as a whole. The thesis can usually be found at the end of the introduction, or it may be unstated. Reread the first six paragraphs of the selection and decide whether the thesis statement is stated or unstated.

B. Write the thesis of the article in your own words. Be sure to include all of the important ideas in your thesis (a few sentences).

_____

_____

_____

_____

Compare your thesis with that of a partner and then with the class as a whole.

Understanding the Details in Reports on Medical Treatments

■ *READING TIP: A reader can expect to find certain information in an article that reports the results of new treatments for medical problems. Formulating expectations is an important critical reading skill and helps the reader to locate key information more easily.*

A. Scan the reading, highlight information, and note in the margin where details on each of the following numbered topics are presented.

1. The treatment program offered to drug offenders as an alternative to prison
2. The effect of acupuncture on drug addicts
3. The use of acupuncture in clinics in the South Bronx
4. The success rate for people who take the Drug Court program
5. The long-term success rate for graduates of this program
6. The effect of using acupuncture on alcohol addiction
7. The use of acupuncture for treating people who want to quit smoking
8. The results of a study at Oxford University on the use of acupuncture for treating people with breathing problems
9. The explanation of how acupuncture helps people with asthma
10. Why studying the effectiveness of acupuncture on asthma patients is important

Use your highlighted information to talk about the important details of this information with a partner.

After Reading

APPLYING THE INFORMATION

A. *Interviewing/Becoming an Expert:* Work with a partner. Using the information from the chapter readings, take turns playing the role of a reporter and the role of an expert in two scenarios, a drug clinic and an asthma clinic.

Some sample questions might be:

Could you describe the kinds of problems people who come here have?

Could you describe the kinds of treatments you use?

In the Drug Clinic
Student A: A reporter interviewing the head of a drug clinic on the use of acupuncture
Student B: The head of the drug clinic being interviewed about the treatment patients receive.

In the Asthma Clinic
Student A: The head of a clinic treating patients for asthma
Student B: A reporter interviewing the head of a hospital clinic about the treatment patients receive for asthma, nausea, or other pain problems

To carry out this activity, follow these steps:

1. Decide which role you will take as an expert and which topic you will write questions to use for your role as an interviewer.

   As a reporter
   - Brainstorm a list of five questions to ask an expert in your role as interviewer.
   - Discuss your ideas with others who prepared questions for the same topic in a small group.
   - Try to agree on a common list of five to seven questions.
   - Be prepared to use your questions to interview your expert.

   As an expert
   - Brainstorm a list of facts on your topic from the reading.
   - Discuss your facts with others who prepared facts for the same topic in a small group.
   - Add as much information as you can to your list of facts.
   - Be prepared to be interviewed on your topic.

2. Work with a person who prepared a *different* expert topic and who has questions for *your* topic.

3. Take turns interviewing and giving expert information with your partner.

B. *Giving Your Opinion—Discussion Questions:* **Based on what you have read and talked about so far, discuss your ideas with a partner or in a small group.**

1. Would you ever try an alternative treatment like acupuncture? Why or why not?

2. What advice would you give someone who was thinking of using acupuncture?

3. Will alternative treatments become more popular in the future? Why or why not?

Vocabulary Building

VOCABULARY IN CONTEXT

Looking for Definitions in the Body of a Text

In any new subject that you read about, you will find vocabulary that is particular to that topic. When writers use special terminology, they usually provide a definition or explanation in the same sentence or the one that follows.

In the following example the special terminology is in boldface and the information to explain it is underlined:

*Acupuncturists say that health is simply a matter of tweaking into balance <u>a mysterious life force</u> called **qi**, which is said to <u>move through meridians in the body</u>.*

A. Underline the information that explains or defines the words or phrases in boldface.

1. There are nearly 400 acupuncture points along the body's 14 major **meridians**, or energy-carrying channels, and each has a Chinese name that describes the kind of energy or organ it affects.

2. He was certain that it was a trick of the mind, that it worked only because people believed it would work. "I thought it must be a **placebo**," he said.

3. Scientists discovered **endorphins**, the now famous opiates that are made in the brain in response to pain and that cause "runner's high."

4. Researchers showed that in adults with **osteoarthritis** of the knee—a painful degeneration of the joint lining—twice-weekly acupuncture treatments reduced pain and increased mobility.

5. Benefits have been well documented in people hooked on heroin and crack cocaine through a program called **Drug Court**, in which felony drug offenders are given the chance to enter an intensive program of counseling and daily acupuncture treatments as an alternative to prison.

Compare your answers with those of a partner. Circle any use of punctuation such as commas, dashes, or semicolons that helped you to find the definitions.

B. In your own words, write a synonym or an explanation for each of the following words or phrases in this article. Refer to the reading to help you form your answer.

1. ailments   _____

2. andidote   _____

3. testimonial   _____

4. anecdotal evidence _____

5. pilot study   _____

Check your answers with a partner and with your teacher.

Recognizing Descriptive Language

Writers often use descriptive language that helps the reader understand an idea as it conveys some feeling or impression about that idea. This makes the writing more interesting to the reader. For example in paragraph 25 the writer states "The program *has its roots* in work by Michael Smith." This wording conveys the same meaning as "This program *began with* work by Michael Smith," but has the feeling of a living being.

In the following sentences, suggest a more ordinary wording that has the same meaning for the descriptive language in boldface. Use a dictionary *only* as a last resort.

1. And here it is on the **sprawling** federal campus in Bethesda, Maryland, that Rosenstadt has experienced a recovery.

   _____

2. James Reston wrote a **startling** first-person account of the pain-killing effects of acupuncture.

   _____

3. In a series of **groundbreaking experiments** that followed, he showed that the acupuncture's pain-reducing effects are largely due to its ability to stimulate the release of endorphins.

   _____

4. The finding remained **an enigma** until a few years later.

   _____

5. He smoked several packs a day until five years ago, when he **served the same sentence on himself** that he had just begun serving on convicted felons.

   _____

Check your answer with a partner and with your teacher.

Expanding Your Language

SPEAKING

Discussion: Would you believe?

Look at the following statistics and think about the following questions.

1. What information about healing can help explain these statistics?
2. What questions should people ask before using alternatives? Should alternatives ever be used to replace conventional treatments?
3. After reading about alternatives, would you use any of these treatments? If so, which? To what extent?

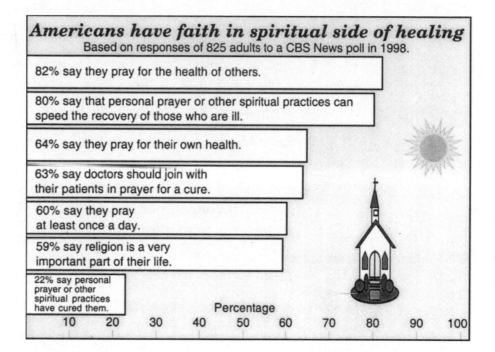

Americans have faith in spiritual side of healing
Based on responses of 825 adults to a CBS News poll in 1998.

82% say they pray for the health of others.

80% say that personal prayer or other spiritual practices can speed the recovery of those who are ill.

64% say they pray for their own health.

63% say doctors should join with their patients in prayer for a cure.

60% say they pray at least once a day.

59% say religion is a very important part of their life.

22% say personal prayer or other spiritual practices have cured them.

Percentage

10   20   30   40   50   60   70   80   90   100

WRITING

Topic Writing: **Based on the information in the chapter readings and discussions, write about the topic of acupuncture and include information about what it is, how it works, what medical problems it can be used to treat, and what your opinion of using this type of treatment is. To do this, follow these steps.**

1. Outline the information about each main idea.

   Example:

   A. What is acupuncture?
      A description
      Where is it from?
      When did it first become known in North America?

   B. How does it work?
      Chinese explanation
      Western explanation

Who practices acupuncture?
What questions do patients and doctors have?

C. Medical problems treated with acupuncture
Addiction
Asthma
Different types of pain

D. Reaction to acupuncture

2. Make an outline for each paragraph that explains a main idea.
3. Use your outline to write a first draft of the essay.
4. Revise the first draft of your paragraphs.
5. Submit the work to your teacher.

CHAPTER 4

Total Fitness: Combining Diet and Exercise

Chapter Openers

DISCUSSION QUESTIONS: KEEPING FIT

Think about these questions. Discuss your ideas with a partner or in a small group.

1. What is your idea of fitness? What people do you think are models of fitness?
2. Why is it important to keep fit?
3. What kind of physical activities can we do to stay fit?
4. What kinds of foods are part of a healthy diet?
5. Is there an age when it is more important to be fit?
6. How easy or difficult is it to stay fit?
7. What do you do to keep fit? What motivates you to stay active?

Exploring and Understanding Reading

PREDICTING: AGREE/DISAGREE

Write *A* if you agree or *D* if you disagree with the statement.

_____ 1. Walking can be one of the most effective forms of exercise.

_____ 2. Eliminating all fat from our diet is a good way to keep fit.

_____ 3. People who aren't used to exercising have to exercise longer and harder at first.

_____ 4. Eating good-tasting food is a good way to reduce weight.

_____ 5. Exercising well requires special training and equipment.

_____ 6. You can eat cake and french fries without gaining weight, if you eat them only in moderation.

_____ 7. It's easy to get motivated to diet and eat right regularly.

Work with a partner or in a small group. You don't have to agree, but explain your ideas as completely as possible.

PAIRED READINGS

The two articles that follow present different avenues to fitness; one focuses on exercise, the other on diet. Choose one of the articles and find out what the authors suggest.

Reading 1: *Walking Your Way to Health*

PREVIEWING

Look at the visuals and read the titles and subtitles as well as any information in bold. What do you think the article is about? Write your ideas in note form.

1. _____

2. _____

3. _____

■ READING TIP:
Previewing is a useful skill to use with newspaper articles. To preview, look at the visuals (photos or diagrams) and read the titles and subtitles. The information you get will give you an idea of what information the article may contain.

SKIMMING

■ READING TIP:
Remember that skimming is reading quickly (5–7 minutes) to get a general idea of what an article is about.

Quickly skim the article and answer the following questions.

1. Why are people counting the number of steps they take in a day?

   _____

2. What would fitness experts like to see people do?

   _____

3. What do most people need to do in addition to their daily routine to keep fit?

   _____

4. How can people lose weight by walking?

   _____

USA TODAY

Journey to better fitness starts with 10,000 steps

By Nanci Hellmich

Mark Fenton, editor at large of *Walking Magazine*, tries to walk at least 10,000 steps during the course of his day, often with his two young children.

Jeffrey Koplan, director of the Centers for Disease Control and Prevention, takes about 12,000 to 13,000 steps on the days he walks for exercise. On other days, he takes 6,000 to 7,000 steps, plus two hours of structured exercise—swimming, rowing or bicycling.

Abby King, an exercise researcher at the Stanford School of Medicine in northern California, usually gets in 10,000 steps, but she has to work at it by holding walking meetings with colleagues and scheduling other forms of activity.

These experts are tracking the number of steps they take in a day partly out of curiosity, partly for scientific reasons.

Exercise scientists across the country, including researchers at Stanford and the Cooper Institute for Aerobics Research in

But scientists believe that people who walk that much are probably meeting the minimum public health guideline of accumulating 30 minutes of moderate activity most days of the week, says Michelle Edwards, a health educator at the Cooper Institute.

Only about 22% of people are active enough to get the general health benefits, including a decreased risk of heart disease, diabetes and some types of cancer.

Walking is the most popular form of physical activity, experts say. As many as 80 million people are recreational or casual walkers, including those who stroll occasionally. Of those about 15 million are serious fitness walkers, who walk for fitness at least two days a week, Fenton says.

Experts would like to see people become more active, but they are struggling for ways to motivate them.

A new hook

Most people have heard the walking message, says cardiologist James Rippe, considered the father of the walking movement.

"If you say to someone, 'Walking is good for you. Go out and walk 2 to 4 miles a day' they'd say, 'Duh.' Everyone knows that. Everyone who doesn't exercise knows they should. And everyone who smokes knows they shouldn't," Rippe says.

But people need motivation, and what these pedometers do is give walking some "pizazz," says Rippe, author of the 1989 book *Complete Book of Fitness Walking*.

King says that counting steps seems to be one concrete way to implement the government recommendation of accumulating 30

Dallas, are having exercise study participants wear sophisticated pedometers on their waistbands to count the number of steps and miles they walk. The pedometers also are used in research in Japan.

The researchers' goal is to get more people to walk at least 10,000 steps a day, which is equivalent to about 5 miles.

A mile walking can be anywhere from about 1,800 to 2,200 steps, depending on stride length and pace, both of which vary widely.

King says there's nothing magical about the 10,000-step goal. Researchers are investigating the number of steps people should take for fitness.

Walk this way

Walking is a movement that comes naturally to most people, and there is no reason to make it overly complex, experts say. However, here are some simple ways to get more out of your walking workout.

Keep good posture

Walk with your head up and your eyes forward. Looking down leads to neck and shoulder tension. Keep your stomach muscles gently contracted. This keeps the lower back flat, not arched, which can lead to back and hamstring tightness.

Bend your arms

Don't walk with straight arms. To help you walk faster and add a bit of an upper body workout, bend your arms at the elbows, at a right angle. Have your hands trace an arc from waistband to chest height. It's not an exaggerated arm swing.

Focus on comfortable steps

Let your foot roll smoothly from heel to toe, pushing off strongly with the toes. Don't reach or lunge with your foot. Imagine placing your foot on the ground beneath you, not out in front. This helps with quicker steps and keeps you from overstriding.

Take quick steps

The faster your steps, the faster your walking speed and the better your workout.

Source: Mark Fenton, editor at large of *Walking Magazine*

minutes of moderate activity most days of the week, which gives people some of the benefits of physical activity.

Too many people misinterpreted the government guideline to mean they could shuffle around the house doing light domestic activities or light gardening, King says. "That's not going to be enough."

Practically speaking, moderate-intensity exercise means that your heart rate and breathing will be faster than during lighter activities, King says.

One simple rule of thumb for walking briskly, Rippe says, is to follow Harry Truman's brisk walking style, which he described as "walking as though I have someplace to go."

But plenty of people move through the day without doing that. Many people who work in offices walk 3,000 to 5,000 steps a day, says Fenton, a former member of the U.S. national racewalking team.

At the end of the day, this group would have to walk another 5,000 to 7,000 steps, or roughly 2 to 3 miles, to reach the 10,000-step goal. In other words, in addition to their daily activity, most people need to get out and do at least a 30-minute brisk walk.

Pedometers

To count steps, a number of pedometers are on the market, some more sophisticated than others.

Edwards says the Cooper Institute has used Digi-Walkers in two studies and is using them in a third study. Exercisers are motivated by them, she says.

"We've had participants who've lost their Digi-Walker, and they're frantic because they want another," she says.

Fenton says that when he started wearing a pedometer and didn't accumulate 10,000 steps by the end of the day, he was ticked off at himself and went out and walked until he had.

He says that wearing it motivates him to take the stairs instead of the elevator, do errands on foot and walk to a farther subway stop.

Setting goals

But how hard is it to walk 10,000 steps a day, and is it really enough?

For some people, it's challenging, King says. Sedentary people in studies walk 3,000 to 4,000 steps in a day, she says.

Scientists initially work them up to 5,000 and 6,000 steps.

"If they jump directly to 10,000 steps a day, they are going to have injuries, strains and muscle soreness from overuse," King says.

The 10,000-step goal is probably enough to get many of the health benefits of walking, Fenton says. Those who want to lose weight, get greater health gains or become more cardiovascularly fit probably need to walk more at a higher intensity.

In a Japanese research project in which subjects were trying to lose weight, they were encouraged to increase their steps to 12,000 to 15,000 a day, Fenton says. He offers these guidelines for walkers:

• An out-of-shape person who is just getting into a walking program should build up to walking 30 minutes a day at 3 to 4 mph. That total would provide the health benefit of physical activity.

• A person who wants to lose weight should walk at 3.5 to 4.5 mph, Fenton says.

"The faster you walk, the more calories you burn per minute. Walk every day for a minimum of 30 minutes. Walk at least 45 to 60 minutes three or four days a week."

• Those who want cardiovascular fitness should aim for 4 to 5 mph or faster if their fitness improves enough. Their goal should be two or three heavy-breathing, sweat-producing, 20-to-40-minute walks a week.

The benefit of cardiovascular fitness is a greatly reduced risk of chronic disease and early death, as well as the increased ability to chase the dog around the yard or play some backyard volleyball and not be wiped out, Fenton says.

SCANNING FOR SPECIFIC INFORMATION

Reexamine the reading to find the answers to these questions. Write your answers in note form.

1. What are pedometers and what are two reasons they are important for walkers to use?

   _____

2. What is the important health reason that scientists want people to walk 10,000 steps?

   _____

3. What is the United States government recommendation for daily physical activity?

   _____

4. What does "moderate-intensity exercise" mean?

   _____

5. What recommendation does Abby King make to sedentary people who are beginning to exercise?

   _____

6. What important guidelines does Mark Fenton offer people who

   a. are out of shape? _____

   b. want to lose weight? _____

   c. want cardiovascular fitness? _____

Compare your answers with those of your partner. Try to agree on the same answer. Look back to the reading if you disagree.

RECAPPING THE INFORMATION: HIGHLIGHTING

■ READING TIP:
Highlighting is a useful strategy for finding and remembering important facts and ideas you read. To highlight, use a colored highlighting pen to mark information. Be careful to mark only the words and phrases that you want to stand out—not the whole sentence.

A. Highlight the facts you read about walking that relate to these ideas:

1. The goal of researchers' work
2. The 10,000 step program, its purposes and benefits
3. The role of the pedometer and how it works
4. How the 10,000 step program works for different types of people

B. Working with a partner who read the *same article*, compare what you highlighted. Discuss whether you highlighted too much or too little. Add any highlighting you need to.

C. Using only what you highlighted, take turns telling each other the important information in the article. Make sure you explain the information as clearly and completely as you can, using your own words when you need to.

REACTING TO THE INFORMATION: DISCUSSION QUESTIONS

Discuss these questions with a partner. Explain your ideas as completely as possible.

1. According to the article, only 22 percent of people are active enough to get health benefits. Why do you think so few people are active?
2. Do you agree that the pedometer is a good motivation technique? Why or why not?
3. Would you incorporate this type of walking into your daily routine? Why or why not?

Reading 2: Eating Your Way to Health

PREVIEWING

■ *READING TIP:*
Previewing is a useful skill to use with newspaper articles. To preview, look at the visuals (photos or diagrams) and read the titles and subtitles. The information you get will give you an idea of what information the article may contain.

Look at the visuals and read the titles and subtitles as well as any information in bold. What do you think the article is about? Write your ideas in note form.

1. _____

2. _____

3. _____

SKIMMING

■ *READING TIP:*
Remember that skimming is reading quickly (5–7 minutes) to get a general idea of what an article is about.

Quickly skim the article and answer the following questions.

1. What is the most important reason people choose to eat healthy food?

   _____

2. What kind of foods do most Americans choose to eat when they eat out?

   _____

3. What are three reasons why people resist eating a healthier diet?

   _____

4. What is one way to change to a healthier diet?

   _____

NEW YORK TIMES

Choosing Right to Make Healthiest and Tastiest One and the Same

By Jane E. Brody

I was at a holiday party last week. As you might guess, there were platters of cookies, cakes and candies to tempt the weak of will. But the three dishes that disappeared the fastest were a lentil soup, a salad of lentils, rice and fresh vegetables and a hot-smoked salmon fillet. Were these downed first because the nutrition police were watching,

because the partygoers were a particularly health-conscious bunch, or because these dishes were simply delicious?

Actually, all three reasons prevailed. I was there, and people assume that I watch what everyone eats. My fellow celebrants were educated, reasonably affluent and aware of the connections between food and health. But to me the most salient explanation was

that the foods that happened to be healthiest were also the best tasting.

Indeed, according to a recently published survey of food choices among nearly 3,000 American adults, taste (surprise, surprise) emerged as the overriding criterion for food choices, regardless of age, income or ethnic background. People simply like to eat what tastes good to them.

Unfortunately, what tastes good *to* most Americans is not exactly good *for* them. What makes food taste good to most people? Fat and sugar. And, predictably, as Americans choose pleasure over nutrition, we are eating more of both. True, the percentage of calories from fats has declined, but because we are eating about 300 calories a day more than we used to, we are actually consuming as much fat as before, primarily in fast foods, restaurant meals and snacks.

Currently, about 60 percent of Americans eat at least one restaurant-prepared meal every day, and most of those meals are made without so much as a nod toward good nutrition. These high-fat, low-fiber meals account for half of our caloric intake. And while the craze for fat-free and low-fat foods has not yet abated, the most popular choices are not fruits, vegetables and whole grains (which are naturally low in fat) but sweet baked goods and frozen desserts, which are loaded with sugar to enhance the flavor lost when fat was reduced.

Only about 15 percent of Americans now consume the recommended minimum of five servings a day of fruits and vegetables, the foods most closely linked to leanness and health. In recent years, there has been no change in consumption of vegetables, particularly the most protective dark green and deep yellow ones.

To no one's surprise, children are not doing any better than adults. With 60 percent of moms working and time pressures on families ever more acute, ready-made and fast-food meals have become the norm in many households with young children. American children are fatter today than ever before, and one in five has a cholesterol level that is setting her or him up for future heart disease. Food specialists at Edelman Public Relations Worldwide have predicted, "In the next 10 years, there will be consumers who have never cooked a meal from basic ingredients, and many of them will have been the children of today."

Obstacles to Change

Now, as the day of grandiose resolutions approaches, the time is ideal for all Americans to [start] making gradual changes toward a healthier diet. It is important to remember that although medical advances are keeping us alive longer than ever before, the goal is not living long per se but living a quality life in one's later years.

Consumer surveys reveal that resistance to adopting a healthier diet can be attributed to a combination of time pressures and false beliefs. Nearly three-quarters of American adults categorize foods as either "good" or "bad," and more than a third think that eating healthier means giving up their favorite foods, i.e., the "bad" foods. Yet, the message nutrition specialists advocate is moderation, not elimination. While some food fanatics may label cake, candy, ice cream, steak, fries or even pizza as poison, most well-schooled and realistic experts say there is room for all of these, in reasonable amounts now and then, in almost everyone's diet.

"Reasonable amounts" is another problem. Anne Wolf, a registered dietitian at the University of Virginia Health Science Center, points out that "our portion sizes have totally changed."

"The original Coke bottle was a six- or eight-ounce bottle," she added. "Then it grew to the 12 ounce can, then the 20-ounce bottle, and then the Big Gulp. And now we have the Double Big Gulp, which has 10 times the calories of a Coke 50 years ago," she said. "Or consider McDonald's. Today, consumers are into value meals, so you not only get your hamburger—which is bigger—but you get more french fries and a bigger soda."

Ms. Wolf laments, "We've internalized these larger portion sizes and, frankly, it's very hard to downsize."

Other obstacles to dietary change include the mistaken belief that eating better is important only for those with serious health risks, resistance to change, and confusion about conflicting information that can emerge from studies on nutrition and health. Is margarine O.K or not? Is a high-carbohydrate diet the right choice, or does it lead to weight gain? Does alcohol protect from heart disease but cause breast cancer? Is olive oil healthy or just another source of fat? A quarter of adults say there are so many conflicting studies they do not know what is good for them, so they have just tossed up their hands and opted to make no changes at all in their eating habits.

Making Painless Changes

Although children learn to like best what they grow up eating, it is also true that peo-ple's tastes can change. After all, few adults of today grew up eating the packaged, fast-food and take-out meals they now consume. But since economic realities combined with on-the-go life styles make it highly unlikely many people will return to cooking most meals from scratch, what are the options?

For one, fresh fruits require no preparation and are ideal snacks and desserts for young and old. Many supermarkets have salad bars or produce sections with cut-up vegetables ready for steaming or stir-frying or use in salads. Or, though not as crunchy or tasty, frozen vegetables (without creamy sauces) are as nutritious as fresh ones.

Fiber-rich whole-grain cereals and breads take no more time to buy or prepare than pasty white ones. Fish fillets and chicken and turkey breasts without skin cook quickly and require only a little seasoning to be moist and delicious. Canned beans are a nutritious, instant addition to salads, soups and pasta sauces. Tuna and sardines packed in water, canned salmon, sliced turkey breast and boiled ham make great sandwiches or salad additions.

My favorite meal plan is to cook a few double recipes on the weekend that can be heated in the microwave for instant meals all week long. To overcome the resistance to change (your own or your family's), it is wise to avoid revolutionary alterations. If you change just one meal a week, or one meal every two weeks, [in a year] your taste buds will have adapted to a whole new and more nutritious diet, achieved painlessly and without the likelihood of relapse into old unhealthy habits.

SCANNING FOR SPECIFIC INFORMATION

Reexamine the reading to find the answers to these questions. Write your answers in note form.

1. What reason does the author say is the most important explanation why people ate the healthiest food at the party she attended?

   _____

2. What types of foods do people most enjoy? Why is that a problem?

   _____

3. What kinds of foods do people eat when they go out for a meal?

   _____

4. What kinds of eating habits do children have? What has happened as a result?

   _____

   _____

5. What are two reasons why people resist adopting a healthier diet?

   a. _____

   b. _____

6. What are three problems that nutrition specialists say people have when it comes to healthier eating?

   a. _____

   b. _____

   c. _____

7. What are three options for people who want to change to a healthier diet?

   a. _____

   b. _____

   c. _____

Compare your answers with those of your partner. Try to agree on the same answer. Look back to the reading if you disagree.

RECAPPING THE INFORMATION: HIGHLIGHTING

A. Highlight the facts you read about choosing a healthy diet that relate to these ideas:

1. The author's observations about why people choose to eat certain food
2. The kinds of foods and eating habits that are not healthy
3. The problems that children face
4. The reasons why it is difficult for people to have healthy eating habits
5. Changes that can make a difference to people's diets

B. Working with a partner who read the *same article*, compare what you highlighted. Discuss whether you highlighted too much or too little. Add any highlighting you need to.

C. Using only what you highlighted, take turns telling each other the important information in the article. Make sure you explain the information as clearly and completely as you can, using your own words when you need to.

REACTING TO THE INFORMATION: DISCUSSION QUESTIONS

Discuss these questions with a partner. Explain your ideas as completely as possible.

1. What are some of your favorite foods? Why do you like them?
2. If you are eating at a restaurant and are served a lot of food at the meal, what do you feel you should do?
3. If you wanted to change your diet, how difficult or easy would it be?

After Reading

RETELLING THE INFORMATION

Work with a partner who read a *different article*.

- Together, use what you highlighted and take turns explaining the information you read. Explain the ideas clearly in your own words.

- Encourage your partner to ask questions or write some of the important facts you explain.

- After you have both explained your information, discuss the questions in "Reacting to the Information."

COMPARING THE INFORMATION

Work with a partner who read a different article.

A. Use the information from both articles to complete the chart:

	Exercise	*Diet*
What to do		
Reasons to follow these suggestions		
People's usual diet and exercise habits		
Ways to become more motivated		

B. Discuss the following questions with your partner. Explain your ideas as completely as possible.

1. What are the benefits of following the advice in these articles?
2. What do you think most motivates people to become fit and maintain fitness?
3. Do you think it is difficult for people to follow the advice given in these articles? Why or why not?

Vocabulary Building

VOCABULARY IN CONTEXT: INFERRING MEANING

A. Choose the statement that best expresses what the writer meant by each of the following sentences.

1. "Everyone who doesn't exercise knows they should. And everyone who smokes knows they shouldn't."
   a. People don't know whether they should exercise and smoke or not.
   b. People have a hard time following good advice.
   c. People aren't sure what advice to follow.

2. Using a pedometer gives walking "some pizazz."
   a. People will use a pedometer on a walk because it makes it easier to count the steps.
   b. People will use a pedometer on a walk because it makes the walk easier to do.
   c. People will use a pedometer on a walk because it is trendy and more motivating.

3. I'm "walking as though I have someplace to go."
   a. I'm deliberately walking quickly.
   b. I have to hurry to get to where I'm going.
   c. I don't have anywhere to go, so I'll take a nice leisurely walk.

4. "One in five [children] has a cholesterol level that is setting her or him up for future heart disease."
   a. Bad childhood eating habits increase the chances of diseases in adulthood.
   b. Bad childhood eating habits decrease the chances of diseases in adulthood.
   c. Bad childhood eating habits have no effect on the chances of diseases in adulthood.

5. "We've internalized these larger portion sizes and, frankly, it's very hard to downsize."
   a. Once you've accepted larger portion sizes, it's hard to refuse them.
   b. Once you've gotten used to larger portion sizes, it's hard to reduce consuming that amount.
   c. Once you've reduced the amount you take, it's easier to get used to larger portion sizes.

B. Insert the following words back into the sentences where they fit best.

only   predictably   simply   unfortunately   yet

1. People _____ like to eat what tastes good to them.

2. _____ what tastes good to most Americans is not exactly good for them.

3. _____ about 15 percent of Americans now consume the recommended minimum of five servings a day of fruits and vegetables.

4. _____ the message nutrition specialists advocate is moderation, not elimination.

5. And, _____ as Americans choose pleasure over nutrition, we are eating more of both sugar and fat.

Check your answers with a partner or with your teacher.

WORD FORMS: NOUNS, ADJECTIVES AND ADVERBS

A. Complete the following sentences with the correct form of the word.

B. Mark the correct part of speech for each by writing *N* for noun, *ADJ* for adjective, *V* for verb and *ADV* for adverb above each word.

1. walk   walking   walkers

   Most people have heard the _____ message. Fifteen

   million Americans are serious _____. But if you say,

   _____ is good for you. Go out and _____
   2 to 4 miles a day, they'd say "Duh." Everyone knows that.

2. research   researchers

   The pedometers are used in _____ in Japan. The

   _____ goal is to get more people to walk. In a

   Japanese _____ project, people were encouraged to
   increase the number of steps done each day.

3. consume   consumer   consumption

   In recent years there has been no change in _____ of
   vegetables. Few adults grew up eating the meals they now

   _____. But in the next ten years there may be

   _____ who have never cooked a meal from basic

   ingredients. _____ surveys reveal that this may be
   due to increasing time pressures.

Check your answers. Work with a partner to take turns reading the completed groups of sentences.

Expanding Your Language

SPEAKING

A. *Speaking from Reading:* The readings in this chapter contain information about diet and exercise habits. Lifestyle and the issue of motivation were both discussed in these readings. In the following selection, you will read about an unusual fitness routine. Find information to discuss these questions:

1. Where did the author go to get fitness advice?
2. What did she have to do to sign up?
3. What services did she get?
4. What results did she get?
5. What made this an effective program for her?
6. Would you use this type of program? Why or why not?

NEW YORK TIMES

Some Shape Up by Surfing the Internet

By Marion Roach

For various reasons, including a busy schedule and two herniated discs in my neck, I got out of shape. Or, more specifically, I got into another shape altogether.

Then, last fall, while doing Internet research for an article about women's body-building, I stumbled onto a site named trulyhuge.com. What this site was selling seemed highly unlikely: on-line training.

Sure, you can get anything on the Internet. But fit? I didn't think so.

These are the words of a changed woman. Seventeen pounds lighter, sleeping through the night for the first time in my life, energetic, fit and strong, I am the worst kind of proselytizer—worse, by far, than the reformed smoker, recovering carbo-loader or even politician. I know on-line fitness when I see it. And I've seen it.

Trulyhuge had a questionnaire that required measuring my height and the size of my body everywhere from my ankles to my wrists. It asked about injuries, access to a gym, pool, weights or any other athletic equipment. I started filling in the boxes on the screen and noticed that I hadn't been tempted to lie. Not for my weight, height, bad habits or goals.

There was something about not being seen by the recipient of these statistics that allowed me to tell the full-sized truth. I think that's when I became intrigued. Already this was a step up from my last personal training experience: No pep talks, no pitches for products I wouldn't feed my septic system and, especially, no welter-weight endomorph lashing my middleweight self with tape measures. That means no on-site humiliation. As for on-line humiliation, who cares?

I wrote that my goals were to lose 15 pounds, increase my aerobic stamina, get back into my clothes (that is, get smaller, not bulk up with muscle), feel better and get a little more energy. I didn't ask about sleep. As a lifelong insomniac, it never occurred to me to include it in my goals.

I wrote that my dream workout would be portable, allowing me to keep up my routine at the gym, at my home in the country (where I have nothing but a few hand weights) and on the road. Being a writer, wife and mother, I have a haphazard schedule, one prone to constant interruption. This had helped me to fail with personal trainers before: keeping those appointments was hard, though paying for them when I canceled was even harder. After I moved upstate, I discovered that the going rate for a personal trainer was only $20 an

hour, much less than what I had been paying in Manhattan. But that's still hefty enough if you train three times a week for the length of time it takes to get in shape, which I figured in my case would be a minimum of eight weeks.

So I signed up for Trulyhuge for 12 weeks, hoping that at the end of it I might be truly small. The total cost was $60; $20 a month for a diet plan, a training regimen and coaching on line. This includes unlimited questions from client and regular check-ins from the trainer.

The man on the other side of Trulyhuge is Paul Becker, who trains bodybuilders in Los Angeles along with running the Web site, which also features products, promotes his training and sells his book, "Trulyhuge."

Within two days of my returning the questionnaire, my complete diet and exercise routine arrived by E-mail. It was portable. It accommodated gym, home and hotel room workouts. The dietary recommendations were for a higher protein–lower carbohydrate routine and included sample menus.

The advice: drink more water and less juice, and cut back on bread—not hard moves to make. His eating regimen was sensible and understandable, calling, for example, for an egg-white omelet in the morning. I don't eat eggs, so now I have a fruit shake with tofu, soy powder or skim milk every morning.

Wanting to track my progress efficiently, I waited until the first day of a new month to go back to the gym. And when it came, I went, armed with nothing more than three pieces of paper from Trulyhuge and my workout clothes.

My program required five days of 30-minute aerobic workouts each week plus three strength sessions. The aerobic exercise recommended was power walking, which I did on a treadmill at the gym. All the exercises, I was instructed, were to be done in sets of 15 repetitions unless otherwise stated.

The three strength days, each separated by a day or two of rest, broke down as follows:

Day One: two sets of leg presses, one set of leg extensions, two sets each of leg curls and seated calf raises, and as many reverse crunches as possible.

Day Two: two sets of bench presses, one set of incline bench presses, one set of flies, two sets of lateral raises, one set of bentover lateral raises, one set of french pressers, one set of triceps pulldowns and as many reverse crunches as possible.

Day Three: two sets of rows and one set each of lat pulldowns, standing barbell curls, incline dumbbell curls, wrist curls, reverse wrist curls and reverse crunches.

The freehand program, or what I call the at-home/on-the-road workout, included push-ups, deep knee bends, calf raises, side leg raises and reverse crunches. By the night of day four I had the sensation that my legs were humming. Lying in bed (not sleeping, of course), I could feel my legs vibrating. Paul replied to my on-line query about this within hours. My legs, he said, were burning fat.

I was hopeful. By the end of the second week, I had lost three pounds. Was I naïve to have hoped for more?

Two and a half weeks into the program, I had dropped four pounds. I E-mailed this progress to Trulyhuge, and Paul wrote me an encouraging note saying I was doing great. I requested a more thorough explanation of the free weight routines. By the end of the day, I had received a completely understandable breakdown of the exercises.

Throughout the weeks, if I didn't E-mail, Paul did. He asked for progress reports or inquired to see if I had questions. I came to appreciate the reminder that someone out there was keeping track of my progress. Weight loss and training, I found out, is not something most friends and relations find terribly interesting.

After 30 days, I cut out all alcohol. Two weeks after that, I started sleeping. No, more than that: I did eight straight hours asleep, for the first time in my life. And every night since I have simply gone right to sleep—face down, face up, it makes no difference. My husband swears that once he thought I was dead. He managed to wake me, but, no matter, I went right back to sleep.

That month I lost five more pounds. But I was frustrated. I had hoped for two pounds a week. So, I tried that time-honored, weight loss motivator: I got an expensive haircut. Eight more pounds were gone by the end of the next month.

I E-mailed Paul Becker and told him how pleased I was: 17 pounds gone in less than three months. I am very pleased to be going into June without that weight. But I had to ask one more question: Why was I sleeping?

In his answer, he used an old English measure, and it was so comforting to see it in this digital age that I've kept his note tacked on my wall: "Lose a stone (14 pounds)," it said. "Sleep like a rock." He's right.

On-line trainers and coaches abound on the Web. While prices vary, expect to pay at least $20 for a one-month workout plan.

Trulyhuge is at www.trulyhuge.com.

B. *Two-Minute Taped Talk:* **Record a two-minute audio tape about one of the stories in this chapter. To make your tape, follow these steps.**

1. Write some notes about the important information in the story.
2. Practice telling the story from your notes. Include as many important facts as possible.
3. Time yourself as you try to speak as clearly and naturally as possible.
4. Record your story. Use your notes to guide your recording.
5. Give the tape to your teacher for feedback.

WRITING

A. *Topic Writing:* **Write two or more paragraphs that describe in detail the complementary processes of diet and exercise and how they can affect our health. Include information about the best recommendations for a healthy lifestyle in this writing.**

B. *Reaction Writing:* **Write about your lifestyle and what you could do in the future to improve or maintain it.**

Read On: Taking It Further

READING JOURNAL

■ *READING TIP:*
Don't forget to write
your reading journal
and vocabulary log
entries in your note-
book. Show the
entries to your
teacher. Arrange to
discuss your
progress in reading.

There are some very interesting biographies of people whose long, healthy, productive lives have been an inspiration to many. Consult with your teacher to choose to read, for example, about the life of Eleanor Roosevelt, or Scott Nearing, or a personality that you know of and are interested in. With your teacher's guidance, choose a story selection to read and report on.

NEWSPAPER ARTICLES

Check the paper over a few days and find an interesting article about alternative therapies, fitness, or a related health topic that interests you. Prepare to present the information in that article to a partner or in a small group. Follow these steps:

1. Skim the article quickly to get a general idea of the information.
2. Ask the journalist's questions—*who, what, where, when,* and *why*—to see if it contains information that will be interesting to your audience and can be readily explained.
3. Highlight the important facts. Make notes if it will help you explain more easily.
4. Practice your presentation.
5. Present your information.

UNIT 3
Memory

Memory is the thing you forget with.
Alexander Chase, Perspectives (1966)

83

Introducing
the Topics

Perhaps because it defines who we are, people have always been fascinated by memory. With some of the most recent research, scientists have begun to understand what it really is. In this unit we will read about some of their findings. Chapter 5 will look at what memory is and how to improve it. Chapter 6 will look at what happens when certain parts of our memory break down.

Points of Interest

PERSONALIZING

A. Read the following incidents. Check (✓) the ones you have experienced.

_____ 1. Somebody comes up to you and greets you by name. You have no idea who he or she is.

_____ 2. You are telling a joke you heard the day before, and suddenly you cannot remember the ending.

_____ 3. You look everywhere for your glasses only to have someone tell you that you are wearing them.

_____ 4. You walk into a room and cannot remember why you went there in the first place.

_____ 5. On your way to work in the morning you realize that your car is low on gas. You make a mental note to stop at the next gas station. Driving home that evening your car stops in the middle of the bridge. Then you remember your mental note about the gas.

_____ 6. You did something really embarrassing during the day and you lie awake at night because you can't seem to forget about it.

Compare your list with a partner or in a small group. Be ready to describe what happened and how you felt in each of the situations you checked.

B. Think of two or three other incidents in which you felt you were having problems with your memory. Take turns explaining these incidents to each other.

USING ANALOGIES

The following terms are often used in connection with memory:

- Short-term memory
- Long-term memory

Discuss what you know about each with a partner or in a small group.

Read the analogy on page 86 and discuss the questions that follow.

1. What do you think determines whether an "animal" (thought) will go into the jungle or go back out of the pass?

2. Refer to the analogy to explain

> ■ **READING TIP:**
> *An analogy is an explanation that is made by comparing one thing with something else that is similar, but easier to understand.*

- why we find it easier to remember certain things, such as our telephone numbers;
- why memory declines with old age;
- what would happen if the entrance into the jungle were "blocked";
- why some people have better memory than others.

Think of your memory as a vast, overgrown jungle. This memory jungle is thick with wild plants, twisted trees and creeping vines. It spreads over thousands of square miles. Imagine that the jungle is bounded on all sides by impassable mountains. There is only one entrance to the jungle, a narrow pass through the mountains that opens into a small grassy area.

In the jungle there are animals, millions of them. The animals represent all the information in your memory. Some animals, like the color of your second-grade teacher's eyes, are well hidden. Other animals, like your telephone number, are easier to find.

There are two rules of the jungle. (1) Each animal (or thought) must pass through the grassy area at the entrance to the memory jungle. (2) Once an animal enters the jungle, it never leaves.

The grassy area represents short-term memory. It's the kind of memory that you use when you look up a telephone number. You can look at seven digits and hold them in your short-term memory long enough to dial them. Short-term memory has limited capacity (the grassy area is small) and short-term memory disappears fast (animals pass through quickly—either into the jungle or out again).

The jungle itself represents long-term memory. This is the kind of memory that allows us to recall information from day to day and year to year. Remember that animals never leave the long-term memory jungle.

–Dave Ellis, *Becoming a Master Student*

CHAPTER **5**

How Memory Works
and How to Improve It

Chapter Openers

DISCUSSION QUESTIONS

Think about these questions. Share your ideas with a partner or with a small group.

1. Why is memory important?
2. What are some factors that can affect memory?
3. What are some ways that you can use to improve your memory?
4. List some of the most significant memories in your life and discuss why they mean so much to you.
5. Do you think having a good memory could be a problem? When? Why?

MEMORY QUIZ

Do you have a good memory? Take the quiz on page 88 and find out!

See page 110, at the end of Chapter 5 for an evaluation of your results.

MEMORY QUIZ

Memory on the fritz? Sometimes it takes a professional to tell you whether you've got a real problem or not. Below is one test the pros use to take the measure of your recall.

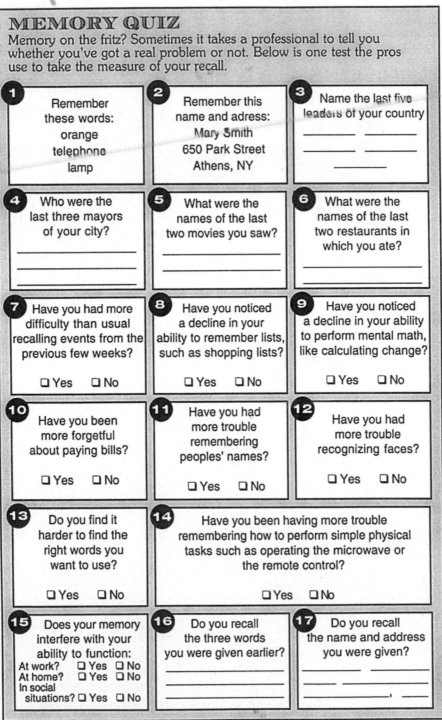

1 Remember these words:
orange
telephone
lamp

2 Remember this name and adress:
Mary Smith
650 Park Street
Athens, NY

3 Name the last five leaders of your country
_____ _____
_____ _____
_____

4 Who were the last three mayors of your city?
_____
_____
_____

5 What were the names of the last two movies you saw?
_____
_____

6 What were the names of the last two restaurants in which you ate?
_____
_____

7 Have you had more difficulty than usual recalling events from the previous few weeks?
❑ Yes   ❑ No

8 Have you noticed a decline in your ability to remember lists, such as shopping lists?
❑ Yes   ❑ No

9 Have you noticed a decline in your ability to perform mental math, like calculating change?
❑ Yes   ❑ No

10 Have you been more forgetful about paying bills?
❑ Yes   ❑ No

11 Have you had more trouble remembering peoples' names?
❑ Yes   ❑ No

12 Have you had more trouble recognizing faces?
❑ Yes   ❑ No

13 Do you find it harder to find the right words you want to use?
❑ Yes   ❑ No

14 Have you been having more trouble remembering how to perform simple physical tasks such as operating the microwave or the remote control?
❑ Yes   ❑ No

15 Does your memory interfere with your ability to function:
At work?   ❑ Yes ❑ No
At home?   ❑ Yes ❑ No
In social situations? ❑ Yes ❑ No

16 Do you recall the three words you were given earlier?
_____
_____
_____

17 Do you recall the name and address you were given?
_____ _____
_____ _____
_____, _____

Exploring and Understanding Reading

PREVIEWING

Read the title and the subtitle only of the following article. Check (✓) the ideas that you expect to find.

_____ Factors that affect memory

_____ Scientific explanation of how memory works

_____ Advantages of having a good memory

_____ Ways to improve memory

_____ Memory-related diseases

_____ Examples of people who feel their memory is declining

List the ideas you checked in the order you expect them to appear in the article.

1. _____

2. _____

3. _____

4. _____

Discuss your work with a partner. Be prepared to support what you did.

SCANNING THE INTRODUCTION

Read the first four paragraphs and answer the following questions.

1. What similarities and differences are there between Stan and Michelle in terms of their age, sex, occupation, and efforts to improve memory?

   _____

   _____

   _____

2. What are Stan and Michelle examples of?

_____

3. Why is it important to have answers to the questions in paragraph four?

_____

4. What two areas are biologists and neuroscientists beginning to learn a lot about?

_____

_____

Check your answers with a partner. Refer to the article if you cannot agree.

Memory

By Geoffrey Cowley and Anne Underwood

Forgetfulness is America's latest health obsession. How much is normal? Can we do anything about it? An explosion of new research offers reassuring insights.

1. Stan Field knows what age can do to a person's memory, and he's not taking any chances with his. He chooses his food carefully and gets plenty of vigorous exercise. He also avoids stress, soda pop and cigarette smoke. But that's just for starters. At breakfast each morning, the 69-year-old chemical engineer downs a plateful of pills in the hope of boosting his brainpower. He starts with deprenyl and piracetam—drugs that are normally used to treat diseases like Parkinson's but that casual users can get from overseas sources—and moves on to a series of amino acids (glutamine, phenylalanine, tyrosine). Then he takes several multivitamins, some ginkgo biloba (a plant extract), 1,000 units of vitamin E and, for good measure, a stiff shot of cod-liver oil.

2. Michelle Arnove is less than half Field's age, but no less concerned about her memory. While working round the clock to finish a degree in film studies, the 33-year-old New Yorker had the alarming sensation that she had stopped retaining anything. "I couldn't even remember names," she says. "I thought, 'Oh no, I'm over 30. It's all downhill from here.'" Besides loading up on supplements (she favors ginseng, choline and St. John's wort), Arnove signed up for a memory-enhancement course at New York's Mount Sinai Medical Center. And when she got there, she found herself surrounded by people who were just as worried as she was.

3. For millions of Americans, and especially for baby boomers, the demands of the Information Age are colliding with a sense of warning vigor. "When boomers were in their 30s and 40s, they launched the fitness boom," says Cynthia Green, the psychologist who teaches Mount Sinai's memory class. "Now we have the mental fitness boom. Memory is the boomers' new life-crisis issue." And, of course, a major marketing opportunity. The demand for books and seminars has never been greater, says Jack Lannom, a Baptist minister and longtime memory trainer whose weekly TV show, "Mind Unlimited," goes out to 33 million homes on the Christian Network. Anxious consumers are rushing to buy do-it-yourself programs like Kevin Trudeau's "Mega Memory," a series of audiotapes that sells for $49.97. And supplement makers are touting everything but sawdust as a brain booster.

4. But before you get out your checkbook, a few questions are in order. Does everyday forgetfulness signal flagging brain func-

tion? Is "megamemory" a realistic goal for normal people? And if you could have a perfect memory, would you really want it? Until recently, no one could address those issues with much authority, but our knowledge of memory is exploding. New imaging techniques are revealing how different parts of the brain interact to preserve meaningful experiences. Biologists are decoding the underlying chemical processes—and neuroscientists are discovering how age, stress and other factors can disrupt them. No one is close to finding the secret to flawless recall, but as you'll see, that may be just as well.

5. To scientists who study the brain, the wonder is that we retain as much as we do. As Harvard psychologist Daniel Schacter observes in his 1996 book, *Searching for Memory*, the simple act of meeting a friend for lunch requires a vast store of memory— a compendium of words, sounds and grammatical rules; a record of the friend's appearance and manner, a catalog of restaurants; a mental map to get you to one, and so on.

6. How do we manage so much information? Brains are different from computers, but the analogy can be helpful. Like the PC on your desk, your mind is equipped with two basic types of memory: "working memory" for juggling information in the present moment, and long-term memory for storing it over extended periods. Contrary to popular wisdom, our brains don't record everything that happens to us and then bury it until a hypnotist or a therapist helps us dredge it up. Most of what we perceive hovers briefly in working memory, a mental play space akin to a computer's RAM (or random-access memory), then simply evaporates. Working memory enables you to perform simple calculations in your head or retain phone numbers long enough to dial them. And like RAM, it lets you analyze and invent things without creating a lasting record.

7. Long-term memory acts more like a hard drive, physically recording past experiences in the brain region known as the cerebral cortex. The cortex, or outer layer of the brain, houses a thicket of 10 billion vinelike nerve cells, which communicate by relaying chemical and electrical impulses. Every time we perceive something—a sight, a sound, an idea—a unique subset of these neurons gets activated. And they don't always return to their original state. Instead, they may strengthen their connections to one another, becoming more densely intertwined. Once that happens,

anything that activates the network will bring back the original perception as a memory. "What we think of as memories are ultimately patterns of connection among nerve cells," says Dr. Barry Gordon, head of the memory-disorders clinic at the Johns Hopkins School of Medicine. A newly encoded memory may involve thousands of neurons spanning the entire cortex. If it doesn't get used, it will quickly fade. But if we activate it repeatedly, the pattern of connection gets more and more deeply embedded in our tissue.

8. We can will things into long-term memory simply by rehearsing them. But the decision to store or discard a piece of information rarely involves any conscious thought. It's usually handled automatically by the hippocampus, a small, two-winged structure nestled deep in the center of the brain. Like the keyboard on your computer, the hippocampus serves as a kind of switching station. As neurons out in the cortex receive sensory information, they relay it to the hippocampus. If the hippocampus responds, the sensory neurons start forming a durable network. But without that act of consent, the experience vanishes forever.

9. The hippocampal verdict seems to hinge on two questions. First, does the information have any emotional significance? The name of a potential lover is more likely to get a rise out of the hippocampus than that of Warren Harding's Agriculture secretary. Like Saul Steinberg's cartoon map of America (showing the Midwest as a sliver between Manhattan and the West Coast), the brain constructs the world according to its own parochial interests. And it's more attuned to the sensational than the mundane. In a 1994 experiment, researchers at the University of California, Irvine, told volunteers alternate versions of a story, then quizzed them on the details. In one version, a boy and his mom pass a junkyard on their way to visit his father. In the other version, the boy is hit by a car. You can guess which one had more staying power.

10. The second question the hippocampus asks is whether the information entering the brain relates to things we already know. Unlike a computer, which stores related facts separately, the brain strives constantly to make associations. If you have already devoted a lot of neural circuitry to American political history, the name of Harding's Agriculture secretary may actually hold some interest. And if the hippocampus marks the name for storage, it will lodge easily among the related bits of information already linked together in the cortex. In short, we use the nets woven by past experience to capture new information. And because our backgrounds vary, we often retain very different aspects of similar experiences.

11. Sophie Calle, a French artist, illustrated the point nicely by removing Magritte's "The Menaced Assassin" from its usual place at New York's Museum of Modern Art and asking museum staffers to describe the painting. One respondent (the janitor?) remembered only "men in dark suits" and some "dashes of red blood." Another (the conservator?) remembered little about the style or content of the painting but readily described the dimensions of the canvas, the condition of the paint and the quality of the frame. Still another respondent (the curator?) held forth on the painting's film noir atmosphere, describing how each figure in the eerie tableau helps convey a sense of mystery.

12. By storing only the information we're most likely to use, our brains make the world manageable. As Columbia University neuroscientist Eric Kandel puts it, "You want to keep the junk of everyday life out of the way so you can focus on what matters." Perfect retention may sound like a godsend, but when the hippocampus gets overly permissive, the results can be devastating. Neurologists sometimes encounter people with superhuman memories. These savants can recite colossal strings of facts, words and numbers. But most are incapable of abstract thought. Lacking a filter on their experience, they're powerless to make sense of it.

13. At the other end of the spectrum stands H.M., a Connecticut factory worker who made medical history in 1953. He was 27 at the time, and suffering from intractable epilepsy. In a desperate bid to stop his seizures, surgeons removed his hippocampus. The operation made his condition manageable without disrupting his existing memories. But H.M. lost the ability to form new ones. To this day, he can't tell you what he had for breakfast, let alone make a new acquaintance. "Nearly 40 years after his surgery," Boston University researchers wrote in 1993, "H.M. does not know his age or the current date [or] where he is living."

14. It doesn't take brain surgery to disrupt the hippocampus. Alzheimer's disease gradually destroys the organ, and the ability to form new memories. Normal aging can cause subtle impairments, too. Autopsy studies suggest that our overall brain mass declines by 5 to 10 percent per decade during our 60s and 70s. And imaging tests show that both the hippocampus and the frontal cortex become less active. As you would expect, young people generally outperform the elderly on tests that gauge encoding and retrieval ability.

15. Fortunately, the differences are minor. Experts now agree that unless you develop a particular condition, such as Alzheimer's or vascular disease, age alone won't ruin your memory. At worst, it will make you a little slower and less precise. "We continue to encode the general features of our experiences," says Schacter, "but we leave off more details." For example, Schacter has found that young adults are usually better than old folks at remembering the details of a picture. But the oldsters quickly catch up when coached to pay more attention. And not everyone needs coaching. Though *average* scores decline with age, some octogenarians remain sharper and quicker than college kids.

16. Whatever their age, people vary widely in recall ability. "Bill Clinton will probably always remember more names than you will," says Gordon. "Unless he has to testify." But that's not to say our abilities are completely fixed. Researchers have identified various influences that can keep the brain from working at full capacity. High blood pressure can impair mental function, even if it doesn't cause a stroke. One study found that over a 25-year period, men with hypertension lost twice as much cognitive ability as those with normal blood pressure. Too little sleep (or too many sleeping

pills) can disrupt the formation of new memories. So can too much alcohol or a dysfunctional thyroid gland. Other memory busters include depression, anxiety and a simple lack of stimulation—all of which keep us from paying full attention to our surroundings.

17. And then there's information overload. "You used to have time to reflect and think," Gordon observes. "Now you're just a conduit for a constant stream of information." It comes at us with terrifying speed—via fax, phone and e-mail, over scores of cable channels—even at the newsstand. And when information bombards us faster than we can assimilate it, we miss out on more than the surplus. As Michelle Arnove (remember her?) discovered, an overwhelmed mind has trouble absorbing anything.

18. The problem often boils down to stress. Besides leaving us sleepless, distractible and more likely to drink, chronic stress can directly affect our brain chemistry. Like a strong cup of coffee, a stressful experience can energize our brains in the short run. It triggers the release of adrenaline and other glucocorticoid hormones, which boost circulation and unleash the energy stored in our tissues as glucose. The stress response is nicely tailored to the environments we evolved in—where surprise encounters with hungry predators were more common than looming deadlines and gridlocked calendars. But this fight-or-flight mechanism causes harm if it's turned on all the time. After about 30 minutes, says Stanford neuroscientist Robert Sapolsky, stress hormones start to knock out the molecules that transport glucose into the hippocampus leaving the brain *low* on energy. And over

longer periods, stress hormones can act like so much battery acid, severing connections among neurons and literally shrinking the hippocampus: "This atrophy is reversible if the stress is short-lived," says Bruce McEwen, a neuroscientist at Rockefeller University. "But stress lasting months or years can kill hippocampal neurons."

19. What, then, are the best ways to protect your memory? Obviously, anyone concerned about staying sharp should make a point of sleeping enough and managing stress. And because the brain is at the mercy of the circulatory system, a heart-healthy lifestyle may have cognitive benefits as well. In a 1997 survey of older adults, researchers in Madrid found an association between high mental-test scores and high intake of fruits, vegetables and fiber. An earlier study, conducted at the University of Southern California, found that people in their 70s were less likely to slip mentally during a three-year period if they stayed physically active. Besides protecting our arteries, exercise may boost the body's production of brain-derived nerve growth factor (BDNF), a molecule that helps keep neurons strong.

20. What about all those seminars and supplements? Can they help, too? The techniques that memory coaches teach can be powerful, but there's nothing magical about them. They work mainly by inspiring us to pay attention, to repeat what's worth remembering and to link what we're trying to remember to things we already know. To remember a new name, says Green of Mount Sinai, listen intently. Then spell it to yourself and make a mental comment about it. Popping vitamins and herbs is easier, but it's no substitute. Preliminary studies suggest that nutritional supplements such as vitamin E and ginkgo biloba may help preserve brain function. But no one has shown convincingly that over-the-counter remedies improve recall in healthy adults.

21. Estrogen is a different story. While the hormone may not supercharge your memory, it clearly supports brain function. Barbara Sherwin, codirector of the McGill University Menopause Clinic, revealed estrogen's importance two years ago, by testing verbal memory in young women before and after they underwent treatment for uterine tumors. The women's estrogen levels plummeted after 12 weeks of chemotherapy—as did their scores on tests of reading retention. But when half of the women added estrogen to their treatment regimen, their performance promptly rebounded. Researchers at the National Institute on Aging have since found that estrogen may affect visual as well as verbal memory (though not as strongly). And other studies suggest that women who take estrogen may lower their risk of Alzheimer's disease. The reasons are still unclear, but the hormone seems to fuel the development of hippocampal neurons and boost the production of acetylcholine, a chemical that helps brain cells communicate. Unfortunately estrogen has risks as well as benefits, especially for women predisposed to breast cancer. For now, few experts recommend it as a memory aid.

22. Estrogen is just one of many compounds that pharmaceutical companies are now eyeing as potential brain savers. "There are so many drugs under study that I have to believe one or more will make it," says James McGaugh, a neuroscientist at the

University of California, Irvine. Most are being developed as treatments for Alzheimer's disease, but researchers foresee a day when people will treat even the minor lapses that come with age. "We want to optimize the opportunity to live a free and independent life," says Columbia's Kandel. "It would be nice to have a little red pill that would take care of it."

23. Kandel has formed a company called Memory Pharmaceuticals to exploit his seminal findings about memory. You'll recall that the brain stores information by strengthening the connections among stimulated neurons. To lock in a memory, the neurons in question actually sprout new branches, creating more avenues for the exchange of chemical signals. Kandel has identified a pair of genes—CREB1 and CREB2—that help regulate that process. CREB1 initiates the growth process, while CREB2 holds it in check. Together, they act as a kind of thermostat. Kandel hopes that by selectively inhibiting one gene or the other, we may be able to change the setting on that thermostat. Partially disabling CREB2 might help anyone retain things more easily, without becoming an indiscriminate sponge. And a drug that *activated* CREB2 (or hogtied CREB1) might help trauma victims avoid having painful experiences seared so vividly into their brains.

24. It's a thrilling enterprise, but fraught with possible pitfalls. New treatments create new expectations, and not just for the infirm. "Suppose the drug raises your score on a job test," says McGaugh. "Who gets hired? Does the other guy file suit? Can the employer fire you if you stop taking the drug?" And suppose parents start feeding the drug to their school-age kids. Others would have to take it just to keep up. Those worries may be vastly premature. Our memory systems have evolved over several million years. If a slight modification made them far more efficient, chances are it would have cropped up naturally by now. The fact is, "maximal memory" and "optimal memory" are not synonymous, says Cesare Mondadori, chief of research for nervous-system drugs at Hoechst Marion Roussel. As any savant can tell you, forgetting is as important as remembering. So be careful what you wish for.

—*Newsweek*

ANALYZING THE INFORMATION

■ *READING TIP:*
Identifying the features of the introduction is an important critical reading skill.

An effective introduction has the following elements:

A. An attention grabber—interesting information in the form of examples, statistics, surprising facts, etc., to make the reader want to continue reading

B. General information—information that provides the reader with background about the topic

C. The major ideas to be discussed in the body of the article

D. A thesis statement—one or two sentences (usually at the end of the introduction) that express the purpose of the article as a whole

Reread paragraphs 1–4 and identify each of these elements. Underline or bracket the section that contains each element and make a note in the margin. Discuss the following questions with a partner.

- Do the authors make the examples interesting and relevant? How?

- Are you given enough background information?

- What are the major ideas that will be discussed?

- Do these ideas match your predictions in the previewing section?

- Using the thesis statement and the major ideas, can you orally summarize what the article will be about?

- What is the point of view of the authors with respect to improving memory? Is it clear?

- Is this an effective introduction? Why or why not?

SURVEYING/CHUNKING

- **READING TIP:**
Chunking means grouping paragraphs that develop the same major idea. It helps you see the general outline of a reading and makes comprehension much easier.

A. Starting with paragraph 5, read the first sentence of every paragraph.

B. Write the main idea of each paragraph in the margin. (Use only two or three words.)

C. Check your main ideas with a partner. You can choose different words, but you should agree on the ideas.

D. Together, group these ideas into three major ideas and list them below. Also list the corresponding paragraphs.

Major Ideas   *Paragraphs*

_____   _____

_____   _____

_____   _____

Check your work with another pair of students. Compare these ideas with the ones you predicted from the introduction and see if they match.

The rest of this section will show you that it is important to use a variety of strategies within the same reading.

SKIMMING FOR SPECIAL TERMS

READING TIP: Use referents to help you. See Chapter 1, Vocabulary Building, page 15.

The first major idea deals with memory-related operations in the brain. It is therefore important to become familiar with terminology specific to the brain in order to fully understand the processes. Skim through paragraphs 5–13 to locate these terms and find definitions for them.

1. Working memory: _____

2. Long-term memory: _____

3. Cerebral cortex: _____

4. Neurons: _____

5. Hippocampus: _____

6. Savant: _____

Check your definitions with a partner. Take turns explaining each one in your own words. Be ready to show how you located each definition.

SCANNING FOR DETAILS

Read through paragraphs 5–13 and find the answers to the following questions. Underline or highlight the relevant information and note the number of the question in the margin for future reference. Write the answer in your own words and in note form.

1. Why is meeting a friend for lunch not a simple act?

_____

_____

2. What misconception exists about what our brain records?

   _____

   _____

   What really happens?

   _____

   _____

3. How do neurons communicate?

   _____

   _____

4. What has to happen for there to be a permanent memory?

   _____

   _____

5. Which part of the brain decides whether or not information is to go into long-term memory?

   _____

   What two questions have to be asked before this decision is made?

   _____

   _____

6. Why is it possible for two people to retain different aspects of similar experiences?

   _____

   _____

7. What are the consequences of

   a. having a hippocampus that allows too much information in?

   _____

   _____

b. having no hippocampus at all?

_____

_____

Check your answers with a partner. Refer to the reading if you do not agree. Take turns telling each other what you now know about how memory is formed. Use your answers to help you but do *not* use the reading.

SKIMMING FOR KEY SUPPORTING IDEAS

The second major idea is about factors that affect memory. Skim paragraphs 14–18. Underline and list six factors that affect memory.

_____

_____

_____

_____

_____

_____

Compare your list with a partner. Add to or change your list if necessary.

NOTE-TAKING

In paragraphs 19–22, the authors look at different ways of improving memory. Identify and list the different methods.

A. _____

B. _____

C. _____

D. _____

Compare your list with a partner and then do the following:

1. Divide the ideas between you and your partner (i.e., take two methods each).

2. Make notes on the ideas you have chosen using the following format.

Main Ideas	**Supporting Ideas and Details**
Method A	1. What it is

_____

_____

2. Evidence that it works

_____

_____

_____

3. Why it works

_____

_____

_____

Use the same format for methods B, C, and D.

Using your notes only, take turns explaining each of the methods to each other.

UNDERSTANDING THE CONCLUSION

Read paragraph 24 and answer these questions.

1. Which of the following statements best describes the authors' point of view?

   a. We should try to make our memory perfect in any way possible.

   b. We should accept our imperfect memory as it is and work with it.

2. Does this point of view agree with the one in the introduction?

3. Is it stated more clearly in the introduction or in the conclusion? Why do you think this is so?

After Reading

GIVING YOUR OPINION

Discuss the following in a small group.

- Which analogy did you find more effective—the one at the beginning of this unit (page 86) where memory is compared to a jungle, or the analogy in the article "Memory," where memory is compared to a computer (paragraphs 6–8)? Why?

- Which memory affecting factors are within our control and which are not? Which do you think are a result of modern life?

- Which of the memory enhancement methods outlined would you use and why?

APPLYING THE INFORMATION

A. Indicate what the authors of "Memory" might suggest to someone who was having trouble remembering each of the following:

- names
- birthdays
- chores for the day
- shopping lists
- appointments

B. Make some suggestions of your own. Share your ideas with a partner or in a small group

C. The following techniques are taken from a study skills book, *Becoming a Master Student*, by David Ellis. Choose *one*. Read and highlight the useful information.

Technique One: Set a Trap for Your Memory

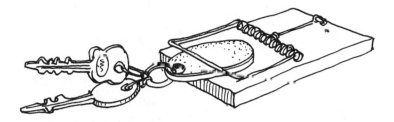

When you want to remind yourself to do something, link that activity to another event that you know will take place.

Say you're walking to work and suddenly you realize that your books are due at the library tomorrow. Switch your watch from your left to your right wrist. Every time you look at your watch it becomes a reminder that you were supposed to remember something. (You can do the same with a ring.)

If you empty your pockets every night, put an unusual item in your pocket to remind yourself to do something before you go to bed. To remember to call your sister for her birthday, pick an object from the kitchen—a fork, perhaps—and put it in your pocket. That evening, when you empty your pocket and find the fork, you're more likely to call your sister.

The key is to pick events that are certain to occur. Rituals like looking at your watch, reaching for car keys, and untying shoes are seldom forgotten. Tie a triple knot in your shoelace to remind you to set the alarm for your early morning jog.

You can even use imaginary cues. To remember to write a check for the phone bill, picture your phone hanging on the front door. In your mind, create the feeling of reaching for the door knob and grabbing the phone cord instead. When you get home and reach to open the front door, the image is apt to return to you. Link two activities together, and make the association unusual.

Another way to remember something is to tell yourself you will remember it. Relax and say, "At any time I choose, I will be able to recall . . . ." The intention to remember can be more powerful than any memory technique.

Technique Two: Remembering Names

Remembering names is an important social skill. Here are some ways to master it.

Recite and repeat in conversation.

When you hear a person's name, repeat it. Immediately say it to yourself several times without moving your lips. You could also repeat the name in a way that does not sound forced or artificial: "I'm pleased to meet you, Maria."

Ask the other person to recite and repeat.

You can let other people help you remember their names. After you've been introduced to someone, ask that person to spell the name and pronounce it correctly for you. Most people will be flattered by the effort you're taking to learn their names.

Visualize.

After the conversation, construct a brief visual image of the person. For a memorable image, make it unusual. Imagine the name painted in hot pink fluorescent letters on the person's forehead.

Admit you don't know.

Admitting that you can't remember someone's name can actually put people at ease. Most of them will sympathize if you say, "I'm working to remember names better. Yours is right on the tip of my tongue. What is it again?" (By the way, that's exactly what psychologists call that feeling—"the tip of the tongue phenomenon.")

Use associations.

Link each person you meet with one characteristic you find interesting or unusual. For example, you could make a mental note: "Vicki Cheng—tall, black hair." To reinforce your associations, write them on a 3 × 5 card as soon as you can.

Limit the number of new names you learn at one time.

When meeting a group of people, concentrate on remembering just two or three names. Free yourself of any obligation to remember every one. Few of the people in mass introductions expect you to remember their names. Another way to avoid memory overload is to limit yourself to learning just first names. Last names can come later.

Go early.

Consider going early to conventions, parties, and classes. Sometimes just a few people show up at these occasions on time. That's fewer names for you to remember. And as more people arrive, you can overhear them being introduced to others—an automatic review for you.

Technique Three: Mnemonic Devices

It's pronounced *ne-man'-ik*. It's a trick that can increase your ability to recall everything from speeches to grocery lists. Some entertainers use mnemonics to perform "impossible" feats of memory, such as recalling the names of everyone in a large audience after hearing them just once. Waiters use them to take orders without the aid of pad and pencil, then serve food correctly without asking. Using mnemonic devices, speakers can go for hours without looking at their notes. The possibilities are endless.

There are three general categories: new words; creative sentences, rhymes and songs; and special systems, including the loci system and the peg system.

If you experiment with each, you just might impress your mother-in-law by remembering her birthday and favorite color.

New words

Acronyms are words created by the first letters of a series of words. Examples include NAFTA (North American Free Trade Agreement), radar (radio detecting and ranging), scuba (self-contained underwater breathing apparatus), and laser (light amplification by stimulated emission of radiation). You can make up your own words to recall series of facts. A common mnemonic acronym is Roy G. Biv, which has helped thousands of people remember the colors of the rainbow.

Rhymes and songs

Madison Avenue advertising executives spend billions of dollars a year on commercials designed to burn their messages in your memory. Coca-Cola's song, "It's the Real Thing," practically stands for Coca-Cola, despite the fact that it contains artificial ingredients.

Rhymes have been used for centuries to teach children basic facts: "In fourteen hundred and ninety two, Columbus sailed the ocean blue," or "Thirty days hath September . . . ."

Systems—loci and peg

The loci system is an old one. Ancient Greek orators used it to remember long speeches. Say that the orator's position was that road taxes must be raised to pay for school equipment. His loci visualizations might have looked like these:

First, as he walked in the door of his house, he imagined a large porpoise (member of the dolphin family) jumping through a hoop. This reminded him to begin by telling the audience the purpose of his speech. Next, he visualized his living room floor covered with paving stones, forming a road leading into the kitchen. In the kitchen, he pictured dozens of school children sitting on the floor because they have no desks.

Now the day of the big speech. The Greek politician is nervous. He is perspiring; his toga sticks to his body. He has cold feet (no socks). He stands up to give his speech and his mind goes blank. "No problem," he thinks to himself "I am so nervous that I can hardly remember my name. But I can remember the rooms in my house. Let's see, I'm walking in the front door and wow! I see, oh, yeah, that reminds me to talk about the purpose of my speech . . . ."

Unusual associations are the easiest to remember. This system can also be adapted to locations in your body. You visually link things you want to remember with places inside your skin. The shopping list is remembered when you recall the visualization of a loaf of bread stuck in your brain cavity, a large can of frozen orange juice in your throat, a bunch of broccoli tucked under your collar bone.

The peg system employs key words represented by numbers. For example, 1 = bun, 2 = shoe, 3 = tree, 4 = door, 5 = hive, 6 = sticks, 7 = heaven, 8 = gate, 9 = wine, and 10 = hen. In order for this system to be effective, these peg words need to be learned well.

You might use the peg system to remember that the speed of light is 186,000 miles per second. Imagine a hotdog bun (1) entering a gate (8) made of sticks (6). Since we tend to remember pictures longer than we do words, it may be easier to recall this weird scene than the numbers one, eight, and six in order.

D. Work with two other people who have chosen different techniques. Using what you underlined, take turns explaining the information to one another.

E. Discuss the following:

- What do you like/dislike about these techniques?
- Which techniques have you used already? Were they helpful?
- Which techniques do you think you might use? Why?

Vocabulary Building

USING QUOTES

An effective way to support a point or idea is to use a quote. In the following exercise, identify the point that is being supported by each quotation from the article "Memory." Then identify the source of the quote. The first one has been done as an example.

1. ". . . Memory is the boomers' new life-crisis issue." (paragraph 3)

   Decline in memory is a popular topic these days.

   source: *Cynthia Green, Psychologist, teaches memory class*

2. "What we think of as memories are ultimately patterns of connection . . . ." (paragraph 7)

   _____

   source: _____

3. "You want to keep the junk of everyday life out of the way so you can focus on what matters." (paragraph 12)

   _____

   source: _____

4. "Nearly 40 years after his surgery, H.M. does not know his age or the current date [or] where he is living." (paragraph 13)

   _____

   source: _____

5. "We continue to encode the general features of our experiences, but we leave off more details." (paragraph 15)

   _____

   source: _____

6. "Bill Clinton will probably always remember more names than you will." (paragraph 16)

_____

source: _____

7. "You used to have time to reflect and think. Now you're just a conduit for a constant stream of information." (paragraph 17)

_____

source: _____

8. "Suppose the drug raises your score on a job test. Who gets hired?" (paragraph 24)

_____

source: _____

Check your answers with a partner or in a small group. Refer to the reading if necessary.

Look back quickly at the sources and comment on the following:

■ Their background
■ Why the authors quote these people

PARAPHRASING

Another effective tool that writers use to support their points or ideas is paraphrasing. Paraphrasing means to express the ideas of someone else in your own words while keeping the meaning intact.

Example (paragraph 3): "The demand for books and seminars has never been greater, says Jack Lannom, a . . . longtime memory trainer. . . ."

The word "says" indicates to the readers that this idea has been paraphrased. Other words that serve this purpose include *observes, indicates, concludes,* and *hopes.*

Find four examples of paraphrasing in the article "Memory." Note them in the following list. In each case also note the source.

1. _____

source: _____

2. _____

source: _____

3. _____

source: _____

4. _____

source: _____

Share your paraphrases with a partner or in a small group. You can add to your list if necessary.

Why do you think the authors use quotes at times and paraphrasing at others?

Is one more effective than the other? Why?

Expanding Your Language

SPEAKING

Reporting Back: **Think of at least three things that you find difficult to remember. Choose any two of the techniques described in the excerpts from *Becoming a Master Student* by David Ellis (pp. 103–106). Use these techniques and report back as follows in your next class**

- Form small groups of three or four.
- Take turns sharing what you did.
- Discuss whether or not the techniques worked.

Compare and Contrast: **Using the information given concerning a "savant" in paragraph 12 of "Memory," try to make a list of everyday problems such a person might have. Share your list with a partner and together compare it with the case of H.M. in paragraph 13. Who do you think would have a harder time in life? Why?**

WRITING

Point of View: **Read the following and write a three- to four-paragraph response.**

It becomes scientifically possible to produce a drug that enhances memory and therefore improves learning. This drug is quite expensive. Under what conditions, if any, should it be made available to the public?

Set up your writing as follows:

- Decide on your point of view.
- List three reasons for your position.
- Note supporting information for each. You can use explanations, examples, etc.
- Discuss your outline with a partner. Make any additions or changes necessary.
- Write a short introduction (three to four sentences) in which you express your point of view. (See pages 96 and 97 for the elements of a good introduction.)
- Write one paragraph for each reason.
- Write a short conclusion (two to three sentences) in which you summarize what you wrote.

Hand your writing to your teacher for feedback.

Evalvation of your answers to the Memory Quiz on page 88.

SCORING	INTERPRETATION
Question 3–6: one point for each correct answer (12 points); **Question 7–15:** one point for each no answer (11 points); **Question 16–17:** one point for each correct answer (9 points).	**28–32 points:** You have a better-than-average memory. **22–27 points:** You may need follow-up. **0–21 points:** You probably need a professional evaluation.

CHAPTER 6

Memory: What Controls It?

◼ Chapter Openers

INTERVIEWING

Think about the following for a few minutes.

- ◼ Your earliest memory
- ◼ A serious quarrel that you had with a parent, spouse, or close friend
- ◼ Three significant events in your life—what happened and why these events are important to you

Work with a partner and interview each other on the preceding topics. Repeat the process two more times with two different partners. Form small groups of three or four and analyze what happened. Use the following questions to guide your analysis.

a. In what way did your information change each time? Was it longer/shorter, more/less detailed?

b. Which version was the most accurate?

c. If your parent, spouse, or close friend were telling the same story would they give the same information? Why?

d. How sure are you now about the accuracy of your information?

e. What are some factors that seem to control or determine what you remember?

QUOTATIONS

Read the following quotations and check those that support the conclusions you came to above.

1. "Memories are like stones, time and distance erode them like acid."
   Ugo Betti

2. "How strange are the tricks of memory, which, often hazy as a dream about the most important events in a man's life, religiously preserve the merest trifles."
   Sir Richard Burton

3. "Not the power to remember, but its very opposite, the power to forget, is a necessary condition for our existence."
   Sholem Asch

4. "The things we remember best are those better forgotten."
   Baltasar Gracian

5. "Better by far that you should forget and smile
   Than that you should remember and be sad."
   Christina Rossetti

6. "A strong memory is commonly coupled with faulty judgment."
   Montaigne

Compare your answers with a partner.

Exploring and Understanding Reading

Many factors affect what and how much we remember. Some factors can even lead us to remember things that never happened.

PREDICTING

The following reading describes a study that explores the connection between stereotyping and what we remember. Check (✔) the statement(s) that you think the reading will support.

_____ Stereotyping does not affect our memory.

_____ Stereotyping makes our memory selective.

_____ Stereotyping creates false memories.

SKIMMING

Read the article quickly in order to verify your predictions. Discuss your answers with a partner.

Self-Fulfilling Stereotypes

By Mark Snyder

1. Having adopted stereotyped ways of thinking about another person, people tend to notice and remember the ways in which that person seems to fit the stereotype while resisting evidence that contradicts the stereotype. In one investigation that I conducted, student subjects read a biography of a fictitious woman named Betty K. We constructed the story of her life so that it would fit the stereotyped images of both lesbians and heterosexuals. Betty, we wrote, never had a steady boyfriend in high school, but did go out on dates. And although we gave her a steady boyfriend in college, we specified that he was more of a close friend than anything else. A week after we had distributed this biography, we gave our subjects some new information about Betty. We told some students that she was now living with another woman in a lesbian relationship; we told others that she was living with her husband.

2. To see what impact stereotypes about sexuality would have on how people remembered the facts of Betty's life, we asked each student to answer a series of questions about her life history. When we examined their answers, we found that the students had reconstructed the events of Betty's past in ways that supported their own stereotyped beliefs about her sexual orientation. Those who believed that Betty was a lesbian remembered that Betty had never had a steady boyfriend in high school, but tended to neglect the fact that she had gone out on many dates in college. Those who believed that Betty was now a heterosexual tended to remember that she had formed a steady relationship with a man in college, but tended to ignore the fact that this relationship was more of a friendship than a romance.

3. The students showed not only selective memories but also a striking facility for interpreting what they remembered in ways that added fresh support for their stereotypes. One student who accurately remembered that Betty never had a steady boyfriend in high school confidently pointed to that fact as an early sign of her lack of romantic or sexual interest in men. A student who correctly remembered that Betty often went out on dates in college was sure that these dates were signs of Betty's early attempts to hide her lesbian interests.

–Psychology Today

REPORTING ON A STUDY

A complete study should have all of the following elements:

- Purpose
- Subjects (on whom the study is being done)
- Method
- Results
- Conclusion

Read the article more carefully, locate each element and highlight or make notes on the relevant information.

A. Working with a partner, use your notes or highlighting in order to talk about the study.

B. Comment on the following points:

- Are the results convincing?
- What conclusions can you draw?
- What could the social consequences of this be?
- In what situations can such a memory lead to problems?

C. Read the following scenario and use the results from the study of Betty K. to predict the ending.

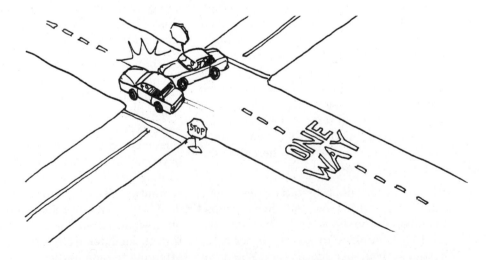

A man in his late 30s is driving on the right side of a one-way street. His two children are in the back. He comes to an intersection for which he does *not* have a stop sign but for which the street on the right does. Just as he is crossing, he notices a car coming from the street on the right. He expects the car to stop but instead it turns right and straight into his lane. The kids in the back yell, "Dad that car is coming straight at us!" The man tries to avoid a collision by veering into the left lane but is unsuccessful. The two cars collide into each other and as a result the windshield shatters leaving glass all over the left side of the road. The driver of the other car turns out to be a woman in her 60s or early 70s. A few pedestrians gather around. The woman gets out of her car. She seems very nervous and shaky. The man also gets out of his car and they argue about who is at fault. The woman claims that she was just driving along in her lane when the man ran into her. Somebody calls the police but they refuse to come because there are no injuries. Finally the man and the woman fill out a joint report on the accident. The phone numbers of two of the pedestrians are included in the report. The report goes to the insurance companies who then call the witnesses. One week later the man gets a letter from his insurance company.

1. Who does the insurance company find at fault?
2. What do you think the witnesses said to the insurance company?
3. What factors do you think influenced them?
4. Would there be any point in questioning the decision made by the insurance company?

PAIRED READINGS

Our memories may be faulty, but at least we have them. Some people are not so lucky. They lose big parts of their memory altogether. These people suffer from amnesia.

DISCUSSION QUESTIONS

Discuss the following questions with a partner or in a small group.

1. What is amnesia?
2. What causes amnesia?
3. Have you or anyone you know ever suffered some form of amnesia? If yes, describe what happened.

A different case of amnesia is discussed in each of the following readings. Choose one of the readings. Work with someone who has chosen the same reading.

Reading 1: The Man Who Vanished Into His Past

PREVIEWING

Read the title of the article. Predict which of the following this man will have a problem remembering.

- His name
- His wife
- His children
- The answer to 2 + 2
- What he had for breakfast
- What he does for a living

Discuss your predictions with your partner.

NEW YORK TIMES

The Man Who Vanished Into His Past

What to do when life resembles a bad "Twilight Zone" episode

By Marcia Sherman, M.D.

Just over a year ago, Terry Dibert got up from his desk in the school district headquarters in Bedford, Pa., and vanished into his past.

That sounds like an opening line to a thriller. But for Mr. Dibert, who left his computer running and his jacket on the back of his chair, it was literally true.

Six days later and 800 miles away, Mr. Dibert, the district's business manager, reappeared near dawn in the midst of a natural disaster. Police officers from Daytona Beach, Fla., found him early on July 6, wandering on Interstate 95 through the blinding smoke from wildfires that had shut the highway and forced the evacuation of much of the area.

Mr. Dibert told the police he was a 23-year-old sergeant trying to rejoin his Army unit at Fort Bragg. He was worried about being separated from his wife, who was pregnant with their first child.

What he said was accurate, but 11 years out of date, as the police discovered when they called Fort Bragg and found that Mr. Dibert's unit had been gone for a decade.

For neurologists, amnesia is a fascinating if generally familiar subject. The most common form is retrograde amnesia, in which some or all recollections seem to have been misplaced, leaving the patients stranded in the present. There is also anterograde amnesia, in which old memories remain intact, but new ones can no longer be formed. Some traumas wipe out the events that led up to them. And some patients lose only stored images and not words.

But Mr. Dibert's case was different, more like "a bad Twilight Zone episode," as he put it in a telephone interview.

"Mistaking the present for the past is not typical of most cases of memory disorder," said Dr. Scott Small, a neurobehaviorist at New York Presbyterian Medical Center in Manhattan. "Most amnesiacs can register the present. What makes this case so curious is its resemblance to a fugue state, and those are generally psychogenic in nature."

In other words, a neurologist encountering Mr. Dibert would have diagnosed his time traveling as the product of emotional stress rather than a brain disorder.

Of course, Daytona Beach was full of people under emotional stress last summer. So the police took him to the logical place: a psychiatric hospital. Still convinced it was 1987, Mr. Dibert eventually mentioned family living in Bedford, Pa., and on July 8, his frantic wife, Julie, received a call from a nurse who had tracked her down.

When Mrs. Dibert arrived at the hospital, her husband recognized her but had trouble recalling her name. He asked how "Bunky" was doing, using the nickname they had invented for the child she was expecting 11 years before. "It was kind of fun for a while, but also scary," Mrs. Dibert said.

She was told that her husband was suffering from stress, and she couldn't disagree. He had been complaining of pressure at his job, and she had seen him taking aspirin for uncharacteristically frequent headaches.

It was not until Mr. Dibert was transferred from the Florida hospital to a hospital in nearby Altoona, where he was unable to recognize his children, that the diagnosis began to unravel.

Mr. Dibert had no previous history of mental illness, and normal people, no matter how stressed, do not suddenly just lose their bearing in time. The Altoona doctors, including Dr. Michael-Gerard Moncman, ordered a CAT scan.

When Dr. Moncman first came to examine Mr. Dibert, he found a patient who had returned to reality enough to be frightened and confused.

"He was pretty much in the present," Dr. Moncman said. "By that time he was aware of gaps in his memory. He could tell me very clearly about his job doing parts inventory at Fort Bragg, but the last four to six weeks were simply gone."

Mr. Dibert describes the time as an "uncomfortable" mix of past and present. "Things would be said that didn't click at first," he said.

The brain scan revealed that Mr. Dibert had a large cyst pushing apart the nerve tissue surrounding it and pressing on a nerve tract, called the fornix, known to play a role in memory retrieval and storage. In one area called the columns of the fornix, tissue had split apart under pressure. There was also brain swelling, explaining the headaches. "There were some parts of the brain that were literally bent around this thing," Dr. Moncman said.

Brain cysts are not unusual. Some never produce symptoms; others cause problems as they grow and push on adjacent structures. Headaches, seizures, weakness, sensory disturbances or dementia may result.

The surgeon who eventually drained Mr. Dibert's cyst, Dr. L. Dade Lunsford, the chairman of the neurologic surgery department at Pittsburgh University, said the cyst had probably been there since birth, growing as spinal fluid seeped in from the base of the brain and never escaped.

As brain cysts go, Mr. Dibert's was not particularly large. But it was in one of the deepest and oldest parts of the brain, where memory, primitive drives and emotions are generated. Fear, aggression, sexuality, eating and drinking all originate from this area, called the limbic system.

It may be hard to think of the self as something so mechanistic that a touch in the right spot can turn the past on or off. But in Mr. Dibert's case, Dr. Lunsford said, the cyst was "perfectly placed" to do just that.

Still, even the most strangely placed cyst with the strangest effects is just a cyst—a sac of fluid that can be drained surgically. On July 16, Dr. Lunsford made a tiny hole in Mr. Dibert's skull and removed 10 to 12 cubic centimeters of spinal fluid. A small hole was left behind in the wall of the cyst, in case fluid reaccumulates.

It was not certain that the surgery would guarantee a happy ending. The nerve tissue that had been bent around the cyst did not simply spring back into place. Scans showed that a large space remained where the cyst had been.

"Nerves don't like to be stretched," Dr. Moncman said. "We tried to restore as much normal anatomy as we could. But it's up to his brain to restore normal function.

"You can't just pat the brain on the head and say 'O.K., you're done.' You've got to stand back and hope for the best."

The scans, of course, gave no clue as to what happened in the period leading up to June 30, when Mr. Dibert suddenly traveled into his past. Dr. Lunsford speculated that up to that point, Mr. Dibert's brain had been able to compensate for the increased pressure exerted by the growing cyst. Perhaps a short-term increase in pressure cut off the flow of memory information along the fornix, or perhaps the compensating mechanisms broke down.

For Mr. Dibert, recovering from the brain surgery was the easy part. He was more worried about how the episode would affect his three children.

"They handled it better than most adults did," he said. "They got out the photo albums and went through them, saying 'Hey, remember this? It was at my birthday party.'"

During Mr. Dibert's initial post-operative checkups, Dr. Lunsford noted a "quizzical" look in his patient, as if he still could not understand or believe what happened to him. But his exam last spring was essentially normal.

Mr. Dibert, who returned to work in the fall, said last week that he felt fine. His missing memories gradually filled in, except for a gap of about 10 days starting "three or four" days before his disappearance, he said. In that interview, Mr. Dibert said that what he had been through had made him and his wife "more aware of little things" like headaches, which he said were no longer just a nuisance to be ignored.

Then over the weekend, Mr. Dibert complained of headaches, said a relative, and yesterday he went to his local hospital for testing. No information was available on his condition.

Dr. Moncman, who is no longer involved in Mr. Dibert's care, said that he thought it likely that his current doctors would move aggressively to test for any recurrence. "After all that he's been through, for the slightest thing that happens, you'd want to get him in there and go to work," he said.

SKIMMING

Skim the article to check your predictions and answer the following questions.

1. What led to his amnesia?
2. Did he make a full recovery?

SCANNING FOR SPECIFIC INFORMATION

Scan the reading to find the answers for the questions that follow. Underline the relevant information and note the number of the question in the margin for future reference. Write the answers in your own words and in note form.

1. What evidence is there that what happened to Mr. Dibert was sudden?

   _____

   _____

2. How far back in time did Mr. Dibert's memory go?

   _____

3. What are the different kinds of amnesia?

   _____

   _____

   _____

   _____

   Does Mr. Dibert fit any of these types? Explain.

   _____

   _____

4. What explanation was first given for Mr. Dibert's condition?

   _____

Why was this explanation not acceptable?

_____

_____

5. What was the cause of Mr. Dibert's condition?

_____

How long had it been there?

_____

Why was the effect so sudden?

_____

_____

6. How successful was the operation that Mr. Dibert had to undergo?

_____

_____

Check your answers with a partner. Refer to the reading if you do not agree.

RECAPPING THE INFORMATION

A. Identify the main events in the story and list them in chronological order.

■ *READING TIP:*
Newspaper articles do not always present information in the order in which it happened.

B. Highlight the information corresponding to each event.

C. Use what you highlighted to make notes on each event. Use your own words as much as possible.

D. Working with your partner, compare the notes you made. Discuss whether they are too detailed or too brief. Add to or remove from your notes if necessary.

E. Using your notes, take turns telling each other the important information in the article. Make sure you explain the information as clearly and completely as you can.

REACTING TO THE INFORMATION

Quotes

■ *READING TIP:*
Quotes give a lot of information about how people feel about and react to a situation.

Work with a partner. Find the following quotations in the reading and discuss what they tell us about how Mrs. Dibert, Mr. Dibert, and their children reacted to the situation.

Mrs. Dibert: "It was kind of fun for a while, but also scary."

Mr. Dibert: "Uncomfortable" mix of past and present. "Things would be said that didn't click at first."

Mr. Dibert: "They handled it better than most adults did. They got out the photo albums and went through them, saying 'Hey, remember this? It was at my birthday party.'"

Mr. Dibert: ". . . more aware of little things" like headaches. . .

Predicting the Consequences

Discuss the following.

1. How much trust will Mr. Dibert put in his memory from now on?
2. In what way(s) will this affect him in his life both at home and at work?
3. Will he be treated differently by

   ■ his wife?
   ■ his children?
   ■ his coworkers?
   ■ his supervisor?

Reading 2: Mystery Man Can't Find Key to Unlock His Past

PREVIEWING

Read the title, subtitle, and section headings of the article. Predict which of the following this man will have a problem remembering.

- His name
- His family
- The answer to 2 + 2
- Where he lives
- What he had for breakfast
- What he does for a living

Discuss your predictions with your partner.

THE MONTREAL GAZETTE

Mystery Man Can't Find Key to Unlock His Past

Therapy produces flashes of memory

By Peggy Curan and Paul Tough

Just after midnight on Oct. 12, 1998, a young man woke up beside a dumpster in a deserted parking lot on University Street near St. Jacques Street in Montreal. He had no idea how he got there. He didn't know what city or even what country he was in. He couldn't remember his name.

He had no cuts or bruises, but his head was pounding and he was naked, although he soon found clothes strewn on the ground nearby. The man dressed and wandered across the street to the Radisson Hotel, but a night manager chucked him out.

After that, he walked aimlessly until he reached the Quality Hotel on Park. Avenue, where a sympathetic concierge listened to his story and called an ambulance.

For six weeks neurologists and psychiatrists at the Montreal General Hospital took turns trying to unlock the mystery of the man's identity with little success. He had a lumbar puncture to test for meningitis and a brain scan to detect possible injury or illness. The results were negative.

He underwent hypnotherapy twice and was injected with sodium amytal, a sedative better known as "truth serum." He was believed to be suffering from dissociative amnesia, a condition that can be triggered by mental trauma.

"It was extremely difficult," said the man, his muted accent a blend of American and English intonation and vocabulary. Physically, he felt fine, except for a constant headache, probably caused by stress. He lost about 20 pounds.

"The hardest part was the loneliness. I met some really fine people who helped me, but it was difficult not knowing who I was or where my friends and family were."

Gisela Marler, who works in the department at the General that does brain scans, was one of the people who helped him.

Charmed by his nice manners, she and her husband invited him to their home on weekends and pressed Montreal Urban Community Police to help by sending a missing-persons report with his picture to the FBI and Interpol.

"I thought he needed a friend. He was very likeable, very engaging," said Marler, who has a son about the same age.

"It was very difficult to keep up his morale, because being a 'nobody' is a very depressing situation to be in, particularly on a psychiatry ward."

During one session at the hospital, the man jerked his head when he heard someone on the ward call out the name James, and he began referring to himself as James

Edward Brighton. However, Marler said, checks with the British High Commission, the U.S. consulate, and Canadian authorities found no one with that name born on the day he believed to be his birthday—March 23, 1970.

Scattered Details Emerge

During therapy to jog his memory, scattered details emerged, that he might live or work near Morristown, New Jersey, possibly as a technician in the broadcasting industry, that he might have been born in England and probably moved to the United States as a teenager.

He remembered TV shows and could describe his apartment, recalled flashes of a family vacation in Niagara Falls and a recent trip to Key West, Florida. He said the small scar hidden under an eyebrow dated from a soccer match at school.

One of the few things that "Brighton" knew from the start was that he is gay, which might offer a clue to how he happened to be in Montreal on Thanksgiving weekend, when the annual Black and Blue party was held. So when other efforts to discover his identity failed, a social worker suggested he contact Gay-Line, an information-and-help telephone service. Coordinator Bruce Walsh said the line normally has a strict policy against meeting callers unless they appear suicidal, but this case was unusual enough to make an exception. He said any doubts he might have had that "Brighton" might be faking dissolved when they met. "He was really concerned that I would believe him," Walsh said. "He was a good advocate for himself. He's a good boy. I hoped he would get home for Christmas, that's for sure."

Gay Newspapers Alerted

Walsh prepared a press statement to newspapers across the continent, as well as to gay community groups in and around Morristown in hopes that someone would recognize him. "What we really needed was two minutes on *America's Unsolved Mysteries*."

After 37 days, the Montreal General released "Brighton" and offered to find him a place in a group home for psychiatric outpatients. Instead, Gregg Blachford, a Gay-Line volunteer, agreed to take him in.

Blachford admits some friends warned him not to take a stranger home, but he felt quite safe because there was no evidence of schizophrenia or other types of mental illness. His guest was grateful to be out of the psychiatric ward and finally able to sleep more soundly.

While under hypnosis to try to find out how he arrived in Montreal, he suffered an anxiety attack and snapped awake. "The hypnotherapist said I lunged out of my chair," he said, which deepened his suspicions that he came to Montreal against his will.

He started keeping a journal to record everything he remembered, or thought he remembered. "That way, if I forgot it, I could get it back again," he said. "I wanted to go home. I was willing to do anything."

James spent the winter in a spare bedroom in the apartment of Gregg Blachford. That winter was a long odyssey for both James and the men of Gay-Line. Gregg and Bruce formed the nucleus of the "team," as they came to refer to themselves. They followed every lead, including one that seemed promising: a woman in Hamilton, Ontario, was certain that she had spent a summer in Surrey, British Columbia, with a teenaged

James Brighton—also English, also born about 1970, also, it turned out, gay. But the team's attempts to find the Brightons were fruitless, and they moved on to other clues.

It was a strange process. Bruce and Gregg were spending every free minute trying to find out who James had been, but at the same time, they were becoming friends with the person he had become. There were lots of late-night phone calls and intense dinner conversations. They'd all share jokes about the cultural references that James still remembered: Bette Midler songs, tacky Christmas lights, *Titanic*.

In a way, James's situation felt familiar to the Gay-Line volunteers who helped him. Like him, they'd been through a moment when they'd broken with the past and had been reborn into a new and confusing present. They'd lost touch with family and friends, too, and had struggled to make sense of who they had become. But there's a difference between turning your back on the past and losing sight of it altogether.

The Mystery Unravels

When the answer came, it involved *Hard Copy*, the syndicated American tabloid TV show. A camera crew came up from New York in late December to do a story on the man without a past. A few hours after the show aired in January, James Brighton, British accent and all, had been identified as Matthew Honeycutt, a small-town boy from La Follette, Tennessee.

Things quickly became a little crazy around Gregg's house. The Montreal police concluded that James—Matthew—had been lying about his amnesia, wasting their time, and they reacted to this slight by arresting him and holding him in jail for three days on charges of public mischief and obstruction of justice.

The day after James's release—Gregg bailed him out, and the police seemed ready to drop the charges—Bruce and Gregg and James gathered at Gregg's house. There was still work to do, but it was also the first chance they'd all had to catch their breath and think about the future. Their quest was over: James was found now, which was what he'd said he wanted all along. But the life he had found wasn't necessarily the one they would have chosen for him, or the one he would have chosen for himself. In his Montreal life, the only one he remembered, he had warm friends, a comfortable home in a cosmopolitan city, and a certain air of mystery. In the life he was going to, or going back to, Matthew Honeycutt had a complicated relationship with his fundamentalist family, and no friends, at least not any he could remember. He was going home—they all kept telling themselves that. But it didn't always feel that way.

At the end of January, Matthew's mother and sister came up to Montreal to bring him back to La Follette. Things were a bit awkward. Gregg and Bruce tried to make their southern visitors feel at home, but it was hard—Montreal was so big, and so snowy, and so French, and Matthew didn't recognize them at all.

For Gregg and Bruce, it was a bittersweet period. There was a lot of media attention, which was exciting, and James—Matthew—had found out who he was. There were still unanswered, perhaps unanswerable, questions. But the adventure had come to an end. A friend was leaving town. On the day James left for Tennessee, Gregg noticed that his British accent had started to fade.

(Adapted from "Mystery man can't find key to unlock his past" by Peggy Curan, *The Montreal Gazette*; and "Identity crisis" by Paul Tough, *Saturday Night*.)

SKIMMING

Skim the article to check your predictions and answer the following

1. What led to his amnesia?
2. Did he make a full recovery?

SCANNING FOR SPECIFIC INFORMATION

Scan the reading to find the answers for the questions that follow. Underline the relevant information and note the number of the question in the margin for future reference. Write the answers in your own words and in note form.

1. What "condition" did this man wake up in?

    _____

    _____

2. What two reactions did he get when he asked for help?

    _____

    _____

3. What tests did he have to go through?

    _____

    _____

    _____

    _____

    What did the doctors conclude?

    _____

    What can cause this condition?

    _____

4. Was his name really James? Explain.

    _____

    _____

5. How much did he remember about himself?

_____

_____

_____

6. What did the Gay-Line organization do to help "James" out?

_____

_____

7. What started happening between Bruce, Gregg, and James?

_____

Why?

_____

8. How was James's true identity found?

_____

_____

Check your answers with a partner. Refer to the reading if you do not agree.

RECAPPING THE INFORMATION

A. Identify the main events in the story and list them in chronological order.

B. Highlight the information corresponding to each event.

C. Use what you highlighted to make notes on each event. Use your own words as much as possible.

D. Working with your partner, compare the notes you made. Discuss whether they are too detailed or too brief. Add to or remove from your notes if necessary.

E. Using your notes, take turns telling each other the important information in the article. Make sure you explain the information as clearly and completely as you can.

■ *READING TIP:*
Newspaper articles do not always present information in the order in which it happened.

REACTING TO THE INFORMATION

Quotes

■ *READING TIP:*
Quotes give a lot of information about how people feel about and react to a situation.

Work with a partner. Find the following quotations in the reading and discuss what they tell us about how "James" and the people around him reacted to the situation.

James:	"The hardest part is the loneliness. I've met some really fine people who have helped me, but it's difficult not knowing who I am or where my friends and family are."
Gisela Marler:	"I thought he needed a friend. He's very likeable, very engaging."
Bruce Walsh:	"He was really concerned that I would believe him. He's a good advocate for himself. He's a good boy. I hope he gets home for Christmas that's for sure.'"
James:	"That way, if I do forget it, I can get it back again, I want to go home. I'm willing to do anything."

Predicting the Consequences

Discuss the following.

1. How much trust will Matthew put in his memory from now on?
2. Will he be happy back in his hometown?
3. How will he be treated by

   ■ his mother?   ■ his sister?   ■ his "friends"?

After Reading

RETELLING THE INFORMATION

Work with a partner who read a different article.

- **Use your notes and take turns reporting on the information you read. Explain the ideas clearly in your own words.**
- **Encourage your partner to ask questions or write some of the important facts you explain.**
- **After you have both explained your information, discuss the quotes and questions in "Reacting to the Information" on pages 122 and 124.**

ANALYZING THE INFORMATION

Work with a partner who read a different article. Quickly look through your notes and answers for both readings. Note down the similarities and differences in the two stories using the following framework.

	Mr. Dibert	Matthew
Background		
Initial condition		
Type of amnesia		
Reason		
Consequences		
Recovery		

Use your comparisons to comment on the following

1. Whose life is likely to go back to "normal" sooner?
2. Assuming that both recover their full memory, who is more likely to suffer another attack?
3. Both Matthew and Mr. Dibert suffered a trauma that made them incapable of remembering what happened before the trauma. Imagine a situation in which a person cannot remember what happens *after* a trauma—that is, she cannot remember what happened a minute or an hour ago, although she can remember everything up to the time of the trauma. In what way would that be different? Would it be easier or harder to handle?

APPLYING THE INFORMATION

So far we have looked at how imperfect memory can be. Let's look at memory from a different angle. Think about the following ideas.

1. How can we make use of the imperfections in our memory?
2. What would be the advantages of destroying certain memories?

Read the following article quickly while keeping these two points in mind.

DALLAS MORNING NEWS

The Flaws of Memory

Remembering something from a long time ago may cause you to lose the memory. And it may change when you re-remember it.

By Tom Siegfried

Memory's essential imperfection is no secret. Everybody sometimes suffers from forgetfulness. And psychologists have long known that not only do people forget, they also misremember.

Still, scientists are only beginning to learn just how strangely flawed human memory can be. One new study, for example, suggests that the worst thing you can do for a memory is recall it. In other words, practice makes imperfect. If you use a memory, you can lose it. "Whenever we bring a memory to mind," writes neurobiologist Yadin Dudai, "it may turn shaky and slip into oblivion."

Dudai, of the Weizmann Institute in Israel, cites a new study reported recently in the journal *Nature* by scientists at New York University. In essence, they showed how to erase a rat's memory of a fearful event.

The New York scientists used a standard experimental set-up: playing a short tone followed by an electric shock to the rat's feet. It doesn't take the rat long to remember that a tone means a shock. Bring the rat back the next day, and it will freeze with fear when it hears the tone, even without the accompanying shock.

Biologists have some idea of what happens in the brain to form such a long-term memory. Specific links between nerve cells are somehow strengthened. Part of that process involves the need for the nerve cells to make new proteins. An event is stored in long-term memory only after this protein production, which can take a few hours. "Most memories, like humans and wine, do not mature instantly," Dudai observed.

Before protein production completes the memory maturation, the memory of the event is fragile, subject to change or loss. It's easy to disrupt a rat's memory during the fragile period. Simply injecting a chemical that blocks protein production prevents the rat from forming a long-term memory of its fear: Bring the rat back the next day and the tone doesn't faze it.

Now take a rat that does remember to freeze at the sound of the tone. Inject it with the protein blocker, the New York scientists found, and the rat will lose its fearful memory—but only if it has first been forced to remember its fear. "This effect requires that the memory be actively retrieved," wrote researchers Karim Nader, Glenn Schafe and Joseph Le Doux.

In other words, if you bring a rat back the second day and merely inject the protein blocker, the rat retains its memory of the tone-shock connection. Only if you first play the tone, activating the rat's memory, will the protein blocker erase the fear. "It now appears that new proteins are required to maintain old memories that have been reactivated," the scientists wrote in *Nature*.

These findings imply that calling up a long-term memory exposes that memory to loss. Whenever you recall a memory, it must be re-stored, requiring new protein production in your nerve cells. And restoring a memory means that it must be encoded again, with all the potential for memory error that occurs when memory is encoded the first time.

In a commentary in the same issue of *Nature*, Dudai notes that scientists already knew that memories are reconstructed with use. Any memory, he points out, involves mingling present perceptions with representations of the past stored in our brain.

Two people can bring a different memory away from the same event because they perceived it through different "filters" colored by their personal pasts.

Then, when a person recalls a long-term memory later on, it mixes with an expanded set of additional memories and perceptions. So that memory will be re-stored in a modified way, even without any protein-blocking injections.

Of course it's a little too soon for biologists to erase their memory of what they used to think about memory. Questions remain, Dudai reminds everybody. For one thing, perhaps the protein blocker did not really erase the fear memory but merely covered it up, and maybe there's some way to trigger it again. Furthermore, it may be that other forms of memory don't work the same way as memory of fear. And there's the obvious issue that even though humans mimic rats in many ways, there are differences.

Even so, recent findings about memory and its flaws may have important impacts on various realms of human interaction. Imagine the possible benefit for people traumatized by memories of terror or tragedy. The day may come when the cure is recalling the trauma, and then erasing it with a shot.

New and improved knowledge about how memory works can suggest novel solutions to such problems, and perhaps even make it easier to memorize poetry.

Discuss the following questions in groups of three or four.

1. What "faulty" characteristic of memory is being explored in this article?
2. What was the purpose of the study?
3. Did it succeed?
4. How may this finding be applied to humans in the future?
5. If you had the choice of either retaining your best memories in absolute detail OR forgetting your worst memories entirely, which would you choose? Why?

Vocabulary Building

WORD FORMS

Fill in the blanks with the correct form of the word.

arrived/arriving

1. When Mrs. Dibert _____ at the hospital, her husband had trouble recognizing her.

fascinated/fascinating

2. Amnesia is a _____ subject.

transferred/transferring

3. Mr. Dibert was _____ from the Florida hospital to another hospital.

suffered/suffering

4. She was told her husband _____ from stress.

recovered/recovering

5. For Mr. Dibert, _____ from the surgery was the easy part.

missed/missing

6. His _____ memories gradually filled in.

tried/trying

7. Gregg and Bruce _____ to make their southern visitors at home, but it was hard.

pounded/pounding

8. He had no cuts or bruises, but his head _____ and he was naked.

needed/needing

9. "I thought he _____ a friend. He's very likeable, very engaging."

depressed/depressing

10. Being a "nobody" is a very _____ situation to be in.

Check your answers with a partner. Refer to the paired readings to confirm your answers.

VOCABULARY IN CONTEXT

All words have a basic meaning, but many words take on additional meanings.

A. Find the meaning of the word(s) in boldface as determined by the context in which they are being used.

1. When Mr. Dibert was unable to recognize his children, the diagnosis began to **unravel**.

   _____

2. Things would be said that didn't **click** at first.

   _____

3. The rat will **freeze** with fear when it hears the tone.

   _____

4. You've got to **stand back** and hope for the best.

   _____

5. New and improved knowledge about how memory works can suggest **novel** solutions to such problems.

   _____

6. It is likely that his doctors will move **aggressively** to test for any recurrence.

   _____

7. Retrograde amnesia is when some or all recollections seem to have been misplaced, leaving the patient **stranded** in the present.

   _____

8. During therapy to **jog** his memory, certain details emerged.

   _____

9. That winter was a long **odyssey** for both James and the men of Gay-Line.

   _____

Check your answers with a partner.

B. Look up the same words in the dictionary. Compare the meaning you derived from the contexts above with the original meaning of each word to see if there is a clear connection. Which do you think is more efficient: to use a dictionary first or to guess from context first?

Expanding Your Language

SPEAKING

A. What is your opinion? Think about the following situation:

It might soon be possible to view images held in the brain for a short time after death. This can be used by detectives in murder cases to identify who the murderer was.

Discuss this idea in a small group of three or four students. Use the following questions.

1. How reliable is a dead person's memory?
2. Is it ethical to look into someone's mind even if they are dead?
3. What other ethical considerations might there be?

B. *Oral Presentation:* **Think of a time when you and a friend, sibling, or spouse were discussing an event from the past in which you were both involved. Each of you had a different recollection of what happened and this led to a big argument. Prepare a five-minute talk using the following sequence.**

- Your version of the event
- The other person's version of the event
- Consequences of difference in memory
- How the situation was resolved
- What you would do in the future to avoid having such a thing happen again

Present your story to a group of three or four others.

WRITING

A. *Personal Writing:* **Write about two of the best (or worst) memories of your life. Describe them in detail and explain what effect they still have on you.**

B. *Reaction Writing:* **Write about your reaction to the study in which mice are given electric shocks. Do you agree with such studies? Is it fair that animals suffer so that human lives can be improved?**

Read On: Taking it Further

READING JOURNAL

Memoirs can be fascinating and provide interesting information not only about their authors, but also about the times and countries they lived in. Examples include *Memoirs of a Geisha, Out of Africa,* and *Long Walk to Freedom* (Nelson Mandela). There are many many more.

Ask your teacher to help you find either one of these or a similar book. Choose a section to read and report on.

SURFING THE WEB

There are plenty of memory Web sites now available. Some offer a variety of memory tests as well as advice on how to improve memory. One such site is *mindtools.com.*

Search the Internet for other sites and download some information that you find interesting. Prepare to present the information to a partner or to a small group. Follow the steps outlined in Chapter 4, page 82. Make sure you tell your classmates which sites you found interesting or useful.

The Age of Communications

A civilization is judged by its quality, not by its speed.

—*Edman*

Introducing the Topics

How is today's communications technology changing our world? With cell phones and e-mail ever available, are our private lives and personal time disappearing? In this unit we will find out about some of the new communications technology issues that people are debating today. Chapter 7 explores the spread of cell-phone use in North American society. Why are cell phones popular? How does cell-phone use affect our daily lives? In Chapter 8, we will find out how changing views about privacy have resulted from the e-mail and Internet revolution. With increased use of the Internet, what private information is becoming public? Do the benefits of access outweigh the dangers?

Points of Interest

COMMUNICATIONS QUESTIONNAIRE: MORE OR LESS

Is it *more* or *less* possible for people today to do each of the following than it was twenty years ago? Circle *M* for more or *L* for less. Be prepared to explain your choices.

1. M   L   Make contact with people in different societies.

2. M   L   Find time to write a long letter to a friend.

3. M   L   Find out what your coworker really thinks about your boss.

4. M   L   Overhear a private conversation.

5. M   L   Carry out business on the weekend.

6. M   L   Find out what a person's credit rating is.

7. M   L   Keep personal information about yourself a secret from people you don't know.

Discuss your ideas with a partner or in a small group and answer the following questions:

1. What technology makes it possible to do any of the things in the above list?

2. What are the advantages and disadvantages of today's communications technology?

CHAPTER 7

The Cell-Phone Explosion

Chapter Openers

A. GETTING INFORMATION FROM A GRAPH

Wireless Nation
Finland pushes cell phone to high-tech limit

Cell phone usage
- **Finland: 60%**
- **USA: 28%**

On the Web
- **Finland: 31%**
- **USA: 28%**

Wireless countries

Finland recently announced it now has more mobile than fixed-line telephones. Top cellular /PCS countries in subscribers per 100 population

Country	Subscribers per 100
Finland	50.9
Norway	46.5
Sweden	45.8
Guam	43.0
Hong Kong	39.0
Israel	37.4
Japan	36.7
Australia	31.5
Denmark	31.2
Singapore	30.2

Note: U.S. ranks 14th at 25.0

Source: The Strategis Group

141

Based on the information in these graphs and ideas of your own, answer the following questions.

1. In which areas of the world are cell phones widely used?
2. How quickly is cell-phone use increasing?
3. Will cell-phone use become global? Why or why not?
3. Are cell phones a luxury, a necessity, or both?

Work with others in a small group to discuss your answers.

B. CATEGORIZING

Some say that cell phones are a help, while others feel they just create problems. What do you think? Decide which category each of the following belongs in. Be prepared to give reasons for your choices.

■ Using a cell phone while driving
■ Using a cell phone from a hospital
■ Using a cell phone on an airplane
■ Using a cell phone at school
■ Using a cell phone to organize a protest rally
■ Having a cell phone with you on a late night errand
■ Having a cell phone with you on a long distance trip
■ Having a cell phone with you while hiking in the wilderness
■ Using a cell phone in a public place such as a concert, or a restaurant

Helpful	*Problematic*

C. CELL PHONES IN THE NEWS

There are many reports about cell phones in the news. Scan these short summaries of news reports from NPR (National Public Radio) Online and highlight information that shows that cell phones are

- helpful,
- problematic,
- neither, or
- both.

1. **Cell-Phone Rally:** In an effort to unseat Philippine president Joseph Estrada, Filipinos sent 30 million cell phone "text messages" daily—more than anywhere else in the world. Activists are using the technology to organize rallies and respond instantly to the latest corruption charges.

2. **Cell-Phone Courtesy:** San Diego is trying a new campaign to encourage more courteous use of cell phones. Cell-phone maker Nokia and the San Diego city government are teaming up to post signs asking cell-phone users to turn off their ringers, or their phones, in public places such as churches, libraries, and movie theaters.

3. **The FBI and Cell Phones:** The Federal Bureau of Investigation is trying to gain an extended authority to precisely track cellular phones and where their users are. The FBI says it needs to be able to pinpoint criminal use of cell phones, but industry officials and privacy advocates oppose the plans, citing how much the new measures to track cellular phones would cost, and that it would violate the privacy of cell-phone users.

4. **Cell Phones in Cars:** With cell-phone sales increasing dramatically there has been a sharp rise in the number of car accidents caused by drivers talking on their cell phones. In Brooklyn, Ohio, a new city ordinance is banning motorists from that activity and police will begin ticketing motorists who don't have both hands on the steering wheel.

Work with a partner or in a small group to discuss the reasons for your choices. Decide on the most helpful and the most problematic uses of cell phones.

Be prepared to discuss your ideas with others in the class.

Exploring and Understanding Reading

PAIRED READINGS

Choose one of the readings. Work with a partner who is reading the same article.

Reading 1: Cell-Phone Use in Finland

PREDICTING

Check (✔) the ideas about cell-phone use that you expect to find in the reading.

In Finland it is possible to use cell phones to

1. _____ take orders at a restaurant.

2. _____ have a cell phone for each grade-one student.

3. _____ have a personal phone book inside a phone.

4. _____ send text messages instead of speaking by phone.

5. _____ buy food from a vending machine.

6. _____ pay for your car to be washed.

Work with a partner to compare your answers. Return to these predictions after you have finished reading and verify your answers.

SKIMMING

Skim the entire article quickly and answer the following questions.

1. How widespread and popular is cell-phone use in Finland?

2. How is cell-phone use in Finland different from cell-phone use in other parts of the world?

WASHINGTON POST

Where cell phones get a ringing endorsement

By T.R. Reid

HELSINKI–At the sun-splashed outdoor café beside Hakaniemi harbor, I sat down at a table and the smiling waitress came over. She had a small black pad but no pen or pencil.

I placed a fairly complicated order: soup, entrée, vegetable, salad, dressing and a mug of Finland's famous beer, Lapin Kulta ("The Gold of Lapland"). But the waitress didn't write anything down. Instead, she unfolded that black pad—it turned out to be a cellular phone—and called the kitchen, perhaps 15 meters away, to relay my order: Then she took her phone and her smile and moved on to the next table.

This is evidently a perfectly normal way for a waitress to operate here in the world's most wireless nation, a country that seems to have developed a national consensus that anything worth doing is worth doing by mobile phone.

North Americans often think of themselves as the most technologically advanced people on Earth. But when it comes to incorporating the latest telecommunications technology into daily life, Finland is far ahead of us. The country has 5 million people and 3 million cell phones—a penetration rate of 60 percent, more than twice the U.S. level.

Finland is the first country to have more mobile phones than traditional fixed-line units. But it won't be the last. In telecom circles, it's accepted wisdom that every advanced nation will fairly quickly reach Finnish levels of cell-phone saturation. Finland, then, gives us a chance to see our telephonic future.

Virtually every man, woman and teenager here, from investment bankers in downtown Helsinki to reindeer herders on the arctic tundra, carries a mobile telephone. The most common Finnish word for "cellular phone" is *kannykka*.

That translates roughly to "little hand," so that linguistically, at least, such a phone is now considered a part of the body.

Walk down the street in Helsinki and you'll see phone-carrying window washers, bus drivers, trash collectors, bicyclists and in-line skaters chatting away as they work or play. In a downtown park that curves along the waterfront, a jogger was carrying on a running conversation—literally—with a friend bobbing in a kayak about 60 meters out in the Gulf of Finland.

Mobile phone usage is universal in high school, students say, and some unhappy principals are moving to install metal detectors.

"It's not for guns, like in your American schools," laughs Hanna Riihelainen, a senior at Helsinki's Laajasalon High.

Today in Finland you can use your phone to:
• Send text messages to other users instead of calling them. SMS (Short Message Service) is exploding, particularly among teens, who like its low cost and classroom-friendly silence.
• Purchase items ranging from mints in a vending machine to a car wash by phoning a number that charges the goods to your phone bill.
• Send instant postcards of yourself by shooting a picture with a digital camera, uploading it to a mobile phone with Internet access, then sending it to Sonera, which for $1.50 prints the image with your message and mails it.

The goal of the Finnish mobile providers is to make the portable phone as indispensable as oxygen. No one is betting against them. . . .

—*USA Today*

"They're trying to keep us from using our phones in class. But it doesn't work. We hold the phones in our laps and send text messages back and forth."

At present, the standard age for receiving a phone of one's own here is about 14, says Olli Martikainen, a professor at Helsinki University of Technology.

"But my 7-year-old will start school in the fall," Martikainen continues, "and he's already worried that he'll be the only kid in first grade without a phone. I have a couple of old phones sitting around, so I'll probably give him one."

Like its Scandinavian neighbors, Finland is a fiercely egalitarian nation, and it is important here that rich and poor alike have access to technological advances. Mobile phone rates are low, generally between $10 and $40 per month. To help parents in Martikainen's situation, Finnish telephone companies offer family plans with lower rates for households with multiple phone numbers.

On the other hand, Finnish telephone companies are rapidly phasing out phone booths, on the grounds that hardly anybody uses them any more.

The telephone book, too, is going the way of the dinosaur. When people call for directory information, the operator sends the number in the form of a text message; a touch of a key on the cell phone will save it in memory. As a result, each Finn can carry around a personal phone book inside his phone.

The dark side of telephony, sadly, has also gone mobile. Telemarketers now routinely call cell phones, so that you can be walking down the street and suddenly have a stranger ring up to offer a time share in Lapland. Even worse, people are starting to get "junk text messages"—unsolicited ads and notices that show up on the phone's display screen.

Perhaps the biggest difference in a wireless society, though, is that it becomes hard for people to gain freedom from their phones.

"Life is not so private anymore," laments Timo Kopomaa, a Helsinki sociologist.

"Since everyone is expected to have a phone all the time, the boss can always find you. You can shut it off, but then you have the nagging thought, 'I might be missing something important.'"

SCANNING

Read each of the questions and look for the answers in the article. Mark the question number in the margin to show where the answer is located. Highlight the key words and write the answer in note form.

1. What percentage of Finland's population uses cell phones as compared to that in the United States?

_____

2. Why are high schools installing metal detectors?

_____

3. How affordable are cell phones in Finland?

_____

4. What do Finns think are the advantages of using cell phones?

_____

5. What do Finns think are the disadvantages of using cell phones?

_____

Work with a partner to discuss your answers.

NOTE-TAKING: CHUNKING INFORMATION

■ **READING TIP:**
Chunking paragraphs in a reading involves deciding which sections of a reading develop a Main Idea that links the information. This analysis allows you to identify relationships among ideas.

Step 1: **Skim the reading and find information for the following Main Ideas about cell-phone use in Finland:**

A. Who has these phones

B. How cell-phone use is affecting schools and kids

C. Cell-phone affordability

D. The results of technological change

Underline or highlight this information.

Step 2: **Use brackets [ ] to show the sections that detail the same idea.**

Step 3: **Write the letter (*A*, *B*, *C*, or *D*) that identifies each of these chunks in the margin of the reading.**

Step 4: **Use the following outline to note important details.**

Cell-phone explosion in Finland

MAIN IDEAS	SUPPORTING POINTS AND DETAILS
A. Who has these phones?	1. Statistics 2. Types of people
B. What's the effect on schools and kids?	1. Problems in high school 2. Age of kids with phones at school
C. Affordability	1. Equal access to technology 2. Help for families
D. Results of technological change	1. Removal of old technology 2. Telemarketers 3. Loss of privacy

■ **TIP:** *Remember to speak naturally and not read from notes.*

Work with a partner and compare the details you wrote.

Correct or add any missing information. Refer to the reading if you need to.

Practice explaining the information from your notes.

■ ■
_____

Reading 2: Cell Phones: The End of Privacy

PREDICTING

When is it not acceptable to use a cell phone?

Check (✔) the activities that you expect to find are out of bounds for cell-phone users.

1. _____ When you are at a wedding (your own or other people's)
2. _____ When you are having dinner at a quiet country resort
3. _____ When you are commuting on a bus or metro
4. _____ When you are in a busy city restaurant
5. _____ When you are meeting with other people

Work with a partner to compare your answers. Return to these predictions after you have finished reading and verify your answers.

SKIMMING

Skim the entire article quickly and answer the following questions.

1. How widespread is cell-phone use in New York?
2. What are the different opinions about using cell phones in New York?

NEW YORK TIMES

The Nuisance of Overheard Calls

Cellular phones are everywhere, but good manners may not be

By Joyce Wadler

The setting was bucolic when the high-powered cell-phone couple went away for the weekend to a little inn in Maine.

The inn, said Lisa Linden and Lloyd Kaplan, public relations partners in New York, had great charm, with a barn and a view and Nubian goats munching on the lawn. And, as some other guests were carrying on a rather loud conversation, Ms. Linden felt there would be some understanding when her cell phone rang during dinner. She stayed on for 45 minutes.

Best to skim over the humiliating reprimand from the management that followed and focus on Ms. Linden's defense.

"I spoke very quietly and I thought it would be a brief call, but it was a client in crisis," she said.

"You can't hang up on a client in crisis, even if the only other sound you hear is the goats munching. I certainly apologize to the innkeepers for unintentionally violating the calm, but these days, is speaking quietly on a cell phone in a dining room that is noisy a total breach of etiquette?"

There are several million cellular phone users in the New York City region, according to Bell Atlantic Mobile. Statistics on how many are yelling into their phones are unavailable.

What is known is that the cell-phone people are everywhere: carrying on long, noisy, intrusive conversations on Metro-North; conducting phone meetings in restaurants; dialing up friends when they're sitting behind first base at a Yankee game to report they're on television.

Those in denial often excuse themselves with the big lie. I got it for the car. The hard-core users, who often feel no need to apologize, insist they need the phones for work.

So that now in New York, where space is shared and where cellular conversations take place in the street and the bus and the commuter train and thus often become everyone's conversation, a battle of manners is being waged.

. . .

The Cellular Telecommunications Industry Association, which is based in Washington, asked the advice columnist Judith Martin, who writes under the name Miss Manners, to do an etiquette booklet on cell phones five years ago.

According to the association's spokesman, Tim Ayers, copies are still available.

"I'll be real honest with you," Mr. Ayers said. "There wasn't much demand."

Next week, Omnipoint Communications, a wireless-telephone company based in New Jersey, will be publishing "Wireless Etiquette: A Guide to the Changing World of Instant Communication" by Peter Laufer.

"I don't have a reputation for decorum," Mr. Laufer said this week from his home in Sonoma County, north of San Francisco.

"But it's clear to me people need a little guidance. Like one winter, I'm on the observation deck of the Empire State Building. It was gray and cold and really special, the snow made it quiet, and some guy was yelling into his cell phone. He seemed to be missing the moment."

Does Mr. Laufer believe it is rude to use cell phones on the train?

"There are ways to use them and ways not to use them," Mr. Laufer said. "We need to train ourselves that the devices are

sensitive enough that there is no need to yell into them. We're like our grandmothers using the long distance line; their voices go up unnecessarily high and loud."

. . .

A sports executive who commutes from Westchester and makes phone calls on the train says he is not the problem.

"I've never had anyone other than my wife tell me I'm talking too loud," the executive said. "The people who are shunned are the ones making those loud personal calls."

Then again, what constitutes proper behavior may be determined by where you live.

Alexandra Atkins, an assistant at Dan Klores public relations, attended her sister's wedding in Italy last June in a villa near Florence. Cell phones rang continually. In the middle of the dinner, when the best man was making a toast to the groom, the groom's phone rang.

"He answered it," said Ms. Atkins. "I'm not kidding, I have a picture. It was his Uncle Fredo from wherever, wishing him good luck on his wedding. I don't think my sister cared. She was like: 'Whatever. I'm married.' My family couldn't get over it."

But there is a reason for cell-phone use in Italy, Ms. Atkins discovered. Land lines are taxed at 30 percent; cell phones are taxed at 10 percent, and people use cell phones in their homes.

Sybil Adelman, a New York comedy writer, lived for several years in Los Angeles, where cell phones first became common.

"I was having dinner in L.A. once, there were eight people in a Mexican restaurant and each one of them had a cell phone," Ms. Adelman said. "I looked at them and thought, 'So why did we all have to come here?'"

Now Ms. Adelman is a convert.

Her manners have not always been perfect. There was the time during her visit to her son's Quaker school that her phone rang during the silent meeting.

Still, Ms. Adelman remains a fan.

"The best use I had for the phone was when I was at the Javits center with my sister-in-law and I lost her," Ms. Adelman said. "I picked up the phone and called her." She had another success story: "My brother told me he was in a theater where a man dropped his cell phone before the curtain went up and was frantic. Another guy said, 'Give me your number; when it rings, we'll find it.'"

A woman visiting Ms. Adelman jumps in with her own anecdote: "I had a friend who was hiking in a park in England. He was lost and it was getting dark, and he didn't know what to do. So he called his secretary in New York and she called some park officials, and they called him and told him how to find his way out."

But not all cell-phone stories have happy endings.

An account executive in her 20's has a cautionary tale.

"A girlfriend of mine was out Saturday night with a guy she was dating," she said. "They were with a group of people going to a bar, and my friend got into one cab and the guy got into another. She called him in his cab from her cab and got his voice mail, so she thinks he's ditched her. She tells all her girlfriends in the cab what a jerk he is. She didn't realize she had left her phone on. He called her back and played all seven minutes of it."

It sounds as if there is a lesson in etiquette here.

The account executive agrees.

"Everybody should make sure the phone is turned off before they start tearing into somebody."

SCANNING

Read each of the questions and look for the answers in the article. Mark the question number in the margin to show where the answer is located. Highlight the key words and write the answer in note form.

1. a. Why did inn management reprimand Lisa Linden?

    _____

    b. What was her reaction?

    _____

2. a. How many cell-phone users are there in the New York City area?

_____

   b. Where are cell phones used?

_____

3. According to Peter Laufer, what can people do to use cell phones more politely?

_____

4. What is the reason why cell-phone use is common in Italy?

_____

5. What is one example of how cell phones can be a real help?

_____

6. What is one example of how cell phones can get you into trouble?

_____

Work with a partner to discuss your answers.

NOTE-TAKING: CHUNKING INFORMATION

■ *READING TIP:*
Chunking paragraphs in a reading involves deciding which sections of a reading develop a Main Idea that links the information. This analysis allows you to identify relationships among ideas.

Step 1: **Skim the article and find information for the following Main Ideas about cell-phone use in New York.**

A. Places where cell phones are used in New York
B. A guide to good cell-phone manners
C. Cell-phone use in Italy and Los Angeles
D. Stories of success and caution with cell-phone use

Underline or highlight this information.

Step 2: **Use brackets [ ] to show sections that detail the same idea.**

Step 3: **Write the letter (*A, B, C,* or *D*) that identifies each of these chunks in the margin of the reading.**

Step 4: **Use the following outline to note important details.**

Cell-phone use in New York; what's acceptable and what's not

MAIN IDEAS	SUPPORTING POINTS AND DETAILS
A. Cell-phone use in New York	1. Number of phone users 2. Where people are using their phones
B. Guide to good cell-phone manners	1. Recent publication on cell-phone manners 2. Mr. Laufer's experience at Empire State Building 3. Advice for using cell phones on the train
C. Cell-phone use in Italy and L.A	1. Experience at an Italian wedding 2. Reason for cell-phone popularity in Italy 3. Experience in an L.A. restaurant
D. Cell-phone use; stories of success and caution	1. Stories of use at the theater 2. Rescue in England 3. Sending unintended messages

■ *Tip: Remember to speak naturally and not read from notes.*

Work with a partner and compare the details you wrote. Correct or add any missing information. Refer to the reading if you need to.

Practice explaining the information from your notes.

After Reading

Work with a partner who prepared notes from a *different reading*. Use your notes to explain the information to your partner.

APPLYING THE INFORMATION

■ *RETELLING TIP:*
When talking from notes, remember not to look down and read your notes. Maintain eye contact with your partner. If you should forget some facts, look quickly at the notes to remind yourself of what you want to say. Then look up and talk.

Make a list of the uses of cell phones and decide if these uses are problem solvers, problem makers, or—in certain circumstances—both.

USES OF CELL PHONES

Problem Solvers	*Problem Makers*
1.	
2.	
3.	
4.	
5.	
6.	

REACTING TO THE READING

These two readings combine personal stories with factual information about cell-phone use. Based on the information, and your own opinion, answer these questions.

1. What are the most important reasons for having a cell phone? What reasons are least important?
2. How are cell phones changing our ways of communicating?
3. How are cell phones changing our ways of behaving in public?
4. Are cell phones a nuisance or a convenience? Explain your reasoning.
5. Will cell phones replace land-based phones in the future? Why or why not?

Vocabulary Building

VOCABULARY IN CONTEXT

A. Circle the phrase that is closest in meaning to the words in *boldface* in these sentences. Then, in the reading, find and underline those words. Circle any words or phrases that help make the meaning clear.

1. After talking for a few minutes, they reached a **consensus** on where to go for dinner,

    a. an argument   b. an agreement   c. an advancement

2. They are moving to **install** metal detectors in the school.

    a. remove   b. permit   c. put in

3. The Phone Company is **phasing out** phone booths.

    a. removing over time   b. putting in over time   c. repairing over time

4. **On the other hand**, hardly anyone needs phone booths anymore.

    a. in addition   b. in time   c. in contrast

5. She received a **reprimand** from the management.

    a. reminder   b. recommendation   c. warning

6. I don't have a reputation for **decorum**, but people need a little guidance.

   a. good manners   b. bad manners   c. behavior

7. She was acting in a very **intrusive** manner.

   a. welcoming   b. inquisitive   c. unwelcoming

8. Cell-phone use in Finland has very quickly reached its **saturation point**.

   a. complete use   b. partial use   c. overuse

B. Complete each sentence with one of the following adverbs that fits it best.

a. linguistically   b. literally   c. rapidly   d. routinely
e. virtually

1. They were _____ running while carrying on a running conversation.

2. Finland is _____ becoming a country where everyone has a cell phone.

3. I _____ call five or six people I'm close to every day.

4. _____ speaking, this was the most interesting article I've read so far.

5. They were _____ the only people not to purchase a cell phone.

Check your answers. Work with a partner and take turns reading your sentences. Together, find three other sentences that contain adverbs and discuss the meanings of each.

JIGSAW SENTENCES

Match each of the clauses in Column A with those in Column B that would best complete them.

Column A

_____ 1. As some of the guests were carrying on a loud conversation,

_____ 2. I have a couple of old phones sitting around,

_____ 3. When people call for directory assistance,

_____ 4. Since everyone is expected to have a phone all the time,

Column B

a. the boss can always find you.

b. so I'll probably give him one.

c. the operator sends the number in the form of a text message.

d. she thought they wouldn't be disturbed by the cell phone.

Check the answers. Work with a partner to take turns reading your completed sentences.

Expanding Your Language

SPEAKING

A. Giving Advice

Read each of the following scenarios. How would you handle or give advice on handling the situation? Use the suggestions that are given, or decide on a solution of your own. Write your ideas in note form.

1. You are in a restaurant enjoying an intimate dinner with a friend. A man at the next table is talking on a cell phone so loudly that it is disturbing you. You feel increasingly uncomfortable and would like to get away. You feel that you shouldn't have to listen to this conversation in a public place.

Some possibilities:

a. Ask the person to move or leave and take his phone conversation out of the dining room.

b. Ask the waiter to tell this customer to turn off the cell phone.

c. Ask the waiter to move you to a table far away from this person.

Your action or advice:

_____

2. You are traveling at high speed down a superhighway with your friend at the wheel, when the cell phone rings. Your friend reaches over to answer the phone. You decide to take action.

Some possibilities:

a. Hand the phone over so that your friend can carry on the conversation while driving.
b. Answer the phone yourself and take a message so that your friend can make the call when the car is stopped.
c. Ask your friend to pull over to the side of the highway and stop the car while on the phone.

Your action or advice:

_____

3. You are visiting a wilderness area with a few friends. Your friends suggest climbing a mountain that requires a certain level of expertise. You are afraid that you and your friends do not have enough supplies and other equipment and may not be able to complete the climb safely. Your friends tell you not to worry because they have a cell phone and can call for help if they get in trouble. What is your reaction?

Some possibilities:

a. Insist that they not climb until they have the supplies and equipment they need.
b. Agree to climb with them.
c. Decide to climb only if they talk to a park official for advice before climbing.

Your action or advice:

_____

Discussion: **Work with a partner or a small group to discuss your answers. Explain your choices. Present your suggestions to the class as a whole.**

Role Play: **Choose one of the three scenarios and decide on the roles involved with a partner or others in a small group. Together, write the conversations among the people in their**

roles. Practice your role plays. Prepare to present your role plays to others in a small group.

B. Interviewing

What do people think about the advantages and disadvantages of cell phones? To find out, interview other students or people outside of class. Find out about their cell-phone use and experience. To carry out the interviews, follow these steps.

Step 1: **On your own**	**Make a short list of interesting questions (four or five) on the topic.**
Step 2: **In small groups**	**Choose the five most interesting questions.**
Step 3: **Whole class**	**Compare the questions written in each of the groups.**
Step 4: **In small groups**	**Write the questions you will use on pages of your own. Leave spaces to take notes.**
Step 5: **Interview**	**Alone or with a partner, choose three people to interview.**
Step 6: **Report**	**Discuss the responses with those you worked with in Step 4. Report to the class a few interesting or surprising findings to the questions you asked.**

WRITING

Topic Writing

Write about the growing popularity of cell phones and how this will change our communication and culture both positively and negatively. Follow these steps.

1. Outline the details on the following main ideas of the topic. Use your notes to help you remember important facts.

A. Growing Popularity
    Places
    Statistics

B. Positive Uses
    Personal Communication
    Business Communications
    Other Uses

C. Negative Consequences
    Lack of Privacy
    Annoyance
    Dangerous Habits

2. Using your outline as a guide, write a paragraph about each of the three ideas.

3. Reread this first draft and check to see that the topic of each paragraph is clearly stated in the first sentence. Make any change needed.

4. Reread that draft and change the order of the information— or add information—for a final draft.

5. Submit this writing to your teacher.

Reaction Writing

Some states are considering or have already introduced a ban on using cell phones while driving. Some cities are considering or have instituted bans on cell-phone use in certain public places such as theaters or banks. Do you think there should be legal restrictions such as these? Write your reaction in paragraph form.

CHAPTER 8

Internet Communications: The Disappearance of Privacy

▌Chapter Openers

GIVING OPINIONS: WHAT'S PUBLIC AND WHAT'S PRIVATE

Decide whether the information that follows should be private or public. Circle *PR* for private and *PU* for public. Be prepared to explain or to offer examples that support your opinion.

1. PR PU   The PIN code to access your bank account

2. PR PU   Your social security, medicare, or driver's license number

3. PR PU   Your telephone number and address (including e-mail)

4. PR PU   The amount of money you make on an annual basis

5. PR PU   The types of purchases you make and the amount of money you spend on each type

6. PR PU   Your medical history, including genetic analyses

7. PR PU   Your political or religious affiliation

Do you think that over the past few decades private information has become more open to the public? If so, what are the advantages and disadvantages of this?

QUOTES

Read each of these quotes on the topic of privacy. Decide if you agree or not and why.

"Privacy is not something that I'm merely entitled to. It's an absolute prerequisite."

Marlon Brando, actor

"Today . . . the only place sacred from interruption is the private toilet."

Lewis Mumford, philosopher

"Government has no place in the bedrooms of its citizens."
Pierre Eliot Trudeau, former Canadian Prime Minister

"I am opposed to writing about the private lives of living authors and psychoanalyzing them while they are alive."

Ernest Hemingway, writer

Discuss your ideas with a partner or with others in a small group.

Exploring and Understanding Reading

PREDICTING

Predict whether you think it is easy (*E*) or difficult (*D*) for the following things to happen. Be prepared to give reasons or examples to support your answers.

1. E D   Someone uses your credit card number and charges $3,000 to your account.

2. E D   Someone gets information from your medical files and sends you brochures on health products you may want to buy.

3. E D   Someone uses the motor-vehicle registration records on your car to find your home address.

4. E D   Someone can reroute your telephone calls to another number without your knowledge.

5. E D   Someone sends an e-mail message that destroys the files on your computer.

Compare your answers and explain your reasoning with a partner. Return to these questions after you have finished reading the introduction and rediscuss your answers.

PREVIEWING

Quickly read the title, quotes, and all the boxes and charts contained in the article. Based on your predictions and your preview, make a list of four ideas that you expect will be explained in the article.

1. _____

2. _____

3. _____

4. _____

EXAMINING THE INTRODUCTION

■ *TIP: Remember, one of the purposes of an introduction is to interest you in the topic. Often writers do this by way of a story or striking example told in a personal way.*

The introduction section of this article is set out in the first thirteen paragraphs (1–13). Read the introduction and complete the following tasks.

A. *Highlighting:* **Find and highlight the following facts.**

1. The type of work that the author does
2. The problems that the author experienced with his credit card
3. The type of book that he and his wife wrote
4. The damage that the hacker did to the author's telephone number
5. The measures the phone company took to counteract the hacker
6. The author's feelings about giving out private information
7. The feelings that most people have about privacy
8. Some important questions about the topic of privacy

Invasion of Privacy

By Joshua Quittner

Our right to be left alone has disappeared, bit by bit, in Little Brotherly steps. Still, we've got something in return— and it's not all bad

1. For the longest time, I couldn't get worked up about privacy: my right to it; how it's dying; how we're headed for an even more wired, underregulated, overintrusive, privacy-deprived planet.

2. I mean, I probably have more reason to think this stuff than the average John Q. All Too Public. A few years ago, for instance, after I applied for a credit card at a consumer-electronics store, somebody got hold of my name and vital numbers and used them to get a duplicate card. That somebody ran up a $3,000 bill, but the nice lady from the fraud division of the credit-card company took care of it with steely digital dispatch. (I filed a short report over the phone. I never lost a cent. The end.)

3. I also hang out online a lot, and now and then on the Net someone will impersonate me, spoofing my e-mail address or posting stupid stuff to bulletin boards or behaving in a frightfully un-Quittner-like manner in chat parlors from here to Bianca's Smut Shack. It's annoying, I suppose. But in the end, the faux Quittners get bored and disappear. My reputation, such as it is, survives.

4. I should also point out that as news director for Pathfinder, Time Inc.'s mega info mall, and a guy who makes his living

on the Web, I know better than most people that we're hurtling toward an even more intrusive world. We're all being watched by computers whenever we visit Websites; by the mere act of "browsing" (it sounds so passive!) we're going public in a way that was unimaginable a decade ago. I know this because I'm a watcher too. When people come to my Website, without ever knowing their names, I can peer over their shoulders, recording what they look at, timing how long they stay on a particular page, following them around Pathfinder's sprawling offerings.

5. None of this would bother me in the least, I suspect, if a few years ago, my phone, like Marley's ghost, hadn't given me a glimpse of the nightmares to come. On Thanksgiving weekend in 1995, someone (presumably a critic of a book my wife and I had just written about computer hackers) forwarded my home telephone number to an out-of-state answering machine, where unsuspecting callers trying to reach me heard a male voice identify himself as me and say some extremely rude things. Then, with typical hacker aplomb, the prankster asked people to leave their messages (which to my surprise many callers, including my mother, did). This went on for several days until my wife and I figured out that something was wrong ("Hey . . . why hasn't the phone rung since Wednesday?") and got our phone restored.

6. It seemed funny at first, and it gave us a swell story to tell on our book tour. But the interloper who seized our telephone line continued to hit us even after the tour ended. And hit us again and again for the next six months. The phone company seemed powerless. Its security folks moved us to one unlisted number after another, half a dozen times. They put special PIN codes in place. They put traces on the line. But the troublemaker kept breaking through.

7. If our hacker had been truly evil and omnipotent as only fictional movie hackers are, there would probably have been even worse ways he could have threatened my

privacy. He could have sabotaged my credit rating. He could have eavesdropped on my telephone conversations or siphoned off my e-mail. He could have called in my mortgage, discontinued my health insurance or obliterated my Social Security number. Like Sandra Bullock in *The Net*, I could have been a digital untouchable, wandering the planet without a connection to the rest of humanity. (Although if I didn't have to pay back school loans, it might be worth it. Just a thought.)

8. Still, I remember feeling violated at the time and as powerless as a minnow in a flash flood. Someone was invading my private space—my family's private space—and there was nothing I or the authorities could do. It was as close to a technological epiphany as I have ever been. And as I watched my personal digital hell unfold, it struck me that our privacy—mine and yours—has already disappeared, not in one Big Brotherly blitzkrieg but in Little Brotherly moments, bit by bit.

9. Losing control of your telephone, of course, is the least of it. After all, most of us voluntarily give out our phone number and address when we allow ourselves to be listed in the White Pages. Most of us go a lot further than that. We register our whereabouts whenever we put a bank card in an ATM machine or drive through an E-Z Pass lane on the highway. We submit to being photographed every day—20 times a day on average if you live or work in New York City—by surveillance cameras. We make public our interests and our purchasing habits every time we shop by mail order or visit a commercial Website.

10. I don't know about you, but I do all this willingly because I appreciate what I get in return: the security of a safe parking lot, the convenience of cash when I need it, the improved service of mail-order houses that know me well enough to send me catalogs of stuff that interests me. And while I know we're supposed to feel just awful about giving up our vaunted privacy, I suspect (based on what the pollsters say) that you're as ambivalent about it as I am.

11. Popular culture shines its klieg lights on the most intimate corners of our lives and most of us play right along. If all we really wanted was to be left alone, explain the lasting popularity of Oprah and Sally and Ricki tell-all TV. Memoirs top the best-seller lists, with books about incest and insanity and illness leading the way. Perfect strangers at cocktail parties tell me the most disturbing details of their abusive upbringings. Why?

12. "It's a very schizophrenic time," says Sherry Turkle, professor of sociology at the Massachusetts Institute of Technology, who writes books about how computers and online communication are transforming society. She believes our culture is undergoing a kind of mass identity crisis, trying to hang on to a sense of privacy and intimacy in a global village of tens of millions. "We have very unstable notions about the boundaries of the individual," she says.

13. If things seem crazy now, think how much crazier they will be when everybody is as wired as I am. We're in the midst of a global interconnection that is happening much faster than electrification did a century ago and is expected to have consequences at least as profound. What would happen if all the information stored on the world's computers were accessible via the Internet to anyone? Who would own it? Who would control it? Who would protect it from abuse?

14. Small-scale privacy atrocities take place every day. Ask Dr. Denise Nagel, executive director of the National Coalition for Patient Rights, about medical privacy, for example, and she rattles off a list of abuses that would make Big Brother blush. She talks about how two years ago, a convicted child rapist working as a technician in a Boston hospital riffled through 1,000 computerized records looking for potential victims (and was caught when the father of a nine-year-old girl used caller ID to trace the call back to the hospital). How a banker on Maryland's state health commission pulled up a list of cancer patients, cross-checked it against the names of his bank's customers

---

It's a very schizophrenic time. We have very unstable notions about the boundaries of the individual.

—Sherry Turkle, Massachusetts Institute of Technology

HOW YOU'RE SPIED ON
Everyday events that can make your life a little less private

BANK MACHINES
Every time you use an auto-mated teller, the bank records the time, date, and location of your transaction.

PRESCRIPTION DRUGS
If you use your company health insurance to purchase drugs, your employer may have access to the details.

EMPLOYEE ID SCANNERS
If you rely on a magnetic-stripe pass to enter the office, your whereabouts are automatically recorded.

BROWSING ON THE WEB
Many sites tag visitors with "magic cookies" that record what you're looking at and when you have been surfing.

CELLULAR TELEPHONE
Your calls can be intercepted and your access numbers cribbed by eavesdroppers with police scanners.

CREDIT CARDS
Everything you charge is in a database that police, among others, could look at.

REGISTERING TO VOTE
In most states, voter-registration records are pub-lic and online. They typically list your address and birth date.

MAKING A PHONE CALL
The phone company doesn't need a court order to note the number you're calling—or who's calling you.

SUPERMARKET SCANNERS
Many grocery stores let you register for discount coupons that are used to track what you purchase.

SWEEPSTAKES
These are bonanzas for mar-keters. Every time you enter one, you add an electronic brushstroke to your digital portrait.

SATELLITES
Commercial satellites are coming online that are eagle-eyed enough to spot you—and maybe a companion—in a hot tub.

ELECTRONIC TOLLS
In many places, drivers can pay tolls electronically with passes that tip off your whereabouts.

SURVEILLANCE CAMERAS
They're in banks, federal office buildings, 7-Elevens, even houses of worship; New Yorkers are on camera up to 20 times a day.

MAIL-ORDER TRANSACTIONS
Many companies, including mail-order houses and pub-lishers, sell lists of their cus-tomers. Why do you think you're getting that Victoria's Secret catalog?

SENDING E-MAIL
In offices, e-mail is consid-ered part of your work. Your employer is allowed to read it—and many bosses do.

and revoked the loans of the matches. How Sara Lee bakeries planned to collaborate with Lovelace Health Systems, a subsidiary of Cigna, to match employee health records with work-performance reports to find workers who might benefit from antidepressants.

15. Not to pick on Sara Lee. At least a third of all Fortune 500 companies regularly review health information before making hiring decisions. And that's nothing com-pared with what awaits us when employers and insurance companies start testing our DNA for possible imperfections.

Farfetched? More than 200 subjects in a case study published last January in the journal *Science and Engineering Ethics* reported that they had been discriminated against as a result of genetic testing. None of them were actually sick, but DNA analysis suggested that they might become sick someday. "The technology is getting ahead of our ethics," says Nagel, and the Clinton Administration clearly agrees. It is about to propose a federal law that would protect medical and health-insurance records from such abuses.

16. But how did we arrive at this point, where so much about what we do and own and think is an open book?

17. It all started in the 1950s, when, in order to administer Social Security funds, the U.S. government began entering records on big mainframe computers, using nine-digit identification numbers as data points. Then, even more than today, the citizenry instinctively loathed the computer and its injunctions against folding, spindling and mutilating. We were not numbers! We were human beings! These fears came to a head in the late 1960s, recalls Alan Westin, a retired Columbia University professor who publishes a quarterly report *Privacy and American Business*. "The techniques of intrusion and data surveillance had overcome the weak law and social mores that we had built up in the pre-World War II era," says Westin.

18. The public rebelled, and Congress took up the question of how much the government and private companies should be permitted to know about us. A privacy bill of rights was drafted. "What we did," says Westin, "was to basically redefine what we meant by 'reasonable expectations of privacy'"—a guarantee, by the way, that comes from the Supreme Court and not from any constitutional "right to privacy."

19. The result was a flurry of new legislation that clarified and defined consumer and citizen rights. The first Fair Credit Reporting Act, passed in 1970, overhauled what had once been a secret, unregulated industry with no provisions for due process. The new law gave consumers the right to know what was in their credit files and to demand corrections. Other financial and health privacy acts followed, although to this day no federal law protects the confidentiality of medical records.

DISABLE YOUR COOKIE
Go to *www.luckman.com* and get a free "anonymous cookie," a program that disables cookies, among other things.

KNOW WHAT YOUR BOSS KNOWS
On Netscape's browser, in the Location field, type *about:global*. This shows every place you've visited, in some cases going back months. In Microsoft's Internet Explorer, you can list every site you've visited for the past 20 days by opening the Go menu and choosing the Open History item. You can erase this stuff by selecting the Clean Cache option on either browser.

SURF THE WEB ANONYMOUSLY
You can browse the Web from behind a privacy curtain by first connecting to *www.anonymizer.com*. The free account imposes a 60-second delay on all browsing; a pay option lifts that annoying restriction.

20. As Westin sees it, the public and private sectors took two very different approaches. Congress passed legislation requiring that the government tell citizens what records it keeps on them while insisting that the information itself not be released unless required by law. The private sector responded by letting each industry—credit-card companies, banking, insurance, marketing, advertising—create its own guidelines.

21. That approach worked—to a point. And that point came when mainframes started giving way to desktop computers. In the old days, information stored in government databases was relatively inaccessible. Now, however, with PCs on every desktop linked to office networks and then to the Internet, data that were once carefully hidden may be only a few keystrokes away.

22. Suddenly someone could run motor-vehicle-registration records against voting registrations to find 6-ft.-tall Republicans who were arrested during the past year for drunk driving—and who own a gun. The genie was not only out of the bottle, he was also peering into everyone's bedroom window. (Except the windows of the very rich, who can afford to screen themselves.)

23. "Most people would be astounded to know what's out there," says Carole Lane, author of *Naked in Cyberspace: How to Find Personal Information Online*. "In a few hours, sitting at my computer, beginning with no more than your name and address, I can find out what you do for a living, the names and ages of your spouse and children, what kind of car you drive, the value of your house and how much taxes you pay on it."

24. Lane is a member of a new trade: paid Internet searcher, which already has its own professional group, the Association of

---

PROTECT YOURSELF

• **Just say no to telemarketers**
If you don't want to get an unlisted telephone number (cost: $1.50 a month), practice the mantra "I don't take phone solicitations." Once you buy, you're put on a chump list that's sold to other marketers.

• **Consider removing your name from many direct-mail and telemarketing lists**
Write to:
Direct Marketing Association
Mail/Telephone Preference Service
P.O. Box 9008 (mail)
or P.O. Box 9014 (phone)
Farmingdale, NY 11735

• **Pay cash whenever possible**
The less you put on your credit cards, the fewer details anyone has about your buying habits.

• **Be wary about buying mail order**
Many mail-order companies sell their customer lists. So call the company to check its procedures (unless you like catalogs).

• **Give your Social Security number only when required by law**
Many organizations, from school to work, use it as your ID number. Resist them. (Experts say it often helps if you can tell someone in authority about your concerns.)

• **Think twice before filling out warranty cards or entering sweepstakes**
These are data mines for marketers. Besides, most products are guaranteed by your sales receipt. And have you ever won anything in a sweepstakes?

• **Be careful when using "free blood-pressure clinics"**
Typically, your data will be used by marketers and pharmaceutical companies.

• **Avoid leaving footprints on the Net**
You're being watched even as you browse. And search engines index your postings to public forums such as Usenet by your name.

> *We think that privacy is about information—it's not.*
> *It's about relationships.*
>
> –Kevin Kelly, Executive editor, *Wired* magazine

Independent Information Professionals. Her career has given her a fresh appreciation for what's going on. "Real privacy as we've known it," she says, "is fleeting."

25. Now, there are plenty of things you could do to protect yourself. You could get an unlisted telephone number, as I was forced to do. You could cut up your credit card and pay cash for everything. You could rip your E-Z Pass off the windshield and use quarters at tolls. You could refuse to divulge your Social Security number except for Social Security purposes, which is all that the law requires. You'd be surprised how often you're asked to provide it by people who have no right to see it.

26. That might make your life a bit less comfortable, of course. As in the case of Bob Bruen, who went into a barbershop in Watertown, Mass., recently. "When I was asked for my phone number, I refused to give them the last four digits," Bruen says. "I was also asked for my name, and I also refused. The girl at the counter called her supervisor, who told me I could not get a haircut in their shop." Why? The barbershop uses a computer to record all transactions. Bruen went elsewhere to get his locks shorn.

27. But can we do that all the time? Only the Unabomber would seriously suggest that we cut all ties to the wired world. The computer and its spreading networks convey status and bring opportunity. They empower us. They allow an information economy to thrive and grow. They make life easier. Hence the dilemma.

28. The real problem, says Kevin Kelly, executive editor of *Wired* magazine, is that although we say we value our privacy, what we really want is something very different: "We think that privacy is about information, but it's not—it's about relationships." The way Kelly sees it, there was no privacy in the traditional village or small town; everyone knew everyone else's secrets. And that was comfortable. I knew about you, and you knew about me. "There was a symmetry to the knowledge," he says. "What's gone out of whack is we don't know who knows about us anymore. Privacy has become asymmetrical."

29. The trick, says Kelly, is to restore that balance. And not surprisingly, he and others point out that what technology has taken, technology can restore. Take the problem of "magic cookies"—those little bits of code most Websites use to track visitors. We set up a system at Pathfinder in which, when you visit our site, we drop a cookie into the basket of your browser that tags you like a rare bird. We use that cookie in place of your name, which, needless to say, we never know. If you look up a weather report by keying in a ZIP code, we note that (it tells us where you live or maybe where you wish you lived). We'll mark down whether you look up stock quotes (though we draw the line at capturing the symbols of the specific stocks you found). If you come to the *Netly News*, we'll record your interest in technology. Then, the next time you visit, we might serve up an ad for a modem or an online brokerage firm or a restaurant in Akron, Ohio, depending on what we've managed to glean about you.

30. Some people find the whole process offensive. "Cookies represent a way of watching consumers without their consent, and that is a fairly frightening phenomenon," says Nick Grouf, CEO of Firefly, a Boston company that makes software offering an alternative approach to profiling, known as "intelligent agents."

31. Privacy advocates like Grouf—as well as the two companies that control the online browser market, Microsoft and Netscape—say the answer to the cookie monster is something they call the Open Profiling Standard. The idea is to allow the computer user to create an electronic "passport" that identifies him to online marketers without revealing his name. The user tailors the passport to his own interests, so if he is passionate about fly-fishing and is cruising through L.L. Bean's Website, the passport will steer the electronic-catalog copy toward fishing gear instead of, say, rollerblades.

32. The advantage to computer users is that they can decide how much information they want to reveal while limiting their exposure to intrusive marketing techniques. The advantage to Website entrepreneurs is that they learn about their customers' tastes without intruding on their privacy.

33. Many online consumers, however, are skittish about leaving any footprints in cyberspace. Susan Scott, executive director of TRUSTe, a firm based in Palo Alto, Calif., that rates Websites according to the level of privacy they afford, says a survey her company sponsored found that 41% of respondents would quit a Web page rather than reveal any personal information about themselves. About 25% said when they do volunteer information, they lie. "The users

want access, but they don't want to get correspondence back," she says.

34. But worse things may already be happening to their e-mail. Many office electronic-mail systems warn users that the employer reserves the right to monitor their e-mail. In October software will be available to Wall Street firms that can automatically monitor correspondence between brokers and clients through an artificial-intelligence program that scans for evidence of securities violations.

35. "Technology has outpaced law," says Marc Rotenberg, director of the Washington-based Electronic Privacy Information Center. Rotenberg advocates protecting the privacy of e-mail by encrypting it with secret codes so powerful that even the National Security Agency's supercomputers would have a hard time cracking it. Such codes are legal within the U.S. but cannot be used abroad—where terrorists might use them to protect their secrets—without violating U.S. export laws. The battle between the Clinton Administration and the computer industry over encryption export policy has been raging for six years without resolution, a situation that is making it hard to do business on the Net and is clearly starting to fray some nerves. "The future is in electronic commerce," says Ira Magaziner, Clinton's point man on Net issues. All that's holding it up is "this privacy thing."

36. Rotenberg thinks we need a new government agency—a privacy agency—to sort out the issues. "We need new legal protections," he says, "to enforce the privacy act, to keep federal agencies in line, to act as a spokesperson for the Federal Government and to act on behalf of privacy interests."

37. *Wired*'s Kelly disagrees. "A federal privacy agency would be disastrous! The answer to the whole privacy question is more knowledge," he says. "More knowledge about who's watching you. More knowledge about the information that flows between us—particularly the meta information about who knows what and where it's going."

38. I'm with Kelly. The only guys who insist on perfect privacy are hermits like the Unabomber. I don't want to be cut off from the world. I have nothing to hide. I just want some measure of control over what people know about me. I want to have my magic cookie and eat it too.

–Time

Discuss the facts you highlighted with a partner. What information surprised you or interested you? What ideas do you agree or disagree with?

■ *READING TIP: A writer uses the first person, a personal style, to communicate and establish a connection with the reader. To be effective, the writer must establish a credible identity and use personal experience as a starting point for addressing more general questions.*

B. *Audience and Purpose:* **Answer the following questions.**

1. a. What information does the writer give using the first person "I"?

   _____

   _____

   _____

   b. How many paragraphs are written in the first person?

   _____

2. What information do you learn about the writer that establishes him as an authority on this topic?

   _____

   _____

3. Paraphrase (restate in your own words) the thesis or author's purpose in writing this article.

   _____

   _____

Work with a partner or in a small group to compare your answers.

CHUNKING

Survey the article from paragraphs 14 through 38. Write the idea that links the following groups of paragraphs. Numbers 1 and 5 have been done as examples.

> **■ Tip:** *Remember to use your surveying skills and read the beginning of the paragraphs to quickly see which ones develop a single idea.*

1. Paragraphs 14, 15   *Abuses of privacy in the field of health*

2. Paragraphs 16–20   _____

3. Paragraphs 21–24   _____

4. Paragraphs 25, 26   _____

5. Paragraphs 27–29   *How to have the right amount of privacy*

6. Paragraphs 30–33   _____

7. Paragraphs 34, 35   _____

8. Paragraphs 36–38   _____

Work with a partner to compare your ideas.

NOTE-TAKING: REPORTING THE FACTS

The writer of "Invasion of Privacy" explains a number of important issues and questions through the use of explanations and examples that are central to each.

Choose *one* of the following sets of important ideas:

Paragraphs 16–24
Paragraphs 25–35

> **■ Tip:** *Listing information in note form is a useful reading strategy that sensitizes you to the connections among ideas as you analyze and restate ideas in your own words.*

Step 1: On a separate sheet of paper, prepare notes based on the information in the section of the reading you chose. Use the divided page system of organization shown in the example on page 29 to make your notes.

Step 2: Work with a partner who prepared notes on the *same set of paragraphs*. Take turns verifying the completeness and correctness of your notes. If necessary, refer to the reading.

After Reading

RETELLING THE INFORMATION

Work with a partner who prepared notes for a *different* section of the reading. Use your notes to explain the information to your partner.

ANSWERING QUESTIONS FROM NOTES

Based on the information from both sets of notes, answer the following questions together with your partner.

1. Name three areas in peoples' lives where, because of advances in today's technology, the right to privacy could be compromised.

   a. _____

   b. _____

   c. _____

2. Give two examples of how private information can be discovered and used in a negative way.

   a. _____

   b. _____

3. According to the author, what has been the history of private information gathering? Complete the following timeline.

Time:	1950s	1960s	1970	Intro. of PCs	Today
Info:	*Social Security numbers entered on mainframes by U.S. government*				

4. In the following chart, list the facts that show we have conflicting attitudes toward the need for privacy.

Maintain privacy at all cost	*Forgo privacy for convenience*
a. _____	a. _____
b. _____	b. _____
c. _____	c. _____

DEBATING THE ISSUES

Work with others in a small group to debate the issue of maintaining privacy at all cost. Follow these steps:

1. Choose your position.
2. Work with others who share your position to develop your arguments.
3. Debate against those who prepared opposing arguments.
4. Try to convince each other of your arguments.

APPLYING THE INFORMATION: PROBLEMS AND SOLUTIONS

Discuss each of the following situations with a partner. Analyze the situation and decide whether it is or is not a problem. If it is a problem, brainstorm some possible solutions. If not, give the reasons for your opinion.

1. You subscribe to a cable company that has a monitor program. Using this program, the company can find out exactly what programs and channels you are watching. This information can be checked against your address and other demographic information. With this information, advertisers could direct specific commercials at TV viewers in your house.

2. A politician running for office in an election uses a computer program that can analyze demographic and lifestyle information on voters in a given district. The politician's campaign organization can use this information to tailor the content and style of the politician's message. In addition, the program can help identify people who can make big contributions to the politician's campaign.

3. You have a bankcard that allows you to take money out of the bank at any time of the day or night. You can also use the card to buy things at many different types of stores. The bankcard company automatically records the transaction every time you use the card. A software company has made a program that can analyze this data and make it available to anyone who wants to buy it. With this information, banks or other institutions can rate you and use the ratings to decide your value as a customer.

4. You go to the bank to withdraw money from your account and discover that the bank has frozen your account. Your credit card is no longer valid. It seems that your identity has been stolen and the thief has made thousands of dollars of purchases in your name. The thief even applied for and received a bank loan using your name.

Work with a new partner or partners. Choose one or two of the situations. Compare your ideas and try to agree on ways to handle the situation. Be prepared to present your ideas to others who analyzed different situations.

Vocabulary Building

VOCABULARY IN CONTEXT

Circle the phrase that is closest in meaning to the words in boldface in these sentences. Find and underline the boldface words in the reading. Circle any words or phrases that help make the meaning clear.

1. We are **hurtling** toward a world in which individual privacy no longer exists.

   a. moving at normal speed   b. moving at a very fast speed
   c. moving slowly

2. They showed us the **sprawling** shopping mall that replaced the original, smaller center.

   a. spread out   b. modernized   c. compact

3. They **obliterated** all signs of the buildings that had been there before.

    a. completely changed   b. completely destroyed
    c. completely rebuilt

4. Every day there are reports of **atrocities** that have been committed against innocent people.

    a. generous acts   b. indifferent acts   c. cruel acts

5. They **loathed** the terrible way that she treated her pets.

    a. liked   b. detested   c. ignored

6. I was **astounded** to hear that she had won the award at such a young age.

    a. surprised   b. pleased   c. proud

7. The accident happened so fast that she got only a **fleeting** look at the car.

    a. lasting for a long time   b. lasting for a moment
    c. lasting forever

8. The **asymmetrical** shape of the building made people concerned about its safety.

    a. unbalanced   b. rectangular   c. balanced

Check your answers. Work with a partner to compare what you underlined.

WORD FORMS

In English many nouns and adjectives come from a verb "root." For example, the words *behavior* and *behavioral* come from the verb root *behave*.

Here is a list of verbs from the reading. Write the nouns and adjectives that derive from each. Look in a dictionary to find other possibilities. Note: Sometimes the same word is used for different parts of speech.

PART OF SPEECH

Verb	Noun	Adjective
1. duplicate	_____	_____
2. suspect	_____	_____
3. disappear	_____	_____
4. appreciate	_____	_____
5. transform	_____	_____
6. discriminate	_____	_____
7. clarify	_____	_____
8. provide	_____	_____
9. alternate	_____	_____
10. intrude	_____	_____

A. Work with a partner to compare your answers. Check with the class as a whole.

B. Find five words in the reading and supply the three parts of speech for each. Work with a partner to quiz each other on the words you chose.

WORD CHOICE

The writer uses a different word or words to describe the same person or idea. Find and circle the word or words used for the following:

a. the hacker who changed the telephone number

b. give information quickly

c. look through

d. a haircut

e. record

f. learn

Work with a partner to compare your answers. Check them with your whole class.

Expanding Your Language

A: *Two-Minute Taped Talk:* **Record a two-minute audio tape about the ideas in the set of notes you wrote based on part of this chapter's reading ("Note-Taking: Reporting the Facts" page 174). To make your tape, follow these steps:**

1. Review your notes.
2. Practice explaining the information. Include as many of the important facts as you can within the time frame you have to speak.
3. Time yourself as you try to speak as clearly and naturally as possible.
4. Record yourself telling the information.
5. Give your tape to your teacher for feedback.

B. *Speaking from Reading—Giving Your Opinion:* **Read the following essay on the issue of privacy. Highlight the important ideas it contains. Decide if you agree or disagree in whole or in part with what the writer has to say. Prepare information to explain and defend your own point of view.**

NEW YORK TIMES

Nobody's Business

By William Safire

WASHINGTON–Your right to privacy has been stripped away. You cannot walk into your bank, or apply for a job, or access your personal computer, without undergoing the scrutiny of strangers. You cannot use a credit card to buy clothes to cover your body without baring your soul. Big Brother is watching as never before.

Encouraged by an act of Congress, Texas and California now demand thumbprints of applicants for drivers' licenses—treating all drivers as potential criminals.

Using a phony excuse about airplane security, airlines now demand identification like those licenses to make sure passengers don't exchange tickets to beat the company's rate-cutting promotions.

In the much-applauded pursuit of deadbeat dads, the Feds now demand that all employers inform the Government of every new hire, thereby building a data base of who is working for whom that would be the envy of the K.G.B.

Although it makes it easier to zip through tollbooths at bridges and highways, electric eyes reading license plates help snoopers everywhere follow the movements of each driver and passenger.

Hooked on easy borrowing, consumers turn to plastic for their purchases, making records and sending electronic signals to telemarketers who track them down at home.

Stimulated by this demographic zeroing-in, Internet predators monitor your browsing, detect your interests, measure your purchases and even observe your expressed ideas.

Nor are Big Brothers limited to government and commerce. Your friends and neighbors, the Nosy Parkers, secretly tape regular calls you make to them, and listen in to cellular calls to third parties, enhancing the video surveillance of public streets by government and private driveways by security agencies.

Enough. Fear of crime and terrorism has caused us to let down our guard against excessive intrusion into the lives of the law-abiding. The ease of minor borrowing and the transformation of shopping into recreation has addicted us to credit cards. Taken together, the fear and the ease make a map of our lives available to cops, crazies and con men alike.

(Here comes the "to-be-sure" graph.) Crime is real; some court-ordered taps of Mafiosi and surveillance cameras of high-violence playgrounds are justifiable. So are random drug and alcohol tests of nuclear-response teams. The S.E.C. should monitor insider stock trades, and no sensible passenger minds the frisking for bombs at airports.

But doesn't this creeping confluence of government snooping, commercial tracking and cultural tolerance of eavesdropping threaten each individual American's personal freedom? And isn't it time to reverse that terrible trend toward national nakedness before it replaces privacy as an American value?

Here's how to snatch your identity back from the intruders:

1. *Sign as little as possible.* Warranty postcards are for suckers (your sales receipt is your guarantee), and sweepstakes are devices to show your gullibility to purchasers of your address. Throw away all mail with Ed McMahon's name on it. (I just chucked a document assuring me of being a winner of $10 million. Easy go.)

2. *Write your local legislator* demanding that a Privacy Impact Statement be

required before passage of any new law, and *call on your local U.S. President* to convene a White House Conference on Privacy, thereby demonstrating the sleeper issue's nonpartisan political clout.

3. *Use snail mail*, harder to intercept than e-mail. And resist mightily requests for your Social Security number. If you're a lawyer, take the state to court over drivers' fingerprinting. When a telemarketer calls, shout an imprecation and hang up. Get your kids to show you how to "disable a cookie" and download free software that lets you surf the Web in anonymity.

4. *Persuade a foundation* to issue a quarterly "Intrusion Index," measuring with scholarly authority the degree to which your privacy is being violated by pols, polls and peepers.

Above all—5. *Pay cash*. Costs less than borrowing and keeps you in control of your own records. Remember: Cash is the enemy of the intruders. Use it to buy back your freedom.

Discuss your ideas with others in a small group.

WRITING

Reaction Writing

Take a position: In the future, the Internet will become more present in our lives. Write your opinion about the following question:

What do you think we should do to have both easy access to information and services, and protection from crimes?

Topic Writing

Review the discussion questions and your notes. Use the information from these exercises and from the reading to help focus your ideas.

1. Write a list of ideas for each following:

- The convenience of Internet access for shopping and other services
- The benefits of Internet access for information and communication
- The problem of criminal activity via the Internet
- The problem of access to private information via the Internet

Do this work in your journal notebook.

2. Work with a partner and explain your ideas to each other.

3. Write a draft of a three-paragraph essay.

Paragraph 1: The benefits of the Internet
Paragraph 2: The drawbacks of the Internet
Paragraph 3: Do the benefits outweigh the drawbacks?

4. Show your draft to a partner for peer review.

5. Rewrite your draft and give the final writing to your teacher.

Read On: Taking It Further

READING JOURNAL

Some very interesting books about privacy have been written both in the past and more recently. Some books, such as *1984* and *Brave New World*, present fictional worlds in which people's personal identities and freedoms are threatened. Others, such as *The Cuckoo's Egg*, present incredible stories of hackers who subvert the Internet for their own purposes. Consult with your teacher about these or other topics related to this unit. With your teacher's guidance, choose a story selection to read and report on.

NEWSPAPER/NEWS MAGAZINE ARTICLES

Check the media in print or online over the Internet over a few days and find an interesting article about cell phones, privacy, or a related communications technology topic that interests you. Prepare to present the information in that article to a partner or in a small group. Follow these steps:

1. Skim the article quickly to get the general idea of the information.
2. Ask the journalist's questions—*who, what, where, when* and *why*—to pinpoint information that is interesting for your audience to hear about and that can be readily explained.
3. Highlight the important facts. Make notes if it will help you to explain more easily.
4. Practice your presentation.
5. Present your information.

UNIT 5

Creativity

Creativity involves breaking out of established patterns in order to look at things in a different way.
—*Edward de Bono*

185

Introducing the Topics

Are people naturally creative? The word *creative* has the power to both frighten and excite people. At first glance, creativity seems elusive and mysterious. In the chapters of this unit we will discover some of the processes of creativity and the way the mind operates when we work creatively. Chapter 9 contains readings on creativity and problem solving. What are some of the processes that we can use to boost our creativity? Chapter 10 looks at the role of humor in our lives. We will read about laughter and then compare social attitudes about optimism and pessimism. Do we have to be happy all of the time?

Points of Interest

EXPLORING POINTS OF VIEW: AGREE OR DISAGREE

Circle *A* if you agree or *D* if you disagree with the following statements.

1. A   D   All human beings are capable of being creative; it is part of our nature.

2. A   D   True creativity is the work of genius.

3. A   D   A creative person is a happy individual.

4. A   D   Good work takes 1 percent inspiration and 99 percent perspiration.

5. A   D   People who like to laugh live long lives.

6. A   D   One of the best mottoes for life is "Don't worry, be happy."

7. A   D   When skies are gray, just let a smile be your umbrella.

Work with a partner or in a small group. Explain the reasons for your opinion.

CHAPTER 9

The Creative Brain

Chapter Openers

EXPLORING EMOTIONS

Check (✔) the emotions that you might experience when you begin to work on a new project.

I might feel

_____ 1. joyful.

_____ 2. fearful.

_____ 3. indifferent.

_____ 4. overwhelmed.

_____ 5. liberated.

_____ 6. excited.

_____ 7. traumatized.

_____ 8. powerful.

_____ 9. powerless.

B. Read the short excerpt from "Bird by Bird" by Anne Lamott and name the types of emotions she feels at the beginning of a writing project. What lessons about how to begin working does she offer?

From Bird by Bird

By Anne Lamott

E. L. Doctorow once said that "writing a novel is like driving a car at night. You can see only as far as your headlights, but you can make the whole trip that way." You don't have to see where you're going, you don't have to see your destination or everything you will pass along the way. You just have to see two or three feet ahead of you. This is right up there with the best advice about writing, or life, I have ever heard.

So after I've completely exhausted myself thinking about the people I most resent in the world, and my more arresting financial problems, and, of course, the orthodontia, I remember to pick up the one-inch picture frame and to figure out a one-inch piece of my story to tell, one small scene, one memory, one exchange. I also remember a story that I know I've told elsewhere but that over and over helps me to get a grip: thirty years ago my older brother, who was ten years old at the time, was trying to get a report on birds written that he'd had three months to write, which was due the next day. We were out at our family cabin in Bolinas, and he was at the kitchen table close to tears, surrounded by binder paper and pencils and unopened books on birds, immobilized by the hugeness of the task ahead. Then my father sat down beside him, put his arm around my brother's shoulder, and said, "Bird by bird, buddy. Just take it bird by bird."

Discuss your ideas with a partner or in a small group.

◼ Exploring and Understanding Reading

DISCUSSION QUESTIONS

Think about the following questions before reading. Share your ideas with a partner or in a small group.

1. What is creativity?
2. What are some creative things that you have done?
3. What is the source of an individual's creativity?
4. What kind of process or processes do people go through in producing creative work?
5. At what stages of life is creativity more or less difficult?

PREVIEWING

Quickly read the title, quotes, and the chart contained in this selection. Based on your preview, make a list of four (or more) important ideas that you expect will be explained in the reading.

1. _____

2. _____

◼ **READING TIP:**
Remember that previewing is a critical reading strategy that helps you predict what information the reading will contain.

3. _____

4. _____

Compare your answers with a partner. Highlight the information on which you based your prediction. Return to these predictions after you have finished reading and verify your answers.

Read the selection quickly and answer the following question:

Why is it difficult for many people to feel comfortable with the idea that they might be creative?

List three possible reasons:

- _____

- _____

- _____

The Creative Brain

By Ned Hermann

1. Prevailing mythology has it that creativity is the exclusion domain of artists, scientists, and inventors—a giftedness not available to ordinary people going about the business of daily life. Partly as a result, *ordinary* people often hold the *creative* person in awe, finding little gradation in genius. It's either the Sistine Chapel ceiling or nothing.

Creative? Who, Me?

2. Our awe of creativity is like a dragon that blocks the gate to our personal creativity, and that we must slay before we can enter our own creative realm. For many of us, the dragon is a balloon, one of our own making, like a fugitive from the Macy's Thanksgiving Day parade. It is a fear inflated by our minds into a monster before which we shrink, trembling. We've created this dragon to protect ourselves from something worse: the possibility that we might really go for it, do the very utmost we can do—and find people out there who still don't think it's good enough and reject not only what we've done, but *us* as individuals.

3. What we need to understand is that by refusing to risk being creative at less than genius levels, we are already rejecting ourselves, passing judgment without evidence. While that judgment mechanism may have served to protect us from censure as children, we as adults no longer need to feel as vulnerable as we did when we were young. What we need to do instead is assume full responsibility ourselves: for encouraging our own inner child, for applauding our courage to try something, for praising our own spontaneity, for admiring our own willingness to start again when something comes out differently from the way we expect, and for delighting in our small and humble expressions of creativity, of which there are many every day.

4. In fact, most individual creativity is pretty humble—no Sistine Chapel ceiling, no Beethoven's Ninth Symphony, no Thomas Edison invention, just a solution to such a mundane problem as getting the microwave merry-go-round to work by turning it over and using it upside down, or finding a new way home, or writing a silly verse to a friend, or arranging and decorating a living room. One man got a faulty thermometer to shake down by attaching it to the blades of a fan and running it for a minute; he thinks that's "just technical," but it's fully creative. It's creative to design a house, develop a new business, paint a picture, lay out a garden, solve a new problem, fix a way to feed the cat when you're away for three days. All of these are valid examples of creative behaviors, because the doing of them includes an element of newness, novelty, and difference.

Exposing Myths about Creativity

5. If we understand creativity in this sense, three things are clear:

1. All human beings are capable of being creative—it is part of our birthright.
2. It is not necessary to be a genius to be creative.
3. No matter how severely our creativity may have been repressed in the past, it can be reaccessed, stimulated, and developed through life experiences and specialized programs.

6. I would expect that less than 1 percent of the total population could rank in the genius category, yet of the thousands of people I've worked with (who by and large didn't consider themselves creative), a good 70 to 80 percent have been able to demonstrate to their own satisfaction that: (1) they do have creative abilities, and (2) exercising those abilities can bring them a great deal of joy and profit.

7. This good news isn't only for the creatively uninformed or uninitiated. The same techniques that can open the creative world to a novice can set off a creative explosion in the adept. One GE inventor—with 34 patents to his credit—took our ACT I Workshop and said, "If I had known all this 25 years ago, I would now have a hundred patents!"

Obtaining Keys to Your Creativity

8. What made the difference for this inventor and for thousands of others who've moved into creative functioning? The keys are these:

1. An understanding of the creative process and its component stages, and how the four modes of knowing come into play at each stage

2. An understanding of what hinders each mode at each stage

3. A commitment to heightening one's own creative awareness and functioning

9. This chapter, the first of four devoted to helping people who want to heighten their creativity, elaborates on each of these areas of understanding.

What Is Creativity, Anyway?

10. I resist defining creativity: Each person's experience of it is so unique and individual that no one can formulate a definition that fits everyone else. However, you need to know what I'm talking about, so in this section I will be defining the word. Add to this extended definition in any way that works for you.

11. Many people think of creativity purely in terms of inventiveness, and that is surely part of it. "Hot" ideas are great and we revel in them when they hit. But if the process stops there, the "flash" evaporates. The world goes on, unchanged. The idea is usually lost. What's more—and this is the point— ideas in and of themselves, if they begin and end in our heads, produce neither growth nor full satisfaction because there's no basis for feedback to encourage more ideas. The reinforcement loop doesn't close.

12. My own thinking is that *creativity in its fullest sense involves both generating an idea and manifesting it—making something happen as a result.* To strengthen creative ability, you need to apply the idea in some form that enables both the experience itself and your own reaction and others' to reinforce your performance. As you and others applaud your creative endeavors, you are likely to become more creative.

13. Defining creativity to include application throws the whole subject into a different light, because:

1. While *ideas* can come in seconds, *application* can take days, years, or even a lifetime to realize.

2. While *ideas* can come out of only one quadrant, *application* ultimately calls on specialized mental capabilities in all four quadrants of the brain.

3. While *ideas* can arrive in a single flash, *application* necessarily involves a process consisting of several distinct phases.

14. Defining creativity to include application also makes creativity totally applicable in the world of business, where it tends to go under the label of *problem-solving*.

"Also, creativity can be learned. Once you have become convinced and aware that you can bring new things into being, then it is simply a matter of choosing a particular way to create."

Unknown

"Creativity is so delicate a flower that praise tends to make it bloom, while discouragement often nips it in the bud. Any of us will put out more and better ideas if our efforts are appreciated."

Unknown

"Discipline and focused awareness contribute to the act of creation."

John Poppy

The Source and Process of Creativity

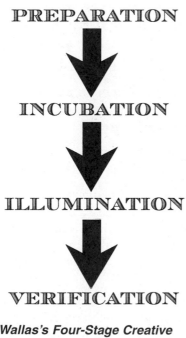

PREPARATION

INCUBATION

ILLUMINATION

VERIFICATION

Wallas's Four-Stage Creative Process

15. *Creativity's source is the brain—not just one part of the brain, but all of it.* Today, this theme song is well established and accepted, but when I first proclaimed it in 1975, it was a new idea and some of my associates in the training field thought I was nuts. Why? Because none of the well-known literature on creativity mentioned the brain once! It simply wasn't part of the prevailing frame of reference regarding creativity. I made the connection when others hadn't simply because: (1) I had specifically been asking about where creativity comes from at the moment of stumbling across the split-brain research, and (2) my awareness of duality had been strong since childhood. Others, whose frame of reference and background differed from mine, simply couldn't relate to what I was saying.

15a. Knowing that creativity arises in the brain makes an enormous contribution to our ability to access, stimulate, develop, and apply the process, because it tells us: (1) what process we need to follow, and (2) how that process calls on the brain's specialized capabilities at each stage.

16. Researcher Graham Wallas, many years ago, set down a description of what happens as people approach problems with the objective of coming up with creative solutions. He described his four-stage process as follows:

1. In the *preparation* stage, we define the problem, need, or desire, gather any information the solution or response needs to account for, and set up criteria for verifying the solution's acceptability.

2. In the *incubation* stage, we step back from the problem and let our minds contemplate and work it through. Like preparation, incubation can last minutes, weeks, even years.

3. In the *illumination* stage, ideas arise from the mind to provide the basis of a creative response. These ideas can be pieces of the whole or the whole itself, i.e., seeing the entire concept or entity all at once. Unlike the other stages, illumination is often very brief, involving a tremendous rush of insights within a few minutes or hours.

4. In *verification*, the final stage, one carries out activities to demonstrate whether or not what emerged in illumination satisfies the need and the criteria defined in the preparation stage.

This four-stage description has helped me define what happens in my own creative endeavors.

> ***"Our creativity is limited only by our beliefs."***
>
> **Willis Harmon**

> ***"Once we are destined to live out our lives in the prison of our mind, our one duty is to furnish it well."***
>
> **Peter Ustinov**

> ***"The weakest among us has a gift; however seemingly trivial, which is peculiar to him and which worthily used will be a gift also to his race."***

Key to Creative Living: Reclaiming Our Passion

17. A major key—perhaps the key—to living creatively is passion. By passion I mean a highly compelling, energetic attention to something. Turned-on people of all kinds are passionate. So are people who've just fallen in love. So are collectors, sports nuts, horse-crazy kids, boys who've just discovered baseball cards or video games, computer hackers.

18. Little children are passionate about almost everything they see. In fact, they are passionate about seeing itself, and feeling, and smelling, and hearing, and tasting, too. Their passion embraces life itself with all its experiences. Even timid children, once they've been reassured, have enormous enthusiasm. They reach out for everything they can—spiders, flowers, butterflies, blocks, hands, eyes, cats, food, wind, water, worms, you, music—everything. They are natural experimenters, dedicated explorers, fascinated examiners of you-name-it. As time goes on, they begin to make connections between things: One child, seeing oil in a puddle of water, exclaimed, "Oh look! A dead rainbow!" So extraordinary and novel are their perceptions that Art Linkletter made his reputation by interviewing children. Apart from committing the indiscretions that horrified their parents and delighted the audience, they resensitized us repeatedly to the wonder of the world around us.

19. The natural passion for life in all its unexpectedness that characterizes children also features strongly in the personalities of people who have chosen to retain or reclaim their own creativity. They are constantly exercising their curiosity, trying new things, and delighting in the experiment for its own sake—even if the results themselves don't please. They are open to the moment for whatever it may bring. They approach life with expectancy, enthusiasm, and energy.

20. How do we reclaim our passion if it has been allowed to dim in our lives? What if we are one of those many people whose zest for life has grown faint or even faded. If we despair of having an original thought all our own? One way—an important way—is to increase the amount of genuine pleasure we allow into our lives. There are many things that make life more pleasurable—listening to good music, exercising, eating what nourishes your body—but I want to concentrate in this section on four things:

1. We can learn—or re-learn—from children.
2. We can affirm ourselves and others, and accept affirmation.
3. We can take stock of our lives—ask if the way we are living truly satisfies us, and if not, what must be changed so it does.
4. We can provide ourselves with proof that reclaiming our passion is worthwhile and possible.

"Play teaches children to master the world."

Jean Piaget

Children Are Our Best Teachers

21. Children have a lot of special talents to offer. Their pursuit of novelty and wonder is both a cause and an effect—a gift of the life fully lived and one of the things that makes life worth living. Anyone who knows children can tell you that they do the following:

22. *Children follow their interests.* If a kid is bored, you know it. None of this polite interest stuff the rest of us get stuck in. What they like, they do, and this teaches them that following what they like makes them happy—so they do it some more.

23. *Children seek out and risk experimenting with new things.* If kids are confronted with something unfamiliar, they will take a chance and try it out. They prod and poke it, smell it, look at it from all angles, try using it in different ways, look to see what you think about it—maybe even give it to you to see what you do with it. We adults, by contrast, slap a label on it, say, "I know what that is," and dismiss it. What we're really saying is, "I know what I already know about that, and there's nothing more worth knowing," which is almost never true of anything or anyone.

24. *Children pay attention to their own rhythms.* We grownups tend to drive ourselves until something's done, or until a certain hour strikes, but children do things when they feel like it. Naturally, since someone else tends to their necessities, they may have more time and freedom to do that, but we would do well to follow their lead where we have the choice. When we work during our most productive times and rest during our other times, we make the most of our energies. That means if we do our best work between 4 P.M. and 2 A.M., then we should strive to arrange our day to make use of those hours. We become more trustworthy to ourselves and others.

25. *Children honor dreams and daydreams.* Children pay attention to, talk about, and follow up on their dreams and fantasies. They may draw pictures they saw in their dreams, conduct conversations with dream characters, and try to recreate something experienced in dreams and daydreams. These are all creative acts. Moreover, they are important: Mankind has learned that dreams are a language the subconscious uses to communicate to the conscious. Many people say they don't remember their dreams, but I know of no serious effort to connect with one's dream life that hasn't succeeded. Those who succeed often report an experience of waking and sleeping that is like living two lives, each one feeding and nourishing the other.

26. *Children consider mistakes as information, rather than as something unsuccessful.* "That's a way it doesn't work. I wonder how else it doesn't work?" For children, the process of figuring something out is in itself a win. We, however, are hung up on outcomes, so we lay judgments on our mistakes—"We did it wrong" and what is worse, we take it further—therefore "People won't love us," "We're never good enough," and "We'll be all alone." No wonder mistakes frighten some of us so deeply. Patterns like that aren't learned overnight, and changing them may take more than a few tries, but they can be changed.

27. *Children play.* Kids make a game out of everything. Their essential business is play, so to speak. They delight in spoofing each other, parents, and personalities. They love to mimic, pretend, wrestle, hide and seek, surprise, play practical jokes. They love to laugh, tell secrets, devise stories of goblins and fairies and giants and monsters and heroes. They're not hung up on accuracy. When in doubt, they know they can always make it up. Many adults, however, have withdrawn permission from themselves to be silly, to expose the part of themselves that feels young.

TELLBACK

A. Work with a partner, read a section, and then take turns explaining from memory what you read. Use the following sequence of steps.

Step 1. Read the first section.

Step 2. Close the book and tell as much of the information as you remember. Explain in your own words, if necessary.

Step 3. Ask your partner to add any information you may have forgotten.

Step 4. Repeat Steps 1–3 for the remaining sections, taking turns telling the information.

B. Choose three important ideas that are interesting or new to you. Explain why these are important with a partner.

Understanding and Paraphrasing Suggestions

Paraphrase the writer's suggestions to answer the following questions. To do this, highlight the information and then restate the ideas in your own words.

1. What does the writer believe are the three keys to creativity?

   a. _____

   b. _____

   c. _____

2. What has to happen for a creative idea to be fully realized?

   _____

   _____

3. Why is the understanding that creativity arises in the brain an important idea?

   _____

   _____

4. What characterizes creative people and why is this quality important?

   _____

   _____

■ *READING TIP:*
Using this technique helps you to paraphrase what you read and to speak more easily.

■ *READING TIP:*
Paraphrasing is the process of putting the writer's ideas into your own words. To paraphrase, you change the wording and the order of ideas you read. Be careful not to lose or change any of the ideas you paraphrase.

5. What do children do that adults should rediscover? Why?

a. _____

b. _____

c. _____

d. _____

e. _____

f. _____

Work with a partner to compare your answers. Your wording will be different but the ideas should be the same. Check to see if you have highlighted the same information. Share your answers with others in the class.

Understanding the Uses of Imagery and Example

In "The Creative Brain," the writer makes use of imagery and example to describe people's attitudes toward creativity.

Scan the reading and underline the images and examples that the writer uses to describe the following:

a. What people think about being creative

b. What prevents people from being creative

c. How children make connections between things

Work with a partner or in a small group and compare your answers. Discuss how effective these images and examples are in conveying the writer's ideas.

After Reading

WRITING

Summarizing Information from a Text

A summary is a brief piece of writing that explains the author's purpose in a larger work by identifying the main ideas and important details expressed therein. Summaries are useful for work in both academic and professional spheres.

Use the information from "Understanding and Paraphrasing Suggestions" on page 197 to make an outline that includes the following:

- The author's purpose in writing "The Creative Brain"
- The important ideas he expresses
- Important details or examples critical to the understanding of these ideas

Use your outline to write a short summary of about 100–150 words on separate pages of your own. Give your summary to a partner. As you read each other's writing do the following:

- Highlight the ideas from the reading that are included in the summary.
- Ask yourself whether or not all the important ideas are included.
- Ask yourself if these ideas are paraphrased.
- Are any ideas left out?
- Are any unnecessary details included?
- How would you rate this summary? 5—excellent, 4—very good, 3—good, 2—incomplete, 1—very incomplete.

Use the feedback from your partner to rewrite your summary.

Give the summary to your teacher for feedback.

■ *READING TIP:*
Summarizing is a strategy that helps you to convey the writer's purpose in conveying information in a reading selection. It is a technique that helps us identify what is important from what is secondary.

APPLYING THE INFORMATION TO ANALYZE A SITUATION

Read the following short article that presents some techniques for increasing creativity.

Based on the four-step process explained in the preceding reading selection, identify the following:

1. What steps in the process are described?
2. What steps in the process are not included?
3. What further steps would you suggest to complete the process?

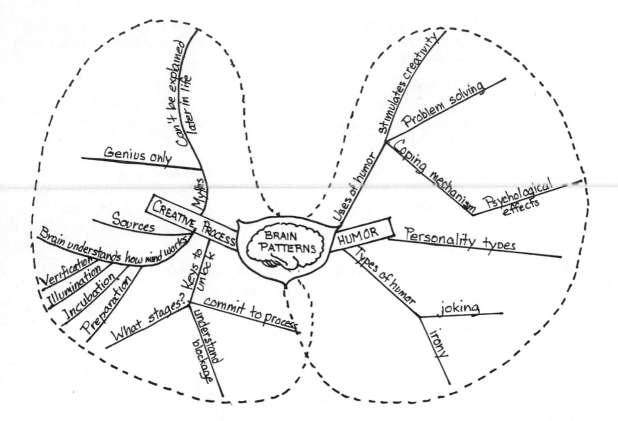

KNIGHT-RIDDER NEWSPAPERS

Mental Breakout

"Mind mapping" tries to tap the creative problem-solving potential of employees

By Tawn Nhan

CHARLOTTE, N.C.—About a dozen IBM executives, engineers and computer programmers walked into a meeting and almost immediately began breaking the rules of corporate etiquette.

Like children, each ripped open a pack of brightly colored pens and began doodling. Instead of taking notes, they drew large circles, arrows and stars.

They were mind mapping, an alternative note-taking technique that doubles as a creative thinking tool. It's the latest training trend to hit the corporate circuit, with companies such as IBM hoping to get an edge on competitors by improving the thinking skills of their workers.

Mind mapping was introduced about 20 years ago by Tony Buzan, an English creativity consultant who explained the concept in his book, *Using Both Sides of Your Brain*. But it's only gained popularity in the last couple of years.

Unlike conventional note-taking, mind mapping maximizes the strengths of both sides of the human brain because it uses words as well as images, according to Anne Durrum Robinson, a mind-mapping consultant training IBM workers.

Mind mapping allows you to personalize your notes.

Instead of using the conventional Roman numerals and letters, you use pictures and color. You start by jotting down a main idea or creating an image in the middle of the page. Then you add ideas by drawing branches from the main idea. Icons, sketches and color are used to highlight priorities. The words are generated from the left brain. The shapes and images come from the right side.

But mind mapping is more than just a way to take notes. Robinson said it's really a way to develop the right side of the brain, which few people fully tap.

"It's a wonderful way to explore mental diversity," Robinson said. "Mind mapping gets people to tap into their whole mind, and we use so little of the marvelous minds we have."

Robinson should know. The 81-year-old owner of Creativity, Communication and Common Sense, a workplace consulting firm in Austin, Tex., began using mind maps in the early 1970s to improve her efficiency as a writer.

Today, Robinson said she writes entire articles using a mind map. While waiting for her flight to Charlotte this week, Robinson said she wrote the bulk of a journal article using a mind map.

"It worked for me and I decided that it had so much value that it would be helpful to others," Robinson said.

Executives use it to write speeches, and workers use it to plan and execute projects and solve problems, Robinson said.

Boeing, 3M, British Petroleum and Fluor Daniel are among the companies that use mind mapping, said Robinson, who leads 10 to 12 mind-mapping seminars a year.

James Donahue, an IBM project executive, said the mind-mapping exercise made him aware of how little he uses his right brain.

"My brain is very left-brained. I have a lot of 'to do' lists. Lotus 1-2-3 is my friend. . . . I keep a lot of checklists," he said. "I don't tap into the right side of my mind enough. That's why I'm here.

"If you spend more than 20 years in a company, you begin to think in a rigid way," Donahue said. "My view of this is that it's a good investment of my time to find out new ways to think and do things differently."

Discuss your ideas with a partner or in a small group.

Vocabulary Building

FIGURING OUT THE REFERENT

In English, you will find that in complex sentences pronouns are often used to refer to ideas given in a preceding sentence or part of the sentence. In the following sentences taken from "The Creative Brain," decide what idea the pronoun in bold refers to. Look at the reading to help you decide.

1. Paragraph 2   Our awe of creativity is like a dragon **that** blocks the gate to our personal creativity.

   _____

2. Paragraph 7   **This** good news isn't only for the creatively uninformed or uninitiated.

   _____

3. Paragraph 11   Many people think of creativity purely in terms of inventiveness, and **that** is surely part of **it**.

   a. _____.

   b. _____

4. Paragraph 13   Defining creativity to include application also makes creativity totally applicable in the world of business, **where it** tends to go under the label of problem-solving.

   a. _____

   b. _____

5. Paragraph 20   **There** are many things **that** make life more pleasurable—listening to good music, exercising, eating what nourishes your body—but I want to concentrate in this section on four things:

   a. _____

   b. _____

6. Paragraph 24   **That** means if we do our best work between 4 P.M. and 2 A.M., then we should strive to arrange our day to make use of those hours.

Check your answers.

JIGSAW SENTENCES

Match the beginning of the sentences in Column A with the best completion of the sentence in Column B.

Column A

_____ 1. If we understand creativity in this sense,

_____ 2. If kids are confronted with something unfamiliar,

_____ 3. If I had known this 25 years ago,

_____ 4. If the process stops there,

Column B

a. they will take a chance and try it out.

b. the flash evaporates.

c. three things are clear.

d. I would now have a hundred patents.

Check your answers. Take turns reading the completed sentences.

WORD FORMS

Read each sentence and circle the correct word to use in the sentence. Write *N* if the word is a noun or *ADJ* if the word is an adjective.

1. _____ What made the **different/difference** for this inventor and for thousands of others who've moved into creative functioning?

2. _____ There's no **basis/basic** for feedback to encourage more ideas.

3. _____ Defining **creativity/creative** to include application throws the whole subject into a **different/difference** light.

4. _____ Little children are **passion/passionate** about almost everything they see.

5. _____ Their **passion/passionate** embraces life itself with all its experiences.

6. _____ The **natural/nature** passion for life in all its **unexpected/unexpectedness** that characterizes children also features strongly in the personalities of people who have chosen to retain or reclaim their own creativity.

Check your answers. Read the sentences with a partner.

Expanding Your Language

SPEAKING

Think of a creative person you are interested in. You may want to focus on a well-known musician, an artist, or a dancer. You may decide to focus on someone who is not well known but whose creative work you admire or who meets the criteria for creativity in everyday life that Herrmann sets out in "The Creative Brain."

Prepare to talk about your subject by researching the following:

- Background or general information about your subject
- Type of work or area of study undertaken
- Important moments in your subject's life
- Difficulties faced
- Reason(s) you admire this person

Using these points prepare notes for a five-minute presentation. Practice your presentation and then give your talk to others in a small group. Prepare three questions to give your audience a focus for discussion after your presentation.

WRITING

Choose a topic related to the discussions in the chapter readings or any other topic that interests you. Try to write about the topic every day for a week. Use the mind-mapping technique to help you develop and expand on your ideas. You can choose a topic in the news or choose to write about the creative person you researched for your oral presentation.

10

Laughter: The Creative Force

▌ Chapter Openers

DISCUSSION QUESTIONS

Think about these questions. Share your ideas with a partner or in a small group.

1. Do you think you have a good sense of humor?
2. What kinds of jokes, films, books, or other entertainment make you laugh?
3. Do you think that a sense of humor helps in life? Explain how this could be.
4. Do you think that a person who acts like a clown is really happy? Why or why not?

AGREE OR DISAGREE

Circle *A* if you agree or *D* if you disagree with the following statements.

1. A D   Wherever there is anxiety in a culture, you'll find humor.

2. A D   It's possible to discover people's values by the jokes they do or don't laugh at.

3. A D Using humor as part of a lecture interferes with people's learning.

4. A D People with a good sense of humor live longer.

5. A D People who laugh a lot do so because they're nervous.

6. A D A sense of humor helps people cope with difficult realities including our mortality.

Work with a partner or in a small group. Explain the reasons for your opinion

CATEGORIZING

How do you feel when someone tells a joke? How do you think your brain and body react? Write *F* for feeling and *B* for a body or brain reaction next to each of the following sentences. Circle the words or phrases that helped you decide.

1. _____ Elation comes from hearing a good joke.

2. _____ The mind associates more broadly after hearing a joke.

3. _____ Four seconds after hearing a joke, a negatively charged wave of electricity sweeps through the cortex.

4. _____ After you laugh, you go into a relaxed state, because your heart rate and blood pressure drop below normal.

5. _____ Telling a joke increases your sense of belonging and social cohesion.

6. _____ Laughter activates T lymphocytes and natural killer cells.

7. _____ People's immunoglobulin A increased when they watched humorous videos.

Check your answers. Work with a partner to compare the words or phrases you circled.

Exploring and Understanding Reading

PAIRED READINGS

Choose *one* of the readings. Work with a partner who is reading *the same* article.

PREDICTING

Check (✔) some of the areas in our lives that humor can affect in an important way.

_____ Good health   _____ Friendships

_____ Problem solving   _____ Academic success

_____ Job promotions   _____ Family relationships

_____ Job satisfaction   _____ Financial success

Work with others in a small group to compare your lists. Explain your choices.

PAIRED READINGS: THE BENEFITS OF HUMOR

Reading 1: Can Humor Help Us Solve Problems?

SKIMMING

Skim (read the complete article quickly) and answer the following question:

What are three areas of human activity that can benefit from a sense of humor?

a. _____

b. _____

c. _____

NEW YORK TIMES

Humor Found to Aid Problem Solving

Creative thinking as well as social bonding are among its benefits, researchers say.

By Daniel Goleman

"In America, everything is permitted that's not forbidden," a European joke has it. "In Germany, everything is forbidden that's not permitted. In France, everything is permitted, even if it's forbidden. And in Russia, everything is forbidden, even if it's permitted."

Such jokes suit the notion that much humor veils aggression, permitting the joke-teller, in Freud's words, "to be malicious with dignity." But Freud's longstanding analysis of humor as the release of repressed feelings is receding as a growing group of social scientists, for whom humor is no joke, make it the focus of serious research. In the new work, humor is seen less as disguised hostility and more as a stimulant to problem-solving and productivity, as an aid to education and as the stuff of social bonds.

Humor and its uses have been a subject of conjecture since Aristotle, and a large body of psychoanalytic literature deals with jokes. But "humor has been a neglected topic among researchers," said Donna Cooper, a psychologist at the University of Connecticut who is a consultant on the uses of humor in organizations. "Most psychologists are preoccupied with grim topics and problems; humor and the positive emotions get little interest or funding."

Of late, though, that has begun to change. Some of the more visible new research, inspired by Norman Cousins' account of how watching Marx Brothers movies and other comedy films helped him recover from a debilitating illness, deals with links between positive feelings and healing.

Less well known is recent research suggesting that putting people in a good mood by telling them jokes makes them think through problems with more ingenuity. Casual joking at work may thus improve people's effectiveness in their tasks.

"Any joke that makes you feel good is likely to help you think more broadly and creatively," said Alice M. Isen, a psychologist at the University of Maryland in Baltimore. The elation that comes from hearing a good joke, Dr. Isen has found, is similar to that which people feel when they receive a small, unexpected gift. Such elation, her research shows, facilitates innovation.

In the research, reported in a recent issue of *The Journal of Personality and Social Psychology,* Dr. Isen found that people who had just watched a short comedy film of television "bloopers" were better able to find a creative solution to a puzzling problem than were people who had watched a film about math or who had exercised.

The problem posed was one frequently used in such research: People were given a candle, matches and a box of tacks and asked to attach the candle to a corkboard wall so that the candle would burn without dripping wax on the floor.

Most people who try to solve this problem fall prey to "functional fixedness," the tendency to see the objects presented them only in terms of their conventional uses. Those who were in a good mood from watching the funny film, however, were generally able to solve the problem by seeing another use for the box holding the tacks: They tacked the box to the wall and used it as a candleholder.

In other studies, Dr. Isen found that the comedy film increased people's ability to think more broadly, seeing relationships that otherwise eluded them. This is a mental skill that is important in finding creative solutions to problems and in foreseeing the consequences of a given decision. The ability to recognize complex relationships and far-flung implications has also been found, in other research, to mark the most successful business executives.

"The mind associates more broadly when people are feeling good after hearing a joke," said Dr. Isen. "They think of things they ordinarily would not and have access to a broader range of mental material. And the more ideas present in your mind, the more ways you see to connect things; you're able to see more solutions."

Beyond Satisfaction

In light of this and other research, joking at work is being appreciated as more than mere diversion. Research to be reported next month at the annual meeting of the American Psychological Association shows that the feeling of having fun at work is more important than overall job satisfaction in workers' effectiveness.

In a survey of 382 people from a wide variety of work places, David Abramis, a psychologist in the School of Business Administration at California State University at Long Beach, found that those who felt their work was fun performed better and got along better with co-workers than did those who were satisfied with their jobs but did not see them as fun.

Traditionally, psychologists have focused on people's sense of satisfaction with their jobs as a measure of their psychological adjustment to work. Dr. Abramis, though, believes that the feeling that one's work is fun is of equal importance and that job satisfaction and having fun at work are independent considerations.

A major source of fun at work, the study showed, is joking with fellow workers, according to Dr. Abramis. "If you are trying to improve people's performance at work, it is not enough to improve their job satisfaction," he said. "Increasing their sense of having a good time at work improves their performance over and above satisfaction."

Joking also has its dangers, particularly carelessness, according to Dr. Isen. "If you want a jocular environment at work, you need to make sure people keep in mind the importance of their work," she said. "If you don't, feeling good may make people sloppy where they should be plodding. But if you tell people who are feeling good that they have made a mistake, they are especially thorough in correcting their errors."

Implications for Children

Although it is a relatively new idea that joking may enhance productivity at work, humor has long been used to make learning more palatable for children, as "Sesame Street" demonstrated. At first, some educators argued that such humor was detrimental to learning, because it drew children's attention away from the serious parts of the material presented. More recently, though, interspersing humor among the serious has been shown to improve children's learning, provided the humor is of the right sort.

New research on which sorts of humor aid learning and which hinder it shows that when the humor distorts the information, it often confuses children. According to findings by Dolf Zillman, a psychologist at Indiana University, irony is particularly confusing to young children, who do not yet have the basic knowledge that would allow them to see what is true and what a distortion. Dr. Zillman cites as an example of distortion a "Sesame Street" depiction of seat belts on an airplane; when the plane turns upside down the seat-belted characters hang from the cockpit as if the belts were rubber.

Children up to fourth grade, and perhaps beyond, are often confused by such distortions, Dr. Zillman reported in the *Handbook of Humor Research* (Springer-Verlag). On the other hand, he has found that humor that does not distort generally enhances children's ability to master new material. The solution he recommends is to use jokes that are unrelated to the topic at hand, rather than jokes about the information itself.

The Maturing Process

By the time students reach college age, though, humor that is unrelated to the educational topic can backfire, Dr. Zillman warns. A lecturer who habitually tells such jokes may be viewed as digressing, according to Dr. Zillman, and the joking asides seem to interfere with the students' grasp of the material presented. On the other hand, lecturers who weave into their material humor about the topic seem to be more effective.

Exactly what people find funny changes as they age, according to a survey of 40 stand-up comedians performed by Lucille Nahemow, a psychologist at the University of Connecticut. "Adults of all ages respond to sexual humor," she said, "while younger audiences like aggressive humor, such as put-down jokes and older audiences like jokes about family life."

Jokes serve an important social function in strengthening the bonds between people, researchers are finding. By laughing at the same things, people let one another know that they have a similar outlook, without having to say so. This makes jokes especially important in communicating about discomforting topics.

"Many jokes are a way to talk about troubling topics like sex and racism," according to Alan Dundes, a folklorist at the University of California at Berkeley, who in *Cracking Jokes* (Ten Speed Press) analyzes the hidden meanings of humor. By laughing at a joke, the listener tacitly signals that he shares the attitude implicit in it, Dr. Dundes argues.

"Wherever there is anxiety in a culture, you find humor," Dr. Dundes said. "In Eastern Europe, for example, you find many more jokes about politics and Russians than you do in the West, where these concerns are not so overriding."

Indeed, Dr. Dundes takes the popular jokes of a people as a barometer of their hidden concerns. Of particular significance, he finds, are "joke cycles," jokes on a single topic that spring up suddenly, have many variations and are extremely popular. Thus, in his view, "Jewish American princess" jokes of the late 1970s were a reaction to feminism.

"All jokes are serious, and anything funny is at someone's expense," Dr. Dundes said. "It is hard to find a truly harmless joke, one without a serious overtone."

SCANNING FOR RESEARCH FINDINGS

Reread the article more carefully and look for the information to answer the following questions. Highlight the information in the text and mark the question number in the margin. Write your answers in note form.

1. What benefits will result from casual joking at work?

_____

_____

2. What example shows that humor aids in problem solving? Explain.

_____

_____

3. What are some possible reasons that humor would help executives become successful?

_____

_____

4. What are the dangers and benefits of joking on the job?

_____

_____

5. a. What kind of humor helps children learn? What kind doesn't?

_____

   b. What solution is proposed to address the problem of using humor in educational material for children?

_____

6. What kind of humor should lecturers use? What kind doesn't work?

_____

_____

7. How do jokes act to strengthen the bonds between people?

_____

_____

8. Why does Alan Dundes think that jokes are really serious?

_____

_____

Work with a partner to ask and answer the questions. Compare the information you highlighted for each of the questions.

NOTE-TAKING

On separate pages, write notes to make an oral presentation of the important information in this reading. Use a divided-page format (see pg. 29) to write supporting points and details for the following main ideas:

A. Introduction; benefits of humor
B. Research about humor in the workplace
C. Research about humor in children's education
D. Research about humor in college education
E: The role of jokes in society

Work with a partner and take turns comparing the notes you wrote for each of the main ideas. Correct or add any missing information. Refer to the reading if you need to.

RECAPPING THE INFORMATION

Practice explaining the information from your notes. Work with a partner and take turns explaining each of the main ideas.

REACTING TO THE INFORMATION

Discuss these questions with others who worked on the *same* reading.

1. How do you react to a lecturer who tells jokes in class?
2. How do you feel when people laugh at jokes that you *don't* think are funny? How do you feel when people laugh at jokes that you *do* think are funny?
3. Does humor help you to think or work more creatively? What examples of this can you think of?
4. Do you think that jokes are a good way to treat troubling topics like sex or racism? Why or why not?

■ ■
_____

Reading 2: Can Humor Enhance Health?

SKIMMING

Skim (read the complete article quickly) and answer the following question:

What are three important areas of human activity that can benefit from laughter?

a. _____

b. _____

c. _____

Happily Ever Laughter

Laughter may help make you happier and healthier.
But not everybody benefits from humor equally.
Here's how to harness laughter's power.

By Peter Doskoch

Laughter is such an intrinsic part of our lives that we sometimes forget how very odd it is. Despite the development of new-fangled imaging machines like MRI and PET scans, neuroscientists still have little idea what's happening in our brain when we laugh. Certainly the brain stem plays a role. People who've suffered strokes in this primitive brain region have been known to have prolonged bouts of pathological laugh- ter. And some anencephalic infants—babies born missing their higher brain circuitry— will, when tickled, make faces that appear to be smiles or laughs, again implicating the primitive brain.

But laughing in response to something funny also calls on more sophisticated brain functions. One of the few brain stud- ies conducted so far in humor research looked at the electrical activity that occurs as we chuckle, giggle, or guffaw. About four-tenths of a second after we hear the punch line of a joke—but before we laugh—a negatively charged wave of electricity sweeps through the cortex, reports Peter Derks, Ph.D., professor of psychology at the College of William and Mary.

What Derks finds most significant about this electrical wave is that it carpets our entire cerebral cortex, rather than just one region. So all or most of our higher brain may play a role in laughter, Derks suggests, perhaps with the left hemisphere working on the joke's verbal content while the analytic right hemisphere attempts to figure out the incongruity that lies at the heart of much humor.

In the Mood

That laughter is a full-cortex experience is only fitting considering the wide-ranging effects it has on us psychologically and physiologically. Perhaps the most obvious effect of laughter is on our mood. After all, with even the most intellectual brands of humor, laughter is ultimately an expression of emotion—joy, surprise, nervousness, amusement. More than a decade of research has begun unraveling the details of the laughter-mood connection

• Stressed-out folks with a strong sense of humor become less depressed and anxious than those whose sense of humor is less well developed, according to a study by psychologists Herbert Lefcourt, Ph.D., of the University of Waterloo, and Rod Martin, Ph.D., now at the University of Western Ontario.

• Researchers at West Chester University in Pennsylvania found that students who used humor as a coping mechanism were more likely to be in a positive mood.

• In a study of depressed and suicidal senior citizens, the patients who recovered were the ones who demonstrated a sense of humor, reports psychiatrist Joseph Richman, M.D., professor emeritus at Albert Einstein Medical Center in Bronx, New York.

All of this makes sense in light of laughter's numerous physiological effects. "After you laugh, you go into a relaxed state," explains John Morreall, Ph.D., president of HUMORWORKS Seminars in Tampa, Florida. "Your blood pressure and heart rate drop below normal, so you feel profoundly relaxed. Laughter also indirectly stimulates endorphins, the brain's natural painkillers."

In addition to its biological effects, laughter may also improve our mood through social means. Telling a joke, particularly one that illuminates a shared experience or problem, increases our sense of "belonging and social cohesion," says Richman. He believes that by psychologically connecting us to others, laughter counteracts "feelings of alienation, a major factor in depression and suicide."

Some of laughter's other psychological effects are less obvious. For one thing, says Morreall it helps us think more creatively. "Humor loosens up the mental gears. It encourages out-of-the-ordinary ways of looking at things."

Humor guru William Fry, M.D., professor emeritus of psychiatry at Stanford University, takes this idea one step further. "Creativity and humor are identical," he contends. "They both involve bringing together two items which do not have an obvious connection, and creating a relationship."

Finally, humor helps us contend with the unthinkable—our mortality. Lefcourt recently found that people's willingness to sign the organ donor consent on their driver's license rises with their tendency to laugh. "Very few people are ready to think, even for a moment, about death," he says. "But those who have a sense of humor are more able to cope with the idea."

A Healthy Sense of Humor

The idea that laughter promotes good health first received widespread attention through Norman Cousins's 1979 best-seller, *Anatomy of an Illness*. But centuries earlier astute observers had ascribed physical benefits to humor. Thomas Sydenham, a seventeenth century British physician, once observed: "The arrival of a good clown into a village does more for its health than 20 asses laden with drugs."

Today, scientific belief in laughter's effects on health rest largely on the shoulders of Lee Berk, M.D., and Stanley Tan, M.D., both of the Loma Linda School of Medicine, in Loma Linda, California. Laughter, they find, sharpens most of the instruments in our immune system's tool kit. It activates T lymphocytes and natural killer cells, both of which help destroy invading microorganisms. Laughter also increases production of immunity-boosting gamma interferon and speeds up the production of new immune cells. And it reduces levels of the stress hormone cortisol, which can weaken the immune response.

Meanwhile, studies by Lefcourt and others have found that levels of immunoglobulin A, an antibody secreted in saliva to protect against respiratory invaders, drops during stress—but it drops far less in people who score high on a humor scale.

While these findings suggest how laughter might benefit our health, nobody has yet proven that these immune effects translate into faster healing, because humor's impact on actual recovery has never been scientifically confirmed.

A study now underway at Columbia Presbyterian Medical Center in New York should shed some more light on this issue. Researchers in the pediatric wards are literally sending in the clowns to see if humor hastens healing in kids with cancer and other serious illnesses. A 35-member Clown Care Unit, composed of members of the Big Apple Circus, makes thrice-weekly visits to Columbia's Babies and Children's Hospital while researchers monitor the kids' vital signs and rate of recovery. Preliminary data should be available early next year.

Laughter: The Proper Dose

Now that we know what laughter can do, it's important to recognize when it's most effective. Here are some things to keep in mind to live life happily ever laughter.

Humor may help some people more than others.

There's one problem with nearly all the research that links humor and mood; it's what scientists call "correlational." The fact that two things happen at the same time doesn't mean one caused the other. So if folks with a strong sense of humor are less affected by stress, "it doesn't mean laughing is what's helping them cope," says Martin. Rather, it could be that if they're coping well, they can laugh a lot.

In Martin's view, by adulthood our sense of humor has essentially reached its final form. And for those of us whose internal humor settings are on the low side, he believes laughter may not help as much. For example, in one study, participants' levels of immunoglobulin A increased when they viewed humorous videos. But they rose most in people whose tendency to laugh was greatest to begin with. So the serious and sober among us may benefit less from laughter.

Others dispute this idea, asserting that humor is an equal-opportunity life enhancer. "Anybody who has normal mental development can engage in and benefit from humor," insists Morreall. "All they have to do is put themselves in this more playful state of mind. We have to give ourselves permission to do something we did very easily when we were three years old."

Martin, though, remains unconvinced. "My sense is that research hasn't been as successful as people had hoped. It seems to be pretty hard to teach someone to change their sense of humor." Nonetheless, if you're a natural humor powerhouse, laughter's force may be especially at your command.

Control and choice may enhance laughter's benefits.

Numerous studies show that psychological and physical health improve when people feel a sense of control in their lives, whether over their jobs, future, relationships, or even their medical treatment. Laughter's benefits may have a similar origin, suggests Morreall.

"When we're stressed, we often feel like we have no control of the situation," he says. "We feel helpless. But when we laugh, at least in our minds, we assume some control. We feel able to handle it."

One implication of this is that the more control people have over the type of humor to which they're exposed, the more they may benefit from it. At least one study bears this out. When patients recovering from surgery at a Florida hospital were allowed to choose the humorous movies they saw, they required less painkillers than a control group that saw no movies. But a third set of patients, force-fed comedies that may not have been to their liking, did worst of all.

Perhaps that should come as no surprise. Humor is intensely personal. Jim Carrey's comedy has little in common with Woody Allen's. "To harness laughter's benefits, it's essential that each person is matched to his or her favorite brand of humor," says Lefcourt. Often, that's remarkably difficult, even for folks close to you. "I'm sometimes very surprised at what people I know find funny," he says.

In the long run, conscientiousness may outperform laughter as a health aid.

Even if laughter proves to aid recovery, it may not be an asset in the long run, contends Howard Friedman, Ph.D., professor of psychology at the University of California at Riverside. Friedman and colleagues have been following the fates of the "Termites," a group of 1,528 eleven-year-olds that the legendary psychologist Louis Terman, Ph.D., began studying in 1921. Terman asked teachers and parents to assess various personality traits of his preteen subjects. Friedman's team found that individuals judged as being cheerful and having a good sense of humor as children have been dying sooner than their less jovial classmates.

The reason, he thinks, is that cheerful people may pay less attention to threats to their physical and psychological well-being. "In the short term, I think it is helpful to be optimistic about a particular illness," says Friedman. But the same good-natured attitude that helps us laugh off the threat of illness ("I'm going to be just fine.") may work against us when we're presented with the opportunity to eat unhealthy foods or light up a cigarette ("I'm going to be just fine.").

In fact, the only personality trait that consistently increased longevity among the Termites, Friedman says, was conscientiousness, possibly because folks with this trait are more likely to avoid hazardous behaviors. So laugh all you like—but temper it with a bit of caution.

Prescription for Happiness

While laughter may not be a panacea, there's still much to be gained from it. And, truth be told, there's room for plenty of additional chortles in our lives. Fry found that by the time the average kid reaches kindergarten, he or she is laughing some 300 times each day. Compare that to the typical adult, whom Martin recently found laughs a paltry 17 times a day (Men and women laugh equally often, Martin adds, but at different things.)

Fortunately, if you're attracted by the idea of using laughter to improve your spirit and health, chances are you've already got a good sense of humor. Meaning, of course, that you're just the type of person who might benefit from what Fry calls "prophylactic humor"—laughter as preventive medicine.

For people who want to inoculate themselves with laughter, Fry recommends this two-step process.

First, figure out your humor profile. Listen to yourself for a few days and see what makes you laugh out loud. Be honest with yourself; don't affect a taste for sophisticated French farces if your heartiest guffaws come from watching Moe, Larry, and Curly.

Next, use your comic profile to start building your own humor library: books, magazines, videos, what have you. If possible, set aside a portion of your bedroom or den as a "humor corner" to house your collection. Then, when life gets you down, don't hesitate to visit. Even a few minutes of laughter, says Fry, will provide some value.

"We're teaching people a skill that they can use when, say, deadline pressures are getting close." explains nurse/clown Patty Wooten, R.N., author of *Compassionate Laughter* (Commune-a-Key) and president of the American Association for Therapeutic Humor.

"The deadline will remain, but by taking time out to laugh, you adjust your mood, your physiology, your immune system. And then you go back to work and face what you have to do."

–Psychology Today

SCANNING FOR RESEARCH FINDINGS

Reread the article more carefully and look for the information to answer the following questions. Highlight the information in the text and mark the question number in the margin. Write your answers in note form.

1. What different parts of the brain are involved when we laugh?

   _____

   _____

2. What examples of biological effects are given to show that laughter affects our mood?

   _____

   _____

3. What are some of the psychological effects of laughter?

   _____

   _____

4. What example shows that humor helps us face our mortality?

   _____

   _____

5. What system of the body can be improved through laughter?

   _____

   _____

   What medical studies show this to be the case?

   _____

   _____

6. Why are correlational studies not enough to prove a link between humor and mood?

   _____

   _____

7. What two views are given about whether adults can develop a sense of humor or not?

   _____

   _____

8. Why is it important for individuals themselves to choose the funny films they like to watch?

   _____

   _____

9. What could explain why children with a good sense of humor had shorter lifespans than those whose sense of humor was less keen?

   _____

   _____

10. What three things can people do if they want to laugh more?

    _____

    _____

Work with a partner to ask and answer the questions. Compare the information you highlighted for each of the questions.

NOTE-TAKING

On separate pages, write notes to make an oral presentation of the important information in this reading. Use a divided-page format (see pg. 29) to write supporting points and details for the following main ideas:

A. Introduction; laughter and the brain

B. Effects of laughter on our mood

C. Effects of laughter on the immune system

D. Interrelationship of mood and personality

E. Control and choice in humor

F: Laughter and longevity

G. How to increase laughter

Work with a partner and take turns comparing the notes you wrote for each of the main ideas. Correct or add any missing information. Refer to the reading if you need to.

RECAPPING THE INFORMATION

Practice explaining the information from your notes. Work with a partner and take turns explaining each of the main ideas.

REACTING TO THE INFORMATION

Discuss these questions with others who worked on the same reading.

1. Do you think that people can learn to develop a sense of humor? Why or why not?
2. What would you do to try to cheer up someone who was sick?
3. Why do children laugh more than adults? What can adults do to laugh more?
4. What are some of the ways you think are effective to cope with stress?

After Reading

RETELLING THE INFORMATION

Work with a partner who prepared notes from a *different reading*. Use your notes to explain the information to your partner.

REACTING TO THE INFORMATION

■ *RETELLING TIP:*
When talking from notes, remember not to look down and read your notes. Maintain eye contact with your partner. If you should forget some facts, look quickly at the notes to remind yourself of what you want to say. Then look up and talk.

Based on the information from *both* readings and ideas of your own, complete the following.

A. Discuss the questions in the "Reacting to the Information" sections on page 214 and at the top of this page.

B. Decide if there is any information to support each of the following sayings:

1. Laughter is the best medicine.
2. Act happy. Genuine joy will follow.
3. Laugh and the world laughs with you. Cry and you cry alone.
4. You can't teach an old dog new tricks.
5. Pleasantry in pain—that makes humor.
6. Humor is not a gift of the mind, but of the heart.

APPLYING THE INFORMATION: GIVING YOUR OPINION

Must we always approach life with a positive attitude, or is there some merit in having a negative attitude? Is pessimism ever a good thing?

A. Skim the reading that follows and find out if there is any use for negativity.

B. Write one of the advantages of pessimism that is explained in this reading.

NEW YORK TIMES

Seeing Pessimism's Place in a Smiley-Faced World

By Erica Goode

Dr. Barbara Held has had just about enough of accentuating the positive and eliminating the negative.

She does not want to cheer up, look on the bright side or let a smile be her umbrella. And she is not planning to put a smiley face sticker on her car bumper any time soon.

In fact, Dr. Held views such activities as rather worrisome. She is one of a small band of psychologists who believe their profession—and indeed America as a whole—has succumbed to an ethos of unrelenting positivity. This "tyranny of the positive atti-tude," as Dr. Held sees it, prescribes cheerfulness and optimism as a formula for success, resilience and good health, and equates negativity with failure, vulnerability and general unhealthiness.

Positive thinking is a staple of self-help books, popular music and Sunday sermons. And in recent years, it has also found a home in the positive psychology movement, which was founded to correct what its leaders, including Dr. Martin Seligman, a professor of psychology at the University of Pennsylvania and a former president of the American Psychological Association, saw as the field's overly narrow focus on mental illness and human failing.

But Dr. Held and like-minded colleagues, who gathered last week at the psychological association's annual meetings in Washington for a symposium titled "The (Overlooked) Virtues of Negativity," feel that bliss can be taken too far.

While positive thinking has its advantages, they argue, a little whining now and then is not such a bad thing. Pessimism, in some circumstances, may have its place. And the unrelieved pressure to be upbeat, they assert, may gloss over individual needs and differences, and may make some people feel worse instead of better.

"I'm worried that we're not making space for people to feel bad," said Dr. Held, a clinical psychologist at Bowdoin College in Brunswick, Me., and the author of "Stop Smiling Start Kvetching."

"Life is very hard," Dr. Held said. "If you're having a hard time with something, it can make it harder to cope if you feel pressure to act O.K when you're not."

A large body of experimental work has elaborated on the pluses of optimism and positive thinking, which appear to have beneficial effects on performance, social adjustment and some aspects of health. But at least some research supports the notion that in some cases, it may be more useful to see the glass as half empty.

Dr. Julie Norem, a social psychologist at Wellesley College, for example, has studied "defensive pessimism," a coping strategy that involves setting unrealistically low expectations, then mentally playing out all the possible outcomes of a given situation.

For instance, Dr. Norem explained, a defensive pessimist is likely to approach a coming public speaking engagement with

mounting anxiety. But rather than giving herself a pep talk or using positive imagery to calm herself down, the defensive pessimist will picture herself tripping over the microphone cord, dropping her notes and dissolving into a fit of coughing.

Yet this anxious reverie will also include plans for avoiding such humiliation, like wearing low heeled-shoes or having a glass of water on the lectern. "This mental rehearsal tends to make defensive pessimists feel less anxious, and so they actually perform better," Dr. Norem said.

In laboratory experiments, the psychologist and her colleagues have found, defensive pessimists indeed perform as well on tasks as "strategic optimists," who are less anxious, tend to set high expectations for their own performance and avoid thinking about all the things that could go wrong.

But the performance of each group suffers when it is impeded from engaging in its preferred strategies.

In one study, for example, defensive pessimists and strategic optimists participated in a dart throwing exercise. The subjects were randomly assigned to prepare for the task in one of three ways. In one, they engaged in "coping imagery," imagining something going wrong and taking steps to fix it, a strategy close to the natural approach of defensive pessimists. In the second, the subjects practiced "mastery," imagining a flawless performance. In the third, the participants engaged in a relaxation exercise, distracting themselves from the pending dart-throwing by imagining a peaceful scene, perhaps a beach.

Defensive pessimists, the researchers found, did well in the game when they prepared using imagery that mimicked their preferred coping style. But their performance declined when they imagined performing perfectly and they did even worse when asked to act like optimists, distracting themselves with relaxing images. Strategic optimists, in contrast, performed best after the relaxation exercise and worst when they imagined things going wrong.

Other researchers have investigated the benefits of griping (high for those who do it infrequently, lower for frequent complainers) and extent of pessimism in different cultures. (Asian-Americans, one study found, are more pessimistic than Caucasian-Americans, and are more likely to use pessimism as a way of coping.)

Work by Dr. James Pennebaker, a professor of psychology at the University of Texas at Austin, also underlines the positive role of what some might call "constructive negativity."

Obsessively ruminating about how miserable life is, studies show, can have a harmful effect on health. But in a series of studies, Dr. Pennebaker and his colleagues asked subjects to focus on stressful or disturbing life events in a structured way, writing essays about the most traumatic experience of their lives, for example. The subjects' health improved on a variety of measures and this improvement persisted for up to four months after the studies were over.

Dr. Pennebaker said he was happy to be considered part of the positive psychology movement but that "a lot depends on what we mean by positive psychology."

"There's some reasonably compelling evidence to suggest that when people are falsely peppy and upbeat and chipper, it's not very healthy," he said.

And, he added, little data supports the idea that a positive attitude enhances health—something he pointed out repeatedly several years ago when his wife developed breast cancer, and people kept telling her, "You just need to be positive all the time."

In fact, Dr. Pennebaker added, a 1989 study he published with Dr. David Watson, now at the University of Iowa, indicates that even nervous, unhappy people, prone to chronic complaining, appear to be no more unhealthy than their buoyant peers. Subjects in the study who scored high on measures of nervousness, apprehension, irritability and oversensitivity were more likely to complain about physical symptoms. But they were no more likely to visit the doctor, develop high blood pressure or die.

"It's not bad to be nervous and it's not bad to be angry," Dr. Watson said in an interview. "We have these emotions because they serve useful functions for us."

The participants in last week's symposium emphasized that they hoped to temper, not to disparage the field's interest in positive things. "I'm not saying it's good to let people wallow in the negative," said Dr. Arthur Beauhart, a humanistic psychologist at California State University at Dominguez Hills. "I see this as a healthy corrective, or an expanding of the positive psychology movement." But psychologists identified with that movement say that positive psychology already makes clear that at times optimism is neither appropriate nor beneficial.

Dr. Seligman, a founder of positive psychology, expressed amusement that a positive focus could stir controversy. "I'm all for negative psychology," he said. "I spent 35 years of my life doing it. It just seems to me that there's no danger that people are going to be working exclusively on the positive. I think most of psychology has been about going from minus 8 to minus 5."

C. Highlight all of the information that explains the purposes of pessimism. Work with a partner and discuss three interesting ways in which pessimism is useful.

D. Based on the discussion and your own experience, prepare a list of the situations in which pessimism could be useful.

ARGUING YOUR POINT OF VIEW

Compare and contrast the uses of humor and laughter with those of pessimism. Prepare to argue in favor of either the importance of optimism or the importance of pessimism in our attitudes toward life today. To do this, follow these steps:

1. Decide which argument you will make.
2. List the points you think are important for your argument. Give examples for each point from the readings and from your own information or experience.

3. Compare your list with others who are making the same argument.

4. Prepare a list of all the arguments and order them from strongest to weakest.

5. Practice explaining your arguments with a partner.

6. Form a small group with people who prepared a different argument and take turns explaining and defending your argument.

7. Prepare to present your conclusions to others in the class.

Vocabulary Building

VOCABULARY IN CONTEXT

Comparisons

Read each of these sentences and choose one of the following words or phrases to complete the comparison.

a. more as   b. less as   c. the more   d. more   e. most

1. Humor is seen _____ disguised hostility and

   _____ a stimulant to problem solving and productivity.

2. Some of the _____ visible new research deals with links between positive feelings and healing.

3. Any joke that makes you feel good is likely to help you think

   _____ broadly and creatively.

4. _____ people who try to solve this problem fall prey to "functional fixedness."

5. The mind associates _____ broadly when people are feeling good after hearing a joke.

6. _____ ideas present in your mind, _____ ways you see to connect things; you're able to see

   _____ solutions.

7. Lecturers who weave into their material humor about the topic

seem to be _____ effective.

Check your answers. Take turns reading the sentences with a partner.

WORD FORMS

Read each sentence and circle the correct word to use. Write *N* if the word is a noun or *ADJ* if the word is an adjective.

1. _____ The **productivity/productive** one experiences is as a result of using humor.

2. _____ The **elation/elated** that comes from hearing a good joke is similar to what people feel when they receive a small unexpected gift.

3. _____ Joking also has its dangers, particularly **careless/ carelessness**.

4. _____ Irony is particularly **confusing/confusion** to young children.

5. _____ Studies looked at the **electrical/electric** activity that occurs as we chuckle, giggle, or gufffaw.

6. _____ Some of laughter's other **psychology/psychological** effects are less obvious.

7. _____ Laughter counteracts feelings of **alienation/alienating**, a major factor in depression and suicide.

Check your answers. Read the sentences with a partner.

DEFINITIONS

In English the definitions that explain special terms are often given in the sentences that follow the use of the terms. Locate the following special terms in the final chapter reading and highlight or underline the explanations that provide the definition for each. Write a definition for each in your own words.

1. "defensive pessimism" _____

2. "coping imagery" _____

3. "mastery" _____

4. "constructive negativity" _____

5. "strategic optimist" _____

Work with a partner to compare your definitions. Refer to the highlighted information in the text to agree on your answer.

Expanding Your Language

SPEAKING

Two-Minute Taped Talk: **Refer back to the paired readings in this chapter. Choose several compelling life situations in which an optimistic attitude can play a crucial role. Provide supporting information to explain why it works. Use the notes you prepared for the article you read and the information you heard from your partner who read a different article. Make a short outline of the ideas you plan to explain. Practice your talk a few times before you record your tape. Give your tape to your teacher for feedback.**

WRITING

Topic Writing: **Using the information from the readings in this chapter and ideas of your own, compare the benefits of optimistic and pessimistic attitudes toward life. Make an outline or write a draft of this topic. Do this work in your journal notebook.**

1. Work with a partner and explain your ideas to each other.
2. Write a draft of a three-paragraph essay.
   Paragraph 1. The benefits of humor on our lives
   Paragraph 2. The benefits of pessimism on our lives
   Paragraph 3. Your opinion: Do we need to be happy all the time?
3. Show your draft to a partner for peer review.
4. Rewrite your draft and give the final writing to your teacher.

Read On: Taking It Further

READING JOURNAL: RETELLING

■ *READING TIP:*
*Don't forget to write
your reading journal
and vocabulary log
entries in your note-
book. Show the
entries to your
teacher. Arrange to
discuss your
progress in reading.*

Choose a favorite comic book writer, a comic, a writer such as Dr. Seuss (Theodore Geisel), or a cartoonist such as Charles Shultz, the creator of "Peanuts." Read some of this person's work. Alternatively, you could choose a book about attitudes toward life such as *Tuesdays with Morrie* by Mitch Albom. With your teacher's guidance, choose some material to read about and report on.

OTHER SUGGESTIONS

What are some of your favorite comedy films? Choose a comedy film that you would enjoy. After seeing the film, prepare to report on the movie to others in the class.

UNIT 6

Work

One of the saddest things is that the only thing a man can do for eight hours a day, day after day, is work. You can't eat for eight hours a day, nor drink for eight hours a day nor make love for eight hours.

–William Faulkner

231

Introducing the Topics

It may be sad but it is definitely true: we all have to work in one way or another. In many ways this is more of a challenge because, as in other areas of life, the nature of work and the workplace is changing very rapidly. In this unit we will examine several important employment issues. Chapter 11 will look at the recent changes in the workplace and the effect these have on society. Chapter 12 will look at how companies are trying to improve job conditions in ways that are more suited to their employees.

Points of Interest

DISCUSSION QUESTIONS

Think about these questions. Share your ideas with a partner or in a small group.

1. What kind of work do you do? (If you have never worked, describe what you would like to do.)
2. Is it getting easier or harder for people to find jobs that they like? Explain.
3. In today's marketplace what do employers look for when hiring new employees? How does this compare to the past?
4. What are the characteristics of a company that is "good" to work for?

WHAT TYPE OF WORKER ARE YOU?

Barbara Moses, a newspaper columnist as well as the author of several career-planning books, developed the following six work-personality profiles. Which one reflects your personality the most? You can choose more than one if necessary. Be prepared to explain your choice(s).

Knowing Goals Best Way to Build Career

By Fiona McNair

• **Independent Thinkers or Entrepreneurs:** "I need to be in charge of what I do, for whom and when."

Autonomy is the great motivator for these people. They need to feel they are living in a free-form world they can shape. They are impatient with corporate norms and procedures, and are uncomfortable with "received wisdom." They are prepared to take full responsibility for their successes and failures; but to do so, they have to be in charge.

• **Lifestylers:** "I work to live, not live to work. I want the flexibility to pursue my personal passions."

People in this category are prepared to work hard to get the job done. But they expect work to buy them free time which they can enjoy in their own way. For example, some young professionals on the West coast said they would be loath to take a transfer to a bigger job on the East coast, because it would take them away from the mountains and into harsh winters.

233

Thirty-something parents who want to balance their work and family lives would also fall into this category.

- **Personal Developers:** "As long as I am learning, I'm happy."

Personal developers evaluate their work in terms of whether they are acquiring new skills and are quickly bored, especially if they think they are in a dead-end job. Not risk takers by nature, they are only prepared to take risks in their career if it gives them an opportunity to stretch.

- **Careerists:** "I want to get ahead, and I am willing to make the necessary sacrifices."

Most careerists resemble traditional baby boomers, who evaluated their success in terms of opportunities for advancement and increasing work responsibility. Unlike old-style careerists, they do not necessarily see a predictable future within a given organization.

- **Authenticity Seekers:** "I gotta be me."

People who are motivated by authenticity refuse to "hang up their personality" at the door. They won't sacrifice their personal expressiveness in order to play a corporate role. If they run their own business they will typically infuse it with a strong personality to reflect their styles.

- **Collegiality seekers:** "I need to work with people. I am a people-person."

These people derive much of their identity from belonging to a team or work group. For them, fun is going out for a drink after work with other members of the group. They are not happy working by themselves.

–Southam News

Get together in a small group of three or four. Discuss the profile(s) that you chose. Use past or present work experience to explain your choice(s). If you have never worked, discuss which one you think you are and why.

CHAPTER 11

The Changing World of Business

![chapter marker] **Chapter Openers**

WHAT'S YOUR OPINION?

Using your own experience, decide whether the following are on the increase or decrease. Try to think of an explanation in each case.

- Company loyalty
- Absenteeism
- Number of jobs held in a lifetime
- Full-time work
- Job security

Share your ideas with a partner or in a small group.

DEFINING THE TERMS

Match these words with the definitions that follow without looking in a dictionary.

a. merger   b. capitalism   c. welfare   d. blue collar
e. flextime   f. wage

1. _____ Payment made to a worker for work done

2. _____ Receiving regular monetary assistance from the government because of need

3. _____ The union of two or more corporations or organizations

4. _____ Wage earner whose job is performed in work clothes and often involves manual labor

5. _____ An economic system in which the means of production and distribution are privately owned by individuals or groups and competition for business establishes the price of goods and services

6. _____ An arrangement by which employees may set their own work schedules, especially their starting and finishing hours

Check your answers with a partner. Refer to a dictionary if you cannot agree.

Exploring and Understanding Reading

PREDICTING

The reading that follows is entitled "Why Good Workers Make Bad People." Before you read it, take a few minutes to consider how this might be. Do the following exercise.

A. Make two lists of qualities or characteristics, one that defines a "good worker" in today's workplace and another that defines a "bad person" according to your beliefs.

B. Share your lists with a partner. Together, come up with a common list for each category. Using your lists, discuss how being a good worker can make you into a bad person.

SKIMMING

Read the article quickly to find the following information:

1. What is the relationship between the two people described in the article?
2. Which one seems to be more successful economically? Emotionally?
3. What, according to the author, is the most obvious change that has taken place in the workplace?
4. What values have been lost in the process?

Compare your answers with a partner

Why Good Workers Make Bad People

By Richard Sennett

Richard Sennett argues that character and contemporary capitalism don't mix

By Richard Sennett

1. I first met Enrico more than a quarter of a century ago when I was writing a book about blue-collar workers in America. By then he had already spent 20 years cleaning toilets and mopping floors in an office building. His work had one single and durable purpose, the service of his family. It had taken him 15 years to save the money for a house, which he purchased in a suburb near Boston, cutting ties with his old Italian neighborhood because a house in the suburbs was better for the kids. Then when I met him, he and his wife, Flavia, who worked as a presser in a dry-cleaning plant, were saving for the college education of their two sons.

2. What had most struck me about Enrico and his generation was how linear time was in their lives: year after year of working in jobs which seldom varied from day to day. And along that line of time, achievement was cumulative. Enrico and Flavia checked the increase in their savings every week, measured their standard of life by the various improvements and additions they had made to their house. The time in which they lived was predictable too. The upheavals of the Great Depression and the Second World War had faded, and unions protected their jobs; though he was only 40 when I first met him, Enrico knew precisely when he would retire and how much money he would have.

3. Time is the only resource freely available to those at the bottom of society. To make time accumulate, Enrico needed what the sociologist Max Weber called an "iron cage," a bureaucratic structure which rationalized the use of time; the seniority rules of his union about pay and the regulations organizing his government pension provided this scaffolding. When he added to these resources his own self-discipline, the result was more than economic.

4. He carved out a clear story for himself in which his experience accumulated materially and psychically; his life thus made sense to him as a linear narrative. Though a snob might dismiss Enrico as boring, he experienced the years as a dramatic story moving forward repair by repair, interest payment by interest payment. The janitor felt he became the author of his life, and though he was a man low on the social scale, this narrative provided him with a sense of self-respect.

5. But he did not want his sons to repeat his own life. The American dream of upward mobility for the children power-

fully drove Enrico. "I don't understand a word he says," he would boast when one of the boys had come home from school and was at work on math. I heard many other parents say something similar in harder tones, as though the kids had abandoned them. The children of men like Enrico, as they headed up the social ladder, sometimes betrayed shame about their parents' working-class accents and rough manners, but more often felt suffocated by the endless preoccupation with pennies and the reckoning of time in tiny steps. These favored children wanted a less constrained journey.

6. A few years ago, in a chance airport encounter, I met one of Enrico's sons, Rico. We sat next to each other on a long flight from New York to Vienna.

7. Rico, I learnt, has fulfilled his father's desire for upward mobility, but has indeed rejected the way of his father. Rico scorns "timeservers" and others wrapped in the armor of bureaucracy; instead he believes in being open to change and in taking risks. And he has prospered; whereas Enrico had an income in the bottom quarter of the wage scale, Rico's has shot up to the top 5 percent.

8. After graduating from a local university with a degree in electrical engineering, Rico went to a business school in New York, where he married a fellow student. He began as a technology adviser to a venture capital firm on the West Coast in the early heady days of the developing computer industry in Silicon Valley; he then moved to Chicago, where he also did well. The next move was for the sake of his wife's career. He got no larger salary, but whereas Enrico felt somewhat ashamed when Flavia went to work, Rico sees Jeannette, his wife, as an equal working partner. It was at this point, when Jeannette's career took off, that their children began arriving.

9. In Missouri, the uncertainties of the new economy caught up with the young man. While Jeannette was promoted, Rico was downsized—his firm was absorbed by another, larger firm that had its own analysts. So the couple made a fourth move, back East to a suburb outside New York. Jeannette now manages a big team of accountants, and he has started a small consulting firm. So this seemed the very acme of an adaptable, mutually supportive, modern, American Dream couple: ready to move, for different reasons, as many as four times in 14 years since graduation, and being rewarded with prosperity. Yet this was not an entirely happy story. As dinner was served on our flight, I learnt that Rico feared that the kind of life he has to live to survive in the modern economy is setting his emotional inner life adrift.

10. Rico told me that he and Jeannette have made friends mostly with the people they see at work, and have lost many of these friendships during their moves over the years, "though we stay 'netted.' " Rico depends on electronic communications for the sense of community which Enrico most enjoyed when he attended meetings of the janitors' union, but the son finds online communications short and hurried.

11. In each of his four moves, Rico's new neighbors have treated his advent as an arrival which closes past chapters of his life; they ask him about Silicon Valley or the Missouri office park but, Rico says,

"they don't see other places"; their imaginations are not engaged. Rico lives in the new kind of suburb that has arisen in the last generation, more economically independent of the urban core than the classic American bedroom suburb, but not really town or village either; a place springs into life, flourishes, and begins to decay all within a generation. Such communities are not empty of sociability or neighborliness, but no one in them becomes a long-term witness to another person's life.

12. This fugitive quality of friendship and local community form the background to the most important of Rico's inner worries, his family. Like Enrico, Rico views work as his service to the family; unlike Enrico, Rico finds that the demands of the job interfere with achieving the end. At first I thought he was talking about the all-too-familiar conflict between work time and time for family. "We get home at seven, do dinner, try to find an hour for the kids' homework, and then deal with our own paperwork." But though this indeed worried him, his real unease was of a different nature.

13. He had felt smothered by the small-minded rules that had governed his father's life. Now, as a father himself, he was haunted by the fear of a lack of ethical discipline, particularly the fear that his children would become "mall rats," hanging out aimlessly in the parking lots of shopping centers.

14. Rico wants to set for his son and daughters an example of resolution and purpose, "but you can't just tell kids to be like that"; he has to set an example. His deepest worry is that he cannot offer the substance of his work life as an example to his children of how they should conduct themselves ethically. The qualities of good work are not the qualities of good character.

15. The gravity of this fear comes from a gap separating Enrico and Rico's generations. Business leaders and journalists emphasize the global marketplace and the use of new technologies as the hallmarks of the capitalism of our age. This is true enough, but misses another dimension of change: new ways of organizing time, particularly working time.

16. The most tangible sign of that change might be the motto "no long term." In work, the traditional career, progressing step by step through the corridors of one or two institutions, is disappearing; so is the deployment of a single set of skills through the course of a working life. Today, a young American with at least two years of college can expect to change jobs at least 11 times in the course of working, and change his or her skill base at least three times. The fastest-growing sector of the American labor force is people who work for temporary job agencies. Even within the walls of a corporation, "jobs" are being replaced by "projects" and "fields of work."

17. This has been accompanied by a change in the typical corporate organization. It has become a network, not a pyramid. Promotions and dismissals are no longer based on clear, fixed rules, nor are work tasks crisply defined; the network is constantly redefining its structure.

18. For these reasons, Enrico's experience of long-term, narrative time in fixed channels has become dysfunctional. But

Rico's story suggests that the material changes embodied in the motto "no long term" have become dysfunctional for him, too.

19. "No long term" is a principle which destroys trust, loyalty and mutual commitment. Trust can be a purely formal matter, as when people agree to a business deal or rely on one another to observe the rules in a game. But deeper experiences of trust are more informal, as when people learn on whom they can rely when given a difficult or impossible task. Such social bonds take time to develop.

20. The short time frame of modern institutions limits the ripening of informal trust. A particularly serious disregard of mutual commitment often occurs when new enterprises are first sold. In firms starting up, long hours and intense effort are demanded of everyone; when the firms go public—that is, offer publicly traded shares—the founders are likely to sell out and cash in, leaving lower-level employees behind.

21. The sociologist Mark Granovetter says that modern institutional networks are marked by "the strength of weak ties," by which he partly means that fleeting forms of association are more useful to people than long-term connections, and partly that strong social ties like loyalty have ceased to be important. These weak ties are embodied in teamwork, in which the team moves from task to task and the personnel of the team constantly changes.

22. Strong ties depend, by contrast, on long association. And more personally, they depend on a willingness to make commitments to others. Given the typically short, weak ties in institutions today, John Kotter, a Harvard Business School professor, counsels the young to "work on the outside rather than on the inside" of organizations. He advocates consulting rather than becoming "entangled" in long-term employment; institutional loyalty is a trap in an economy where "business concepts, product designs, competitor intelligence, capital equipment, and all kinds of knowledge have shorter life-spans." Detachment and superficial cooperativeness are better armor for dealing with current realities than behavior based on values of loyalty and service.

23. It is the time dimension of the new capitalism, rather than hi-tech data transmission, global stock markets or free trade, that most directly affects people's emotional lives outside the workplace. Transposed to the family realm, "no long term" means keep moving, don't commit yourself and don't sacrifice. Rico suddenly erupted on the plane: "You can't imagine how stupid I feel when I talk to my kids about commitment. It's an abstract virtue to them; they don't see it anywhere." In place of the chameleon values of the new economy, the family—as Rico sees it—should emphasize instead formal obligation, trustworthiness, commitment and purpose. These are all long-term virtues.

24. This conflict between family and work poses some questions about adult experience itself. How can long-term purposes be pursued in a short-term society? How can durable social relations be sustained? How can a human being develop a narrative of identity and life history in a society composed of episodes and fragments? The new economy feeds on experience which drifts in time, from place to place, from job to job. If I could state Rico's dilemma more largely, short-term capitalism threatens to corrode his character, particularly those qualities of character that bind human beings to one another and furnish each with a sense of sustainable self. Rico is trying to affirm timeless values that characterize who he is—for good, permanently, essentially.

25. What is missing is a narrative that could organize his conduct. Narratives are more than simple chronicles of events; they give shape to the forward movement of time, suggesting reasons why things happen, showing their consequences. Enrico had a narrative for his life, linear and cumulative, a narrative that made sense in a highly bureaucratic world. Rico lives in a world marked instead by short-term flexibility and flux; this world does not offer much, either economically or socially, in the way of narrative. Corporations break up or join together, jobs appear and disappear, as events lacking connections. Creative destruction, Schumpeter said, thinking about entrepreneurs, requires people at ease about not reckoning the consequences of change, or not knowing what comes next. Most people, though, are not at ease with change in this careless way.

26. I think Rico knows he is both a successful and a confused man. The flexible behavior which has brought him success is weakening his own character in ways for which there exists no practical remedy.

—New Statesman

SURVEYING/CHUNKING

Can this article be surveyed in the same way as other articles in this book?

To answer this question, use the information you got from skimming to analyze the organization of the reading by commenting on the following.

- Is there an introduction? If yes, where?
- Is there a clear thesis? If yes, where?
- Is the author's point of view stated clearly? If yes, where?

What conclusions can you draw about the organization of this article as opposed to most of the articles you have read so far? Compare your answers with a partner.

This article is indeed different. The author does not state his point of view from the beginning. He builds up the case gradually by going from point to point until finally he leads the readers to what he wants to say. Therefore the surveying should be done as follows:

■ **READING TIP:** *The last sentence is important in this type of writing because the writer will often conclude a paragraph by introducing the next to help the reader follow his train of thought.*

- **Read the first and last sentence of every paragraph.**
- **Note the main idea of each paragraph in the margin.**
- **Read the last four paragraphs.**
- **Identify the author's point of view.**
- **Identify the major ideas in the article as well as the corresponding paragraphs and list them in the following chart.**

Some have been done as examples.

Major Ideas	Paragraphs
Enrico	1–5
	6–9
	10–11
	12–14
"no long term"	15–18
	19–22

Compare your answers with a partner.

SCANNING FOR DETAILS

Read through the entire selection more carefully to find the answers for these questions. Note the question number in the margin for future reference. Write the answers in note form and in your own words as much as possible.

1. What was Enrico's main purpose for working?

   _____

   Did he accomplish his purpose? Explain.

   _____

   _____

   _____

   What characteristics of Enrico's generation helped him do this?

   _____

   _____

   _____

2. What are Rico's beliefs as compared with his father's beliefs?

   _____

   _____

   Give examples from the lives of both to show how their different beliefs have been reflected in their lives.

   _____

   _____

   _____

3. In what way has the kind of life Rico leads affected his friendships?

   _____

   _____

4. What are the characteristics of the communities in which Rico lives?

_____

_____

5. What is Rico's greatest worry?

_____

In what way is his work responsible for this?

_____

_____

6. Identify three changes that have taken place as a result of the motto "no long term."

_____

_____

_____

What values have been affected as a result?

_____

_____

7. What advice does John Kotter give to young workers?

_____

_____

8. What does the idea "no long term" mean when translated into the family?

_____

_____

9. What contradiction is suggested in the very last sentence?

_____

Check your answers with a partner.

Talk about the article using the ideas you have identified. Take turns explaining each idea. Refer to your answers for details when necessary.

SUMMARIZING THE ARGUMENT

Show how the author leads us to his point of view by outlining the steps he goes through starting from Enrico's story. Give an example whenever possible

- *Enrico's story: success at work comes from commitment to one job.*

  Example: *20 years same job, same place*

- _____

  _____

- _____

  _____

- _____

  _____

- _____

  _____

Discuss your steps with a partner.

■ After Reading

REACTING TO THE INFORMATION: ORGANIZATION

Do you find this way of presenting information easy or hard to read? Why or why not?

Do you find it more or less interesting than the more common way of presenting information? Why or why not?

Would it have been more effective for the writer to state his point of view first and then support it? Why or why not?

REACTING TO THE INFORMATION: CONTENT

A. *Quotes*. **The following quotes are taken from "Why Good Workers Make Bad People." Work with a partner. Locate and read the quotes in the context in which they appear. Discuss what is implied in each and whether or not you agree with this implication.**

1. "I don't understand a word he says" (paragraph 5)
2. "though we stay 'netted'" (paragraph 10)
3. "they don't see other places" (paragraph 11)
4. "but you can't just tell kids to be like that" (paragraph 14)
5. "work on the outside rather than on the inside" (paragraph 22)
6. "You can't imagine how stupid I feel when I talk to my kids about commitment. It's an abstract virtue to them; they don't see it anywhere." (paragraph 23)

B. *Discussion*. **Think about the following and share your ideas with a partner.**

1. Overall, what has changed in the importance of the role that work plays in our lives?
2. What effects will this change have on people's lives in the future?

APPLYING THE INFORMATION

Discuss the following questions.

1. What are the consequences, in terms of behavior and attitude toward employers, when employees feel they can move from job to job?
2. How do employers react to this?

Read the following article quickly and highlight the examples that would help answer these questions.

NEW YORK TIMES

To Shirkers, the Days of Whine and Roses

By Eve Tahmincioglu

For more than three months, Kevin Meeker, owner of Philadelphia Fish and Company, a restaurant and bar, put up with a cook whose obsession with the stock market often took his mind away from the soup. The 22-year-old employee checked his Motorola shares every half-hour on his pager and periodically slipped out to the dining room to get the bartender to turn on CNBC.

Not so long ago, Mr. Meeker says, he would have warned the cook to knock it off and fired him if he did not comply. But not in this job market. Instead, he turned a blind eye to the goofing off, and says he would probably still have the man on the payroll if he had not quit on Mother's Day after being asked to work beyond his eight-hour shift.

"I think the attitude among workers right now is, 'I could always go and get another job,'" Mr. Meeker said. "Now, that cook's working for another restaurant around the corner."

Checking on stock prices is the least of it. Increasingly, employees are testing the boundaries of the American work ethic as employers, hammered by recruiting and training expenses and fearful that they will be unable to fill job openings, make allowances for just about every form of misconduct. Offenses like frequent tardiness or absenteeism, apathy and even insubordination that would have merited a pink slip a

few years ago are now being shrugged off as inconveniences.

The new management rule of thumb, it seems, is that a warm body is better than no body.

Take Suzan Windnagel, director of human resources for a credit union in San Jose, Calif. A woman who worked for her was frequently late, gave customers incorrect information and just did not feel like learning new computer skills.

If not for the tight labor market, Ms. Windnagel says, she would have dismissed the slacker within four months. Instead, she spent a year and a half counseling her, lecturing her and desperately trying to train her. Nothing worked, and, finally, she had to let her go.

But she says she is neither surprised nor particularly upset about the sloppy work habits she sees around her these days. "Workers, not bosses, have the upper hand," said Ms. Windnagel, who has been a human resources manager for 22 years. "Managers today know how hard it is to recruit people, so they put up with more. I don't blame workers at all."

Most people still put in an honest day's work, of course. It is just that the lazy, the rude and the nonproductive have an easier time of it.

Doug Peterson, vice president for human resources at the Shape Corporation, an automotive supplier in Grand Haven, Mich., for example, says most of the company's 1,000 workers are productive and disciplined. Yet Mr. Peterson acknowledges that he harbors under-performers.

"Have we held on to people where in years past, we would have fired them?" he said. "The answer is yes."

The reason for the leniency is that at any given time, the company has an average of 40 unfilled jobs.

Because skilled trades are such tough positions to fill, Mr. Peterson said, he tolerated for nearly a year a hot-tempered staff electrician who often threatened co-workers. The company tried to counsel him and even signed him up for anger-management training, but finally dismissed him. "Five or six years ago, we would have not put up with that," Mr. Peterson said. "The person would have been gone immediately."

To combat worsening tardiness and absenteeism, he said, Shape has chosen the carrot over the stick. Last year, it decided to give workers 17 hours of personal time off a year on top of their vacation days—and to pay them $10 for each of those hours they do not use. "We're giving incentives for people to be at work," he said.

Adaptec Inc., a maker of software and computer components in Milpitas, Calif., illustrates the starkness of the change taking place in the workplace. Six years ago, almost one-third of the people who left the company had been fired, according to Rick Olivieri, the director of compensation and benefits. Today, that proportion is down to 2 percent. "It's a real war for people out there right now," Mr. Olivieri said.

But leniency carries risks, warns DeAnne Rosenberg, author of *Hiring the Best Person for Every Job* (John Wiley & Sons, 2000). Most notably, accommodating shirkers can hurt office morale, she says.

Ms. Rosenberg cites the case of a home-health care administrator in Boston who yelled constantly at her co-workers, fobbed off work on colleagues and treated clients disrespectfully. Over eight months, 10 co-workers complained to her supervisor, but he refused to reprimand her, much less fire her. "He kept saying: 'It's a hard labor market. At least the little she does, she does,'" Ms. Rosenberg said.

Ultimately, the co-workers took matters into their own hands. They came in on a weekend, packed up the administrator's belongings and moved her desk and chair to another floor, she said. When the administrator came to work on Monday, they pretended she was not there and talked about her as if she had gone to another company.

She quit that day.

Obnoxious behavior is one thing. Illegal behavior is another.

Mark Spring, a labor and employment lawyer in Sacramento, Calif., says that executives at one of his client companies, a national book and music chain, merely gave a written warning to a manager who had ordered two subordinates to move a marijuana plant from his office to his home during work hours, he said.

In another case, a bank slapped the wrist of an employee who had been caught downloading pornography from the Internet, revoking his Internet privileges for 30 days and sending him to a sensitivity-training course.

Both the book and music chain and the bank exposed themselves to potential litigation by their inaction, Mr. Spring said.

Referring to the bank employee, he said, "If this had happened in the early 90's, he would have been fired because of the recession and because at the time everyone was nervous over sexual harassment."

Barring blatant wrongdoing, though, many companies are pursuing the path of least resistance.

"If a slacker comes in to work at 10 a.m. instead of 8 a.m., maybe the company needs to rethink that worker's schedule," said Erisn Ojimba, compensation expert for Salary.com, a salary-resource Web site based in Wellesley, Mass. "Maybe they're not their most productive before 10 a.m."

Work with a partner. Use what you highlighted to talk about the article. For each example that you highlighted, discuss

- what the worker did;
- what the response from the company was;
- how you think the other employees felt.

Do you agree that companies should take the path of least resistance? Why or why not?

Does this article support the idea that good workers make bad people?

Explain your opinion.

Vocabulary Building

LOADED WORDS

In presenting or arguing a point of view, writers often choose words that carry negative or positive meanings depending on how they want the reader to react. Examine these sentences or clauses taken from "Why Good Workers Make Bad People" and write *N* if the words in bold carry a negative meaning, and *P* if they carry a positive meaning.

1. _____ Though a snob might **dismiss** Enrico as boring . . .

2. _____ . . . he experienced the years as a **dramatic** story . . .

3. _____ The children . . . often felt **suffocated** by the endless preoccupation with pennies . . .

4. _____ His work had one single and **durable** purpose. . .

Check your answers with a partner. Using the preceding as examples, find at least two more negative and two more positive words. Present your examples to another student or to the class.

VOCABULARY IN CONTEXT

Locate the following sentences in the reading "Why Good Workers Make Bad People" and use the context to explain the meaning of the words in bold.

1. And along that line of time, achievement was **cumulative**. (paragraph 2)

   _____

2. So this seemed the very **acme** of an adaptable, mutually supportive, modern, American Dream couple . . . (paragraph 9)

   _____

3. In each of his four moves, Rico's new neighbors have treated his **advent** as an arrival which closes past chapters of his life . . . (paragraph 11)

   _____

4. This **fugitive** quality of friendship and local community form the background to the most important of Rico's inner worries, his family. (paragraph 12)

   _____

5. Business leaders and journalists emphasize the global marketplace and the use of new technologies as the **hallmarks** of the capitalism of our age. (paragraph 15)

   _____

6. The most **tangible** sign of that change might be the motto "no long term." (paragraph 16)

   _____

7. . . . by which he partly means that **fleeting** forms of association are more useful to people than long-term connections . . . (paragraph 21)

   _____

8. He **advocates** consulting rather than becoming "entangled" in long-term employment . . . (paragraph 22)

   _____

9. How can durable social relations be **sustained**? (paragraph 24)

   _____

10. Narratives are more than simple **chronicles** of events . . . (paragraph 25)

   _____

Check your explanations with a partner. If you are still not sure, consult a dictionary or ask your teacher.

FIGURING OUT THE REFERENT

A. Use your understanding of key words to identify the referent for each of the words in boldface.

■ **NOTE:** *In English, writers often use pronouns and/or synonyms to refer to ideas that have just been or will be mentioned. These ideas are known as referents.*

1. When he added to **these** resources his own self-discipline, **the result** was more than economic. (paragraph 3)

   these: _____

   the result: _____

2. **These** favored children wanted a less constrained journey. (paragraph 5)

   these: _____

3. So **this** seemed the very acme of an adaptable, mutually supportive, modern, American Dream couple. (paragraph 9)

   this: _____

4. Rico lives in **the new kind of suburb** that has arisen in the last generation . . . (paragraph 11)

   the new kind of suburb: _____

   _____

5. But though **this** indeed worried him, **his real unease** was of a different nature. (paragraph 12)

   this: _____

   his real unease: _____

6. For **these** reasons . . . (paragraph 18)

   these: _____

B. Scan the reading and find two other sentences with words that have referents. Write the sentences and underline the words as well as the referents. Compare your answers with a partner.

◼ Expanding Your Language

SPEAKING

Role Play: **Work with a partner. Set up a role play as follows.**

- Read the following scenario:

   A husband and wife both have stable jobs as well as family within 300 miles. They also have two children aged seven and ten. One of them has been offered a job that would entail traveling abroad and staying in different countries for periods of two to three years at a time.

- Choose to be either the person who has been offered the job or a friend to whom this person has gone to for advice.

- Decide on whether the job has been offered to the male or female member of the couple.

- As the friend, make a list of reasons that support accepting the job.

- As the person offered the job, make a list of reasons that support refusing the job.

- To make it as realistic as possible, carry out the role play *without* looking at the other person's arguments. Be ready to change or adapt what you have prepared.

Present your role play to other groups in the class or to the class as a whole.

WRITING

Reaction Writing: **Write on whether you prefer the predictable—maybe boring—life led by Enrico or the uncertain life led by his son Rico. Also include your own feelings about the future. Are you comfortable with what seems to be happening or has the information in the chapter readings made you apprehensive?**

CHAPTER **12**

Can Companies Keep their Employees?

Chapter Openers

GETTING INFORMATION FROM TABLES, CHARTS, AND GRAPHS

Quickly look through the following table, charts, and graph. Answer the questions.

Employee Attitudes toward Work

Attitude	%Response
It's O.K to take a day off if feeling overworked	28
Poor attendance should not be grounds for getting fired	25
It's O.K to call in sick and get the day off	10

–Robert Scally, *Discount News*

Research on employee retention from the American Management Association (AMA) Human Resources Conference, which included data from 352 companies, showed that corporate concern about employee retention is growing.

- 46% felt retention very significant issue
- 27.6% felt retention significant issue
- 91.2% expected more concern one year later
- 66.2 felt scarce supply of workers by 2001
- 2/3 have 10% turnover

–HR Focus

---

1. How do workers seem to be feeling about their jobs these days?
2. What is the major problem companies are having?

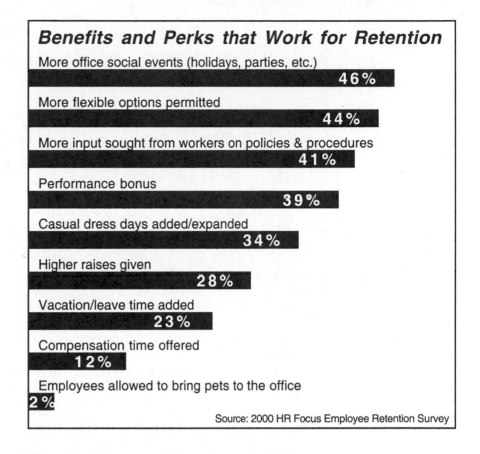

Benefits and Perks that Work for Retention

More office social events (holidays, parties, etc.)
46%

More flexible options permitted
44%

More input sought from workers on policies & procedures
41%

Performance bonus
39%

Casual dress days added/expanded
34%

Higher raises given
28%

Vacation/leave time added
23%

Compensation time offered
12%

Employees allowed to bring pets to the office
2%

Source: 2000 HR Focus Employee Retention Survey

3. What are their predictions for the future?
4. What are they doing about this problem?

PERSONALIZING

Read the following and check (✔) the ones that would be important to you in terms of where you work. In the column at the right, rank the ones you chose in order of importance with "1" being the most important.

_____ Free daycare _____

_____ Sports facilities _____

_____ Medical benefits _____

_____ Tuition-reimbursement programs _____

_____ Shopping center   _____

_____ One hour every week to attend to personal matters   _____

_____ A cafeteria   _____

_____ A party once a month   _____

_____ Performance bonus   _____

Discuss your list with a partner or in a small group.

If you had to choose between having all the extra privileges you consider important or a 10 percent increase in salary, which would you choose? Why?

Exploring and Understanding Reading

PREDICTING

The following quotations have been taken from some of the readings in this chapter. Use them to predict three or four principles employers need to consider in order to retain their employees.

- "The only difference between people who are dead and people who are alive is that dead people do the same thing every day."
- "A business is not a building, it's the people. And people have lives."
- "What we have here is a plan for a complex where technological workers can thrive, grow and enjoy themselves."
- "It was a more relaxed environment and I wasn't feeling guilty about not spending enough time with my children."
- "These teams develop team spirit and allow people to identify with the company."

PREVIEWING

Read the title and the subtitle of the article that follows. Which ideas do you expect to get more information on?

_____ A definition of loyalty

_____ Examples of loyal employees

_____ Examples of disloyal employees

_____ Company characteristics that ensure loyalty

ORLANDO SENTINEL

Loyalty has to be earned

In today's tight job market, if employees aren't satisfied, they leave

By Diane Sears Campbell

ORLANDO, Fla.—How does Mike Freiner define loyalty in the workplace?

He can tell you what it's not. It's not the feeling you get after you've put your heart and soul into a place for seven years—getting pumped for new ideas for weeks—only to be laid off one day at 8 a.m. and out the door by 1:30 p.m.

No, says Freiner, the service manager and education director at Amber Electric in Ocoee, Fla. Loyalty is what comes when your boss involves you in decisions, lets you make a mistake without being publicly humiliated, and gets to know the names of your spouse and your children. It comes after you have a heart attack and your boss holds your job open for you, the CEO calls to see how you're doing and your co-workers throw a little party to welcome you back to the office.

"A business is not a building, it's the people," Freiner said. "And people have lives."

As today's workers define it, loyalty is something you give your employer only if it's earned. And the main person who can earn it is the person who affects your situation directly: your boss.

Unlike generations of the past, employees of the '90s don't sign on to a job for life and commit their loyalty unconditionally. If they don't feel satisfied in their workplace, they leave. And as long as unemployment remains low, the situation is not going to change.

"Loyalty is just not an honored trait the way it used to be," said Maitland, Fla., psychologist Mimi Hull, president of Hull & Associates Human Relations Management and Development. "We value speed, we value change. . . . Loyalty is kind of an anachronism."

Loyalty is a hot topic among employers today. They're all abuzz with strategies for keeping good workers, because it's so hard to replace them.

Besides pay raises, medical benefits, 401(k) plans and even child-care and tuition-reimbursement programs, employers are offering more offbeat perks. Those might include personal valet service to handle a worker's dry-cleaning errands, or on-site manicures and massages paid for by the company, or new policies allowing pets in the office.

But is that what keeps an employee loyal?

No way, employees say.

"It's all those little things called caring," said Freiner, who has worked at Amber Electric for six years and is one of about 250 employees.

"You're not a number here," he said. "When you say this is a caring company, that's true from the floor-sweeper right up the line. I think that's very rare. That's why I'm here."

In interviews with more than 20,000 U.S. workers who were leaving their companies, the Saratoga Institute in Santa Clara, Calif., found that poor supervisory behavior was the top reason for their departure.

Tell that to Orlando resident Don Hepenstal. There was a lot he liked about working for Walgreen Drugs, a company that offered him competitive pay, benefits and opportunity for growth. But he just wasn't happy.

He left the company briefly a year ago to take another job. He returned to Walgreen's, this time at a different store with a different set of managers. Something clicked.

Now, Hepenstal is fiercely loyal to both his supervisors and his company.

"My store manager has a lot to do with that," Hepenstal said. "Every time I look at him, he's smiling. . . . If I had a crummy store manager, that might change the situation."

Workers are loyal to an employer who recognizes the importance of personal and family life, according to the America At Work 1999 study conducted by Aon

Consulting in Chicago. The study found that employees have a higher level of commitment if they're allowed to spend a small amount of their work time each week attending to personal matters, whether it's making alternative arrangements for daycare or scheduling a dental appointment.

It's true, said Linda Goins, a closing agent with Kampf Title in Sanford. When your employer cares about you, it makes you want to reciprocate.

Goins went through a series of family crises during the past couple of years, including her own battle with cervical cancer; and her boss stood by her through it all. The family-owned company of 22 employees paid her for the eight weeks she was out for surgery and recovery. Her job was waiting for her when she came back, and the company didn't dock her pay for the hours she missed for daily radiation treatment.

She has been with Kampf for 14 years, and she has no plans to leave. She pitches in cheerfully when a flurry of activity requires her to work overtime.

"They take care of their people," Goins said. "They more than deserve the loyalty I feel because of what they've done for me. And they're good people."

She credits her boss with creating an atmosphere that keeps people loyal. He lets employees handle things their own way without questioning their judgment. If a customer or client calls with a concern, he doesn't assume the worst of his workers. He asks questions first.

It makes a big difference when employees have a say in how things are run, said Kim Ashby, an attorney with the Akerman, Senterfitt & Eidson law firm in Orlando.

When she came to the firm a year ago, Ashby didn't expect to be treated the same as attorneys who had worked there 30 or 40 years. She was just grateful to land a good position as a litigator specializing in construction and commercial-products liability. Her former employer, another law firm, had merged with another firm after she had been there 17 years.

She was surprised to find that at Akerman, Senterfitt & Eidson, her opinion was valued and even solicited.

The firm's open, friendly atmosphere makes her feel like she's working in a small environment, and her fellow attorneys make up a tight-knit group. They help each other on projects and in personal crises.

Ashby tells a story about a co-worker who was sick with leukemia. The other attorneys in her office spent part of a day taking Polaroid pictures of each other doing goofy things at work and holding up signs that read "Get well," and they sent the photos along with a package to the co-worker's room at a cancer hospital in Houston.

It's those kinds of things that make people stay.

"If it's just a job, there are other jobs," she said.

SURVEYING

Survey the article by reading the introduction and the first sentence of every paragraph after that. Identify

- the thesis;
- the type of information the author will use to support this thesis;
- the main ideas.

Discuss your survey with a partner or with a small group. Which of the ideas listed under "Previewing" will be covered?

INFERRING INFORMATION

Writers do not always express all their ideas clearly. Sometimes they let the reader come to his or her own understanding. Use the introduction to

- define loyalty in your own words;
- explain the changes that have happened to the concept of loyalty.

Compare your work with a partner or in a small group.

SCANNING

A. The next to last paragraph in the article states: "It's those kinds of things that make people stay," in response to a question that was asked in an earlier paragraph. Locate the question and scan the paragraphs in between to determine what "those things" are. Underline the relevant information.

B. Compare what you underlined with a partner. Discuss whether you underlined too much or too little. You may remove or add to your underlining if necessary.

C. Together, determine what basic principle is being used to ensure company loyalty. Use the information you underlined to support this.

PAIRED READINGS: TWO KINDS OF INCENTIVES

Two approaches to keeping employees are discussed in the following readings. Choose one of the readings. Work with someone who has chosen the *same* reading.

Reading 1: A Workplace You Could Live In

PREVIEWING

Read the title and the subtitle of the article. Predict what these companies are doing to hold onto their employees. Compare your predictions with your partner.

SKIMMING

Quickly skim the article and answer the following questions.

1. What extra services are companies offering their employees?

2. Which two countries are being compared? Which one offers better services?

_____

_____

3. How does the number of people leaving such companies compare with the national average?

_____

Compare your answers with your partner.

THE MONTREAL GAZETTE

The Office as Utopia

Free candy? Golf? Anything to keep the staff happy . . .

By Joanne Chianello

OTTAWA—When several women at SAS Institute were facing the tough issues about how to balance their careers and young families, they approached their boss with their problem.

James Goodnight, founder of the world's largest privately owned software company, decided to set up a child-care center at the company. The first class had only six children in it.

That was in 1981.

Now, SAS has two on-site day-care centers and one across the street from its headquarters near the technology center of Raleigh, N.C. The company-sponsored day-care costs parents $200 U.S. a month and can accommodate about 600 children.

Child-care centers, athletic facilities, comfortable indoor and outdoor meeting areas, cafés and even retail outlets are becoming not only more common in the corporate world, but are being demanded by employees so stressed out about their jobs that they can barely get the rest of their lives in order.

Nowhere is this more apparent than in the expanding high-technology sector, where there is a shortage of highly skilled and educated people.

High-tech corporations are looking at ways to keep the talented employees they have happy, and for ways to attract new recruits.

And technology campuses—as the facilities are known in the industry—have their own special problems, because they are typically located outside of city centers, often in areas where there are no nearby shopping malls, restaurants or facilities of any kind.

It's a problem Newbridge Networks Corp. of Kanata, Ont. has decided to deal with head on.

Newbridge chief executive Terry Matthews plans to build an impressive array of new facilities, including a hotel, athletic club, conference center, 18-hole golf course, tennis and racquetball courts, retail center and day care.

While many high-tech firms provide small gyms or beer parties for employees, our own [Canadian] companies generally lag behind their U.S. counterparts in the trend toward providing more for employees.

Clearly, SAS is a leader in this field and its 1981 day care was well ahead of its time.

But many other U.S. high-tech firms have picked up on the theme.

Novell Corp. provides a three-hole golf course. Cisco Systems offers one hour of calisthenics every morning, and the 12 cafeterias at Bill Gates's Microsoft Corp. serve as many as 10 different dishes a day, from Cooper River salmon from British Columbia to Thai stir-fry.

Matthews of Newbridge wants to emulate some of his U.S. colleagues.

"What we have here is a plan for a complex where technological workers can thrive, grow and enjoy themselves," he said at the project's unveiling.

What we actually have is the new reality of North America's corporate culture.

Nortel, which has redesigned many of its facilities in the past few years to better address the morale and needs of employees, has definitely heard the call.

Its one-million-square-foot world headquarters in Brampton, northwest of Toronto, won a design award from *BusinessWeek* magazine last year as "The City" because the interior is set up with streets and plazas, the Brampton facility houses a full bank branch, automated-teller machines capable of dispensing U.S. dollars, dry-cleaning services, convenience stores, athletic facilities and cafés.

"It's a reflection of the understanding of how human dynamics, ergonomics and physical well-being contribute to over-all morale," said Nortel spokesman Jacques Guerette.

But Guerette said employees don't stay at Nortel simply because it has a great gym or because they can easily do their banking. These things are part of a bigger package that, the company hopes, improves the job satisfaction of employees.

The SAS facilities and services offered—from a medical clinic with two full-time doctors to an expanded athletic center—are definitely time- and money-savers for employees. Workers can even take home any leftovers from the two campus cafés every day.

But even the company's less magnanimous practice of giving its 2,500 employees fresh fruit on Mondays, M&Ms on Wednesdays and bakery treats on Fridays tells workers that they are valued, that the company is always thinking of them.

"We have a very forward-thinking CEO," Fried said of Goodnight, who has headed the company for more than 20 years.

"He believes in treating people the way he'd like to be treated. We look at the demographics of our population and try to figure out what makes their lives easier."

The result: only 4 percent of employees leave the company every year, compared to the 15 percent national average in the U.S. And some high-tech companies report turnover rates of more than 30 percent.

At Microsoft's 300-acre campus in Redmond, Wash., employees who need to clear their minds can go for a run or walk their dogs along the miles of trails set through a beautifully landscaped campus that includes a waterfall.

A project team that might need a break will go outside to play pick-up basketball.

The best part about it is that no one asks these workers where they are going or when they'll be back.

"There's an enormous amount of autonomy here," said Microsoft spokesman Mark Murray. "The organization is built around setting goals."

How employees reach that goal is up to them.

"There's very attractive landscaping here and we're well-known for our cafeterias," said Murray.

But it's the fact that employees are free to use these facilities whenever they want that makes employees feel appreciated, contributing to the reasons why only 7 percent of employees leave the company each year.

"That's why people love to work here."

SCANNING FOR SPECIFIC INFORMATION

Reexamine the reading to find the answers to these questions. Note the number of the question in the margin for future reference. Write the answer in note form and in your own words as much as possible.

1. When was the first child-care center set up at SAS Institute?

   _____

   Why was it set up?

   _____

2. Which business sector is SAS an example of?

   _____

   What special problems does this sector have?

   _____

3. How big is the Nortel headquarters?

_____

Why is it known as "The City"?

_____

4. What two functions do the facilities offered at SAS serve?

_____

5. Is there a limit to how much time employees can spend on recreational activities?

_____

What is the reasoning behind that?

_____

Compare your answers with your partner. Try to agree on the answers. Refer to the article if you disagree.

RECAPPING THE INFORMATION: HIGHLIGHTING/NOTE-TAKING

A. Identify the main ideas of the article. Highlight the information corresponding to each main idea.

■ *READING TIP: In newspaper articles the writer often goes back and forth between ideas, i.e., information on one main idea can often be found in more than one place.*

B. Use what you highlighted to make notes on each main idea. Use your own words and include as many examples as possible.

C. Working with your partner, compare the notes you made. Discuss whether they are too detailed or too brief. Add to or remove from your notes if necessary.

D. Using only your notes, take turns telling each other the important information in the article. Make sure you explain the information as clearly and completely as you can.

REACTING TO THE INFORMATION

Discuss these questions with another person who read the *same* article. Explain your ideas as completely as possible.

1. According to the article, it is the high-technology sector that suffers the most from a shortage of qualified employees. Why do you think this is so?

2. Which of the services offered would attract you the most? Why?

3. Why would being able to use the facilities whenever they want make the employees feel appreciated? What is the potential for abuse with such a system?

4. What benefits would a project team get from playing basketball?

I love our new flexible policy!

■ ■
_____

Reading 2: A Schedule You Could Live With

PREVIEWING

Read the title and the subtitle of the article. Predict what these companies are doing to hold on to their employees. Compare your prediction with your partner.

SKIMMING

Quickly skim the article and answer the following questions.

1. Does accepting a flexible schedule hold a person back from being promoted?
2. Who takes more advantage of flexible schedules, men or women?
3. What benefits do companies get by offering flexible schedules?

Compare your answers with your partner.

THE MONTREAL GAZETTE

How Less Can Mean More

Professionals who work fewer hours can still succeed, study indicates

By Rex Huppke

Charlotte Hawthorne advanced her high-powered career with Eli Lilly and Co. by working fewer hours and spending more time with her family.

Sound like a pipe dream? Researchers at McGill University and Indiana's Purdue University say that in many large North American corporations, that dream has become reality. In fact, some corporations predict that customized work arrangements—which help employees balance careers and family life—will be the key to managing the modern work force and keeping the best workers.

"I was able to keep my career on track," said Hawthorne, who reduced her schedule with the drug company in 1993 when she had her first child.

"It was a more relaxed environment and I wasn't feeling guilty about not spending enough time with my children."

Hawthorne had a second child, continued her work as an industrial engineer and won a promotion to a managerial position before returning to full-time work in 1998.

Her success is not uncommon.

The universities performed a two-year study of 87 corporate professionals and managers who by choice work less than full time and have their wages reduced proportionately.

The results showed that the scaled-back work weeks slowed employees' careers down, but didn't stop them. About 35 percent had actually been promoted since they started working less.

The adjusted schedules made about 90 percent of the respondents happier with the way they balanced work and home life, and only 10 percent of the people interviewed planned to return to full-time work within the next three years. Some of the respondents were women starting families, while others were men seeking more time with their kids or greater community involvement, said Shelley MacDermid, director of the Purdue Center for Families.

"We had a substantial number of cases where both the boss and the worker thought that performance had improved," said MacDermid, who is also an associate professor of child development and family studies.

Sometimes even over-all performance was better among the respondents who were, on average, 39 years old.

"They were actually getting as much or more done working fewer hours."

Customized work arrangements are changing because the work force is changing, said Mary Dean Lee, McGill's associate professor of organizational behavior and human resource management.

"My view is that the way jobs got set up, the way careers got structured decades ago, was based on the old sort of society where men were the ones who had the professional and managerial jobs and they had wives who took care of the family work," said Lee, who was director of the joint project. "Even though the traditional family structure has more or less disappeared, there really hasn't been any reexamination of how we think about professional work and careers."

Not every company offers flexibility for part-time workers. And employees on non-traditional schedules still bump up against systems where success is judged by the number of hours workers are in the office, said a 1997 study by the New York-based Catalyst research group.

Still, there are indications that companies are beginning to change.

Candi Lange, director of work force partnering initiatives for the Indianapolis-based Eli Lilly, said 200 of her company's 14,000 U.S. employees have schedules adjusted to fit their needs.

"For the manager to say, 'Do this and everything else has to take second place,' is no longer realistic given the needs of the current work force," Lange said. "I think to be able to meet these real needs of the workplace, companies will have to become flexible."

Hawthorne believes Eli Lilly's flexibility helped her improve time management skills. "I think I was probably most efficient when I was working three days a week," she said.

Susan Thomas, director of employment policies and programs for the Philadelphia-based Cigna Corp., said flexibility is key for competitive companies to retain quality workers.

"I think it's absolutely terrific because it enables us to retain people who we otherwise might lose," she said.

MacDermid said the study did have some negative results. Some people found it hard to set boundaries between home life and work, and started using their extra free time to keep working.

But both researchers agree that the positive results of their study foreshadow the future of successful labor management.

"Any sort of work arrangement that makes it possible for people to afford to put bread on the table and to spend time with their family members, I would think is a good thing," MacDermid said.

SCANNING FOR SPECIFIC INFORMATION

Reexamine the reading to find the answers to these questions. Note the number of the question in the margin for future reference. Write the answer in note form and in your own words as much as possible.

1. What dream is becoming a reality in today's workforce?

    _____

    Give an example.

    _____

2. What did the study show about

    promotions? _____

    employee satisfaction? _____

    _____

3. What are the reasons both men and women seek flexible schedules?

_____

_____

4. In what way has the workplace not caught up with changes in the family structure?

_____

_____

5. What problem do some people experience with flexible schedules?

_____

_____

Compare your answers with your partner. Try to agree on the answers. Refer to the article if you disagree.

RECAPPING THE INFORMATION: HIGHLIGHTING/NOTE-TAKING

A. Identify the main ideas of the article. Highlight the information corresponding to each main idea.

■ *READING TIP: In newspaper articles the writer often goes back and forth between ideas; i.e., information on one main idea can often be found in more than one place.*

B. Use what you highlighted to make notes on each main idea. Use your own words and as many examples as possible.

C. Working with your partner, compare the notes you made. Discuss whether they are too detailed or too brief. Add to or remove from your notes if necessary.

D. Using only your notes, take turns telling each other the important information in the article. Make sure you explain the information as clearly and completely as you can.

REACTING TO THE INFORMATION

Discuss these questions with another person who read the *same* article. Explain your ideas as completely as possible.

1. How can you explain the fact that some people produced more when they worked less time?

2. How should somebody who is working fewer hours be paid if he or she is accomplishing the same amount of work as somebody who is working normal hours?

3. What are some other reasons why it would be hard to implement a flexible schedule?

4. Should everyone be offered the choice of working fewer hours or only those who need this option?

After Reading

RETELLING THE INFORMATION

Work with a partner who read a *different* article.

- Use your notes and take turns reporting on the information you read. Explain the ideas clearly in your own words.
- Encourage your partner to ask questions or write some of the important facts you explain.
- After you have both explained your information, discuss the questions in "Reacting to the Information" on pages 266 and 270.

ANALYZING THE INFORMATION

A. Work with a partner who read a *different* article. Quickly review your notes and answers for all three readings. Identify the specific employee needs that the employers are trying to meet. List these needs.

Example: *exercise*
_____

consideration when sick
_____

_____

_____

_____

_____

Think about the following questions and discuss them with your partner.

- What do all these needs have in common?
- What other needs do employees have?

B. The following is a letter concerning a dissatisfied reporter. Predict why a reporter would be unhappy with his job. Read the letter quickly to determine whether your prediction is correct.

Open Letter to an Editor

By Joe Grimm

I had an intriguing conversation with a reporter recently—one who works for you. In fact, he's one of your best reporters. It's the type of conversation you probably wish he hadn't had. He wants to leave.

I wish I could say that I initiated our conversation, but I didn't. He got in touch with me.

Oh, did I tell you? I recruit for another newspaper.

Your reporter gave me a copy of his resume and photocopies of six stories that he wrote for you. The headlines showed you played them proudly. With a simmering passion, he talked about how he finds issues, approaches them, and writes about them. His fire, his clips, and his beat tell me he is one of your best. He fills your front page with important, compelling stories. And the guy can write. I'm sure you would hate to lose him.

He doesn't want you to know we talked, of course, so I can't say who he is. I'm writing this letter because he speaks for many people—even some at my own paper, I'm afraid—and we, as editors, really need to do better by him and others like him.

It's funny, really. Your reporter is not unhappy, dead-ended, burned-out, tapped-out, or on the outs. In fact, he told me he really likes his job. He has a great assignment, and said you run a great paper. It would be easy for you to keep him, he said. He knows that the paper values him. He appreciates the responsibility you've given him, takes ownership of his career, and savors his freedom. He knows how unusual it is to enjoy as much freedom as you've given him, and he's smart enough to know he's earned it by producing, producing, producing—for Page One.

Self-starting reporters like this are to be prized. I know.

So why is he looking for a way out? The answer to that question would help your paper hold on to him.

He talked to me because he wants his editors to demand so much more of him. What's good enough for his editors is not good enough for him. He wants to be pushed, challenged, coached to new heights. He wants to soar.

"This is a story I did," he said, handing me a photocopied clip from a recent issue

Copyright © Houghton Mifflin Company. All rights reserved.

of your paper. It would have made any paper proud. Yet he wasn't as proud of it as he wanted to be. "I wish I had gotten more guidance from my editors," he said. Even so, he was happy that "because of my story, people's lives got better." Think how many more lives might have gotten better with some real conversation from an editor. Think how much better the reporter's life would have been. I bet he wouldn't have sought out a recruiter from some other paper.

Your reporter is looking outside because of what he sees in your newsroom. What he sees is editors who have too much to do. "They're very busy. They're always putting out fires," he said.

So, what is going on out there in your newsroom when this reporter is talking with your editors? Isn't he getting the coaching he craves? Not really. The reporter believes that good stories spring from good questions, and his editors don't ask good questions. Usually, they ask how long the story will be, when it will be in, where it can play, and what budget line they can take into a meeting for you to read. There is almost no talk about what else could be, what the story means, or what other approaches might exist.

He craves an occasional conversation with an editor who will help him turn his good ideas into great ones. He wants someone to get excited about what he's doing and to help him turn his story idea upside down and inside out, exploring the best ways to report and tell it. He wants to get better. He wants to be better. He wants to be even more valuable for your paper. That's what you want for him, too, isn't it?

He understands how the system should work: "A reporter comes up with an idea, but a good editor helps sharpen the idea. I need someone who can ask me the real questions about my stories." Although he knows that's what should happen, it never really does, he sadly said. He seemed to think that any of your editors has the talent to help him—they just don't have the time.

As I listened to your reporter, wondering what might be a good spot for him among our reporters, I had to wonder about them, too. Which of my own paper's good reporters are feeling less-than-challenged, and talking to someone else—maybe even you—looking for editors who will help them achieve greatness?

So, your reporter has me thinking.

Our best hope in keeping our best reporters, copy editors, photographers, artists—everyone—is to work harder to make sure they get the help they are demanding to reach their potential and to be fulfilled. If we can't do it, they'll find someone who can.

*—**Editor & Publisher***

Read the letter again and highlight the sections that give information about

- the reporter's ability as a reporter;
- what he likes about his job;
- how appreciated he is by his paper;
- what he needs in order to do a better job.

Use what you highlighted and your own experience to answer these questions:

1. Is the reporter being realistic in what he is asking for?
2. Would this reporter want to become an editor one day?
3. If you were an editor, would you hire this reporter? Why or why not?

Vocabulary Building

VOCABULARY IN CONTEXT

A. *Jigsaw Sentences:* **Match one part of an idea in column A with the remaining part in column B.**
Decide if part A should be placed *before* **or** *after* **part B.**

Column A

_____ 1. Candi Lange said 200 of her company's 14,000 employees have schedules adjusted to fit their needs.

_____ 2. She pitches in cheerfully when a flurry of activity requires her to work overtime.

_____ 3. When she came to the firm a year ago, Ashby didn't expect to be treated the same as attorneys who had worked for 30 years.

_____ 4. Technology campuses have their own special problems

_____ 5. He believes in treating people the way he would like to be treated

Column B

a. When your employer cares about you, it makes you want to reciprocate.

b. They are typically located outside of city centers.

Copyright © Houghton Mifflin Company. All rights reserved.

c. Still, there are indications that companies are beginning to change.

d. We have a very forward-thinking CEO.

e. She was surprised to find her opinion valued and even solicited.

Compare your combinations with a partner.

B. *Expressions:* **These sentences have been taken from the readings in this chapter. Use the context to understand the meaning of the expressions in bold. Use each expression in a sentence of your own.**

1. Loyalty is not the feeling you get after you have **put your heart and soul** into a place for seven years.

   _____

   _____

2. Besides pay raises, medical benefits . . . employers are offering more **offbeat perks**. These might include . . . allowing pets in the office.

   _____

   _____

3. "You are **not a number** here," he said.

   _____

   _____

4. He returned to Walgreens, this time . . . with a different set of managers. **Something clicked**.

   _____

   _____

5. Employees who need to **clear their minds** can go for a run.

   _____

   _____

Copyright © Houghton Mifflin Company. All rights reserved.

6. "They (editors) are very busy, They're always **putting out fires**."

   _____

   _____

7. He wants someone to . . . help him turn his story idea **upside down and inside out**.

   _____

   _____

▮ Expanding Your Language

SPEAKING

A. *Choosing the Best:* **Four different approaches toward keeping employees happy have been presented in this chapter. Evaluate each and choose the best as follows:**

1. Select four criteria that you consider important. You may choose from the ones listed here, make up your own, or use a combination of both.

   - Benefits to employees
   - Cost of implementation
   - Ease of implementation
   - Equally applicable in both small and large companies
   - Long-term consequences (*Example: A long-term consequence of making the workplace so comfortable would be encouraging employees to actually spend more time at work and less with their families.*)

2. Evaluate each approach using the criteria you selected.
3. Rank them in descending order. Be ready to support your decision.
4. Present your ranking to a pair or group that came up with a different ranking and try to convince them why yours is better.

Copyright © Houghton Mifflin Company. All rights reserved.

B. *Interviewing:* **How do people feel about where they work? To find out, conduct a few interviews outside the classroom. Follow these steps:**

Step 1: Individually	Use the ideas generated in this chapter to make five interesting questions on the topic.
Step 2: In groups	Get together with two or three other students. Pool the questions and choose the best five.
Step 3: Individually	Write down the questions.
Step 4: Individually	Find three people to interview outside the class. These could be family members, friends, or coworkers.
Step 5: Individually	Conduct the interviews and bring the responses to class.
Step 6: In groups	Discuss the responses with the same people you worked with in step 2.
Step 7: In groups	Report the results of your survey to the class.

WRITING

Letter Writing: **You have recently resigned from your job and you are now very happy in a different company. Write a letter or an e-mail message in which you try to convince a close colleague at the previous company to also resign and apply for a position at your present company. Use the following procedure:**

- Make a list of all the reasons why you left.
- Make a list of all the benefits at the new place.
- Write a paragraph on each followed by a paragraph on why you think the move would be a good idea.

Show your letter to your teacher for feedback.

Copyright © Houghton Mifflin Company. All rights reserved.

Read On: Taking it Further

NEWSPAPER ARTICLES

Pick a work-related topic that has not been discussed in this unit (entrepreneurs, team work, mergers, stress at work, etc.). Check the newspaper over the next few days and find an article that interests you. Prepare to present the information in that article to a small group. Follow these steps:

1. Skim the article quickly to get the general idea of the information.
2. Identify the thesis/point of view of the article
3. Identify the main ideas and make notes on the supporting information.
4. Practice your presentation.
5. Prepare three questions that you could ask your group to discuss *before* you present.
6. Present your information.

READING JOURNAL

Report on what you presented in your journal.

Copyright © Houghton Mifflin Company. All rights reserved.

Answer Key

UNIT 1 Birthrights

CHAPTER 1: The Family: Moving in Many Directions
Understanding Details, page 10

1. a. The majority of women with children under six are working.   **b.** There is very little family time.   **2.** One in every five   **3. a.** Artificial insemination   **b.** Sperm can be collected from dead men.   **c.** Older women can be enabled to give birth.   **4. a.** Many more gay parents then in the past   **b.** Their community is very supportive and accepting.   **5.** Much easier for women to go back to work after childbirth with the changes to job security and childcare.
6. a. caterers   **b.** dry cleaners   **7.** Children also lead much busier lives, they are constantly scheduled in various activities.

Looking Back; Highlighting, page 11

(sample answers)
a. flexibility for working mothers   **b.** new fertility techniques   **c.** new types of families
d. children also very busy   **e.** better communication technology

Vocabulary Building, page 15

A. 1. the plane crash   **2.** Parents   **3.** Teacher, child   **4.** The teacher lecturing the student about academic promotion   **5.** Parents telling children how they [children] should feel
6. The little boy crossing his legs because he had put his shoes on the wrong foot

B. (sample answers)
"We need to allow **them** to be children." children
"Why are **we** rushing our children to become adults?" parents

Vocabulary in Context, page 16

A. 1. d   **2.** b   **3.** e   **4.** f   **5.** g   **6.** c   **7.** h   **8.** a

B. 1. evolution, evolved   **2.** consulted, consultation, consultant   **3.** migrated, migrants, migration   **4.** establishment, established, establishing

CHAPTER 2: Cheaper by the Dozen
Finding the Main Points of an Argument, page 27

1. c   **2.** e   **3.** a   **4.** g   **5.** d   **6.** b   **7.** f

Fact and Opinion, page 28

1. O   **2.** F   **3.** O   **4.** O   **5.** F   **6.** F   **7.** O

Copyright © Houghton Mifflin Company. All rights reserved.

Vocabulary Building, page 32

1. N   **2.** N   **3.** NE   **4.** P   **5.** NE   **6.** N

Signal Words/Markers, pages 33–34

1. a. "first and most obvious . . . " (paragraph 3)

   b. "equally important . . . " (paragraph 5)

2. a. ". . . enormously wonderful and rewarding. But it is also hard work." (paragraph 5)

   b. "The McCaughey septuplets and Chukwu octuplets, however, represent too much of a good thing." (paragraph 2)

3. a. "Regardless of the motivation, dedication . . ." (paragraph 7)

   b. "Yet this is clearly not an option . . ." (paragraph 12)

4. a. "For these reasons . . ." (paragraph 12)

   b. "In the end . . ." (paragraph 14)

UNIT 2 Health: Moving in New Directions

CHAPTER 3: Alternative Healing

Predicting: Getting Information from a Diagram, page 43

needles; "meridians"; needles; painkilling and inflammation-reducing substances; nerve cells, midbrain, pituitary gland; asthma, headaches, alcohol abuse; neck pain, painful menstruation, paralysis, tennis elbow

Chunking, page 52

PARAGRAPH GROUPS	MAIN IDEAS
2. 12–16	Example of the success of acupuncture
3. 17–22	Studies done about acupuncture and why it is successful
4. 23–27	How acupuncture helps with addictions
5. 28–30	How acupuncture helps with asthma and other problems
6. 31–35	The critics of acupuncture

Analyzing Chunks of Text, page 53

1. Some results of treatment with acupuncture (paragraph 11)
   Introduction of acupuncture to North America (paragraph 7)
   Popularity of acupuncture (paragraph 10)
   Safety of acupuncture (paragraph 9)

Copyright © Houghton Mifflin Company. All rights reserved.

Vocabulary in Context, page 56

A. 1. energy-carrying channels

    2. trick of the mind

    3. opiates made in the brain

    4. degeneration of the joint lining

    5. program that felony drug offenders can enter into which includes acupuncture and serves as an alternative to prison.

B. (sample answers)

1. sicknesses   **2.** counter-effect   **3.** personal experience   **4.** proof from a personal experience   **5.** a test study

Recognizing Descriptive Language, pages 57–58

(sample answers)

1. big

2. extraordinary

3. new and effective tests

4. a mystery

5. imposed the same on himself

CHAPTER 4: Total Fitness: Combining Diet and Exercise

Skimming, page 63

1. They are counting the number of steps that they take for curiosity and for scientific purposes.

2. Fitness experts would like to see people become more active.

3. People need to go out for a 30-minute brisk walk.

4. People can lose weight by walking 30 minutes a day and 45–60 minutes at least 3 or 4 times a week.

Scanning for Specific Information, page 67

1. Pedometers measure the number of steps and miles that a person walks. Pedometers give people "pizazz" and motivate them to walk rather than take an easier alternative.

2. To meet minimum health requirements.

3. The government regulation is 30 minutes of moderate activity most days of the week.

4. Heart rate and breathing will be faster than when doing normal activities.

Copyright © Houghton Mifflin Company. All rights reserved.

5. They need to start with a lower number of steps, about 3,000 to 4,000.

6. a. Build up to walking 30 minutes a day at 3 to 4 mph.

   b. Need to walk 30 minutes, some days 45–60 minutes at 3.5–4.5 mph.

   c. Need to walk at 4–5 mph, three times a week for 20–40 minutes.

Skimming, page 69

1. The healthiest food is often the best tasting.   **2.** High fat, low fiber meals   **3.** Time pressure, false beliefs and myth that eating better is only for people with serious health risks
4. Start switching to fresh fruits, which are widely available and make good, healthy snacks

Scanning for Specific Information, page 73

1. It tasted better.   **2.** People enjoy foods that taste good. Those foods contain a great deal of fat and sugar.   **3.** High fat and low fiber   **4.** Children eat ready-made foods and fast foods. They are fatter and have high cholesterol.   **5. a.** Time pressure   **b.** False beliefs.

6. a. People label food as either good or bad.

   b. People think it means giving up favorite foods.

   c. Problem with eating a "reasonable amount"

7. a. Eat fresh fruit

   b. Eat fiber-rich whole-grain cereals and breads.

   c. Eat low-fat meats, i.e., fish and chicken without skin.

Vocabulary Building in Context: Inferring Meaning, page 75

A. 1. b   **2.** c   **3.** a   **4.** a   **5.** b

B. 1. simply   **2.** unfortunately   **3.** only   **4.** yet   **5.** predictably

Word Forms: Nouns, Adjectives and Adverbs, page 77

A. 1. walking, walkers, walking, walk

   2. research, researchers, research

   3. consumption, consume, consumers, consumer

B. 1. ADJ, N, N, V

   2. N, N, ADJ

   3. N, V, N, ADJ

Copyright © Houghton Mifflin Company. All rights reserved.

UNIT 3 Memory

CHAPTER 5: How Memory Works and How to Improve It
Scanning the Introduction, pages 89–90

1. Stan is 69 and Michelle is 33. Stan is a man and Michelle is a woman. Stan is a chemical engineer and Michelle is a film student. Both take pills to help improve their memory, but Michelle also attends a memory improvement class.

2. They are examples of millions of Americans who are trying to keep up their memories with the demands of the information age.

3. Because people are aging and as they age are worried about their memory.

4. a. How different parts of the brain interact and how age and stress as well as other factors affect these processes

Surveying and Chunking, page 97

D. (sample answers)
How the brain processes memory (paragraphs 6–13)
Influences on our memory's ability to function well (paragraphs 14–18)
How to protect our ability to keep memory function high (paragraphs 19–24)

Skimming for Special Terms, page 98

1. Working memory: part of the memory that juggles information in the present moment

2. Long-term memory: stores information for extended periods of time

3. Cerebral cortex: outer region of the brain, which stores long-term memory

4. Neurons: "vinelike" nerve cells that communicate using chemical and electrical impulses

5. Hippocampus: The "keyboard" of the brain, which responds to the neurons to allow them to build a sensory network, determines whether or not information is kept in the memory.

6. Savant: person who can retain a great deal of facts but has difficulty with abstract thinking.

Scanning for Details, pages 99–100

1. Because it requires your memory to recall name, friend's appearance, location of restaurant, and how to get there.

2. Our brains don't record everything that happens to us and then bury it. Most of what our working memory absorbs, quickly evaporates.

3. They relay chemical and electrical impulses.

4. Permanent memory is when a particular memory is constantly activated and becomes embedded into the brain tissue.

5. The hippocampus. Does the information have emotional significance? Does the information entering the brain relate to something we already know?

Copyright © Houghton Mifflin Company. All rights reserved.

A-6 Answer Key

6. Because they have different backgrounds, retain different information, and have different experiences that new facts build on.

7. a. A super-human memory develops and the person retains a huge number of facts but is incapable of abstract thought.

b. There is no ability to form new memories.

Skimming for Key Supporting Ideas, page 100

High blood pressure, too little sleep, too much alcohol, dysfunctional thyroid gland, information overload, stress

Note-Taking, page 100

A. healthy lifestyle

B. seminars and supplements

C. estrogen

D. other drugs

Vocabulary Building, pages 107–108

2. Memory is created through a complex system in the brain. Dr. Barry Gordon, head of memory-disorders clinic at Johns Hopkins School of Medicine.

3. Memory serves as a filter so that people retain important information. Neuroscientist Eric Kandel.

4. The importance of the hippocampus. Boston University researchers.

5. Memory is constantly at work even in old age, although it is a little slower. Daniel Schacter, Harvard psychologist.

6. Recall ability varies quite a bit. Dr. Barry Gordon, head of memory-disorders clinic at Johns Hopkins School of Medicine.

7. Information is coming at record speeds and amounts. Dr. Barry Gordon, head of memory-disorders clinic at Johns Hopkins School of Medicine.

8. Memory-enhancing drugs have disadvantages. James McGaugh, neuroscientist at University of California, Irvine.

Paraphrasing, page 108

1. "For example Schacter has found that young adults are usually better than old folks at remembering details of a picture." (paragraph 15)

2. "As Harvard psychologist Daniel Schacter observes in his 1998 book . . . the simple act of meeting a friend for lunch requires a vast store of memory." (paragraph 5)

3. "As Michelle Arnove discovered, an overwhelmed mind has trouble absorbing anything."

Copyright © Houghton Mifflin Company. All rights reserved.

(paragraph 17)

4. "Barbara Sherwin, codirector of the McGill University Menopause Clinic revealed estrogen's importance two years ago. . . ." (paragraph 21)

CHAPTER 6: Memory: What Controls It?

Scanning for Specific Information, page 120

1. He left his computer on and his jacket on the back of his chair at work.

2. Eleven years

3. Retrograde amnesia, in which some or all memories are "misplaced"; anterograde amnesia, in which only old memories remain.
Anterograde amnesia

4. Stress. It was not acceptable because people under stress do not suddenly lose their memory and bearing in time.

5. A cyst pushing on a nerve tract. It had been there since birth. It was perfectly placed for it to affect the key areas of the brain.

6. It was extremely successful, Mr. Dilbert regained most of his memory except for the 10 days surrounding his disappearance.

Scanning for Specific Information, page 127

1. Confused, couldn't remember his name, headache, naked.

2. One person threw him out.
Another person listened to story and called ambulance.

3. Meningitis test, brain scan, hypnotherapy, injection with truth serum.
Dissociative amnesia.
Mental trauma.

4. No, only thought so because he jerked when someone said name.

5. Lived in NJ, worked as a technician, TV shows, apartment, trips with family, being gay.

6. Sent press statement to newspapers all over continent and to gay communities in Morristown, NJ.

7. They became very good friends. They shared similar experience of having to start new life.

8. TV show did story on him that was aired across the country.

Word Forms, page 133

1. arrived **2.** fascinating **3.** transferred **4.** suffered **5.** recovering **6.** missing
7. tried **8.** pounded **9.** needed **10.** depressing

Copyright © Houghton Mifflin Company. All rights reserved.

Vocabulary in Context, page 134

1. fall apart

2. make sense

3. be paralyzed/stop

4. stop doing anything about it

5. new, unique

6. faster

7. stuck

8. bring back

9. process

UNIT 4 The Age of Communications

CHAPTER 7: The Cell-Phone Explosion

Skimming, page 147

1. extremely, everyone from bankers to trash collectors . . .

2. ahead of everyone, first country to have more mobile phones than fixed phones

Scanning, page 147

1. 60%, which is twice the U.S. percentage

2. Teachers object to cell-phone use in school because students send text messages to each other in class.

3. Extremely affordable for all types of budgets ($10–$40)

4. They can create personal phone books, send e-mails, and buy things.

5. Life is not as private as it used to be; telemarketers call their cell phones, and advertisements appear on their text messages.

Note-Taking: Chunking Information, page 148 (only partial details provided)

Cell-phone explosion in Finland

MAIN IDEAS	SUPPORTING POINTS/DETAILS
A. Who has these phones?	1. Statistics: By the year 2000, 100% penetration rate; twice the number as the U.S.
	2. Types of people: Everybody has these phones—rich, poor, old and young.

Copyright © Houghton Mifflin Company. All rights reserved.

B. What's the effect on schools and kids?

    1. Problems in high school: Students send text messages to each other in class.

    2. Age of kids with phones at school: Average age of getting a phone is 14, but age is getting younger and younger (grade 1).

C. Affordability

    1. Equal access to technology: Rich and poor can have access because all types of plans available.

    2. Help for families: Phone companies make special family phone packages.

D. Results of technological change

    1. Removal of old technology. Telephone booths are being taken off the streets; telephone books are a thing of the past.

    2. Telemarketers: Starting to call cell phones to solicit.

    3. Loss of privacy: There is no sense of privacy because people are always reachable.

Skimming, page 149

1. noticeably everywhere

2. range from polite to very impolite

Scanning, pages 152–153

1. a. The inn management reprimanded her because her cell phone rang.

    b. She thought that there would be some type of understanding.

2. a. Several million cell phones.

    b. Cell phones are used everywhere.

3. Speak more softly into the phone.

4. Cell phones are cheaper than regular phones.

5. You can find people in a busy place.

6. You can forget to turn them off and say things that you will regret.

Copyright © Houghton Mifflin Company. All rights reserved.

Note-Taking: Chunking Information, pages 153–154 (only partial details provided)

Cell-phone use in New York: what's scceptable and what's not

MAIN IDEAS	SUPPORTING POINTS/DETAILS
A. Cell-phone use in New York	**1.** Number of phone users: Several million.
	2. Where people are using their phones: Everywhere.
B. Guide to good cell-phone manners	**1.** Recent publication on cell-phone manners: "Wireless Etiquette: A Guide to the Changing World of Instant Communication"
	2. Mr. Lauter's experience at Empire State Building: A man ruined the feeling at the top of the building by yelling into his cell phone.
	3. Advice for using cell phones on the train: Don't make personal calls.
C. Cell-phone use in Italy and L.A.	**1.** Experience at an Italian wedding: The groom's cell phone rang.
	2. Reason for cell-phone popularity in Italy: Cheaper rates.
	3. Experience in L.A. restaurant: Everybody at the table had a cell phone.
D. Cell-phone use; stories of success and caution	**1.** Stories of use at the theater: Somebody dropped a phone and another person called the number to be able to locate it in the dark theater.
	2. Rescue in England: Lost hiker called secretary in New York to send park officials in England.
	3. Sending unintended messages: Women forgot to turn cell phone off and a man heard her ranting and raving about him.

Copyright © Houghton Mifflin Company. All rights reserved.

Applying the Information, page 155

(sample answers)

PROBLEM-SOLVERS	PROBLEM MAKERS
1. Can be useful in case of car problems	
	2. Can interrupt at important times
	3. Can disturb those around you
4. Can help you find people	
5. You will always be reachable.	**5.** You will always be reachable.

Vocabulary in Context, pages 156–157

A. 1. b   **2.** c   **3.** a   **4.** c   **5.** c   **6.** a   **7.** b   **8.** a

B. 1. b.   **2.** c   **3.** d   **4.** a   **5.** e

Jigsaw Sentences, pages 157–158

1. d   **2.** b   **3.** c   **4.** a

CHAPTER 8: Internet Communications: The Disappearance of Privacy

Audience and Purpose, page 173

1. a. His own personal experiences with lack of privacy on the Internet   **b.** 9

2. He makes his living off of the Web.

Chunking, page 174

(sample answers)

2. The history of how we progressively lost our privacy

3. Availability of information on the net, thanks to desktop computers

4. Basic ways to protect your privacy

6. How to navigate safely without revealing your name to online marketers

7. Technology moving ahead of law; e-mail monitoring

8. The debate about establishing a federal privacy agency.

Answering Questions from Notes, pages 175–176

1. a. purchasing

   b. telephone use

   c. banking

2. a. Through your cellular phone, calls can be intercepted and eavesdropped on.

   b. Through credit cards, everything you charge entered into a database that many people have access to and can copy your card number from.

Copyright © Houghton Mifflin Company. All rights reserved.

3. 1960s: Data surveillance surpasses the law; privacy bill of rights drafted to try to prevent government and private companies from too much access.

1970s: Fair Credit Reporting Act passed; consumers allowed to know about their credit files.

Introduction of PCs: Data that once was protected now open to anybody.

Today: Many preventative measures are in place to help ensure privacy, but they are insufficient.

4. Maintain privacy:

a. 41% of people would rather leave a Web site then enter personal information.

b. 25% lie when they do fill in Web information.

c. Refused to give social security number in all cases.

Forgo privacy for convenience:

a. Convenience of cash when it is needed

b. Security of a safe parking lot

c. Improved mail-order service that knows your interests

Vocabulary in Context, pages 177–178

1. b   **2.** a   **3.** b   **4.** c   **5.** b   **6.** a   **7.** b   **8.** a

Word Forms, pages 178–179

VERB	NOUN	ADJECTIVE
1. duplicate	duplication	duplicate
2. suspect	suspect	suspicious
3. disappear	disappearance	disappearing
4. appreciate	appreciation	appreciable
5. transform	transformation	transformed
6. discriminate	discrimination	discriminatory
7. clarify	clarification	clarified
8. provide	provider	
9. alternate	alternate	alternating
10. intrude	intruder	intruding

Word Choice, page 179

a. prankster, interloper   **b.** rattles off   **c.** cruise   **d.** locks shorn   **e.** note that   **f.** glean

Copyright © Houghton Mifflin Company. All rights reserved.

UNIT 5 Creativity

CHAPTER 9: The Creative Brain
Skimming, page 190

- People see creativity as reserved for artists, scientists and inventors.
- They don't see it as available for ordinary people.
- They are in awe of the idea of creativity.

Understanding and Paraphrasing Suggestions, page 197

1. a. Understanding the stages of the creative process

   b. Understanding the aspects that hinder the different modes at each stage.

   c. A commitment to improving one's own creativity.

2. An idea has to be generated and something made to happen as a result of the idea.

3. It tells us the process to follow and the role of our brain at each stage of the process.

4. Passion characterizes creative people. This is important because it means that people are energetic toward certain things.

5. a. Children play.

   b. Children pay attention to their own rhythms.

   c. Children seek out and risk experimenting with things.

   d. Children follow their interests.

   e. Children honor dreams and daydreams.

   f. Children consider mistakes as information as opposed to being unsuccessful.

Figuring Out the Referent, page 202

1. that—our idea of creativity.

2. this—70–80% of people who don't consider themselves creative have shown that they do have creative abilities and use them well.

3. a. that—inventiveness

   b. it—creativity

4. a. where—the world of business

   b. it—creativity

5. a. there—good music, exercising, eating nourishing food

   b. that—good music, exercising, eating nourishing food

6. that—know and use our most productive time well

Copyright © Houghton Mifflin Company. All rights reserved.

Jigsaw Sentences, page 203

1. c   **2.** a   **3.** d   **4.** b

Word Forms, pages 203–204

1. difference, N   **2.** basis, N   **3.** creativity, N   **4.** passionate, ADJ   **5.** passion, N
6. natural, ADJ; unexpectedness, N

CHAPTER 10: Laughter: The Creative Force

Skimming, page 208

a. learning

b. problem solving and work

c. social bonding

Scanning for Research Findings, page 212

1. Joking may improve people's problem solving and effectiveness in the tasks they carry out.

2. People who had seen a comedic film clip were able to come up with more creative solutions to a difficult problem.

3. Humor helps executives recognize complex relationships and far flung implications.

4. The benefit is that people's work performance improves because they are having fun doing their jobs. The danger is that is that the work environment may become too relaxed and people too careless.

5. a. Humor that helps children learn is humor that does not distort. Humor that distorts information doesn't help children learn.

   b. Jokes unrelated to the topic under discussion are recommended.

6. Lecturers should use humor about the topic being discussed. They should not use humor outside of the topic because they will be accused of digressing.

7. By laughing at similar things people see that they have similar outlooks on life without having to discuss the matter outright.

8. He does not believe that any joke is truly harmless. Every joke is at someone's expense, he says.

Skimming, page 215

1. a. stress   **b.** depression   **c.** physical health

Scanning for Research Findings, pages 219–221

1. Our entire cerebral cortex: the left side is figuring out the verbal content and the right side is figuring out the humor.

Copyright © Houghton Mifflin Company. All rights reserved.

2. Laughter affects blood pressure and heart rate.

3. Think creatively and makes us feel as though we belong.

4. People with a sense of humor are better at coping with death (e.g., signing organ-donor cards).

5. a. Laughter improves our immune system.

   b. There are no conclusive medical studies yet, but a study is under way at a New York hospital's Clown Care Unit.

6. Just because two things happen at the same time does not necessarily mean that the two are connected in any way.

7. Some argue that internal humor settings are fully developed by adulthood and those with lower settings may not benefit from laughter. Others disagree and say that most people can benefit from humor.

8. The more control people have over the type of humor they are exposed to, the more that they will benefit.

9. People who are more cheerful do not pay as much attention to their physical and psychological health.

10. First, figure out the types of things that make you laugh out loud; then build your own humor library filled with objects that make you laugh, and visit it when you feel down.

Vocabulary in Context, pages 227–228

1. b, a

2. e

3. d

4. e

5. d

6. c, c, d

7. d

Word Forms, page 228

1. productivity, N   **2.** elation, N   **3.** carelessness, N   **4.** confusing, ADJ   **5.** electrical, ADJ
6. psychological, ADJ   **7.** alienation, N

Definitions, pages 228–229

1. a coping strategy that involves setting unrealistically low expectations, then mentally playing out all the possible outcomes of a given situation

2. imagining something going wrong and going over the steps to fix the situation

3. imagining a flawless performance

4. focusing on stressful or disturbing life events in a structured way

5. person who is less anxious, sets high expectations, avoids thinking about what could go wrong

Copyright © Houghton Mifflin Company. All rights reserved.

UNIT 6 Work

CHAPTER 11: The Changing World of Business
Defining the Terms, pages 235–236

1. f   **2.** c   **3.** a   **4.** d   **5.** b   **6.** e

Skimming, page 236

1. They are father and son.   **2.** Rico, the son (economically). Enrico, the father (emotionally). **3.** There is no more long term; people move around from job to job.   **4.** Formal obligation, trustworthiness, commitment, purpose.

Scanning for Details, page 243

1. To provide for his family. Yes, he accomplished his purpose by buying a house in a better neighborhood for his children and saving for them to go to university. For Enrico's generation, time was extremely linear and achievement was cumulative.

2. Rico believes in risk taking and being open to change, whereas his father believed in staying with what he knew and saving for the future. Rico moved around quite a bit and moved up in the business world, living in the moment, whereas Enrico stayed in a steady but not upwardly mobile job and had specific and definite goals set out for himself.

3. His friendships have developed mostly around work and because he and his family have moved a lot, they have lost touch with many of the friends. He depends on technology to stay in touch.

4. The communities are not permanent; people get acquainted on a surface level because they aren't in one place long enough to get to know one another.

5. He worries about his children's values. He feels his work habits do not set a good example.

6. People do not progress step by step in their careers; people use numerous working skills throughout their employment; temporary job placements are the most popular job agencies. Affected values are trust, loyalty, and mutual commitment.

7. He advises them to not become "entangled" by long-term employment and always work on the outside of an organization.

8. Keep moving, don't commit, don't sacrifice.

9. Success, which he wanted so badly, is also causing him pain.

Loaded Words, page 250

1. N   **2.** P   **3.** N   **4.** P

Vocabulary in Context, pages 250–251

1. It added up over the years.   **2.** top, best of   **3.** coming   **4.** impermanent   **5.** characteristics   **6.** easy to understand   **7.** quickly passing   **8.** advises   **9.** continued   **10.** recordings

Copyright © Houghton Mifflin Company. All rights reserved.

Figuring out the Referent, page 252

A. 1. these—use of time, senority, pension   **the result**—a clear story for himself

2. these—children of working class parents

3. this—Jeannette manages big team, he owns a business, modern

4. the new kind of suburb—suburb which arises and decays within one generation

5. this—conflict between work and time and family;
his real unease—fear of lack of ethical discipline for his children.

6. these reasons—organization has become a network, promotion and dismissals no longer based on clear fixed rules, network constantly redefining its structure, people changing jobs eleven times in a lifetime

CHAPTER 12: Can Companies Keep Their Employees?

Skimming, page 261

1. Child-care centers, athletic facilities, comfortable indoor and outdoor meeting areas, cafés, and retail outlets

2. The United States and Canada; the United States

3. 4% leave every year, compared to the 15% national average in the United States

Scanning for Specific Information, pages 264–265

1. It was set up in 1981. Several women at the company were having problems balancing career and young families.

2. SAS is in a high-tech industry. High-tech industries located outside city centers.

3. One million square feet. Its interior is set up with streets and plazas, full bank branch, ATM that dispenses U.S. $, dry-cleaning, convenience stores, athletic facilities, and café.

4. Time and money savers

5. No, no one asks people where they're going or when they'll be back. People have autonomy and can decide how to reach their goals. Makes people feel important.

Skimming, page 267

1. No; actually leads to promotion
2. both men and women
3. performance improves and retention of good employees

Scanning for Specific Information, page 269

1. People are able to get flexible working hours so that they can balance their work and personal lives. Charlotte Hawthorne is able to spend more time with her children and keep her career "on track."

Copyright © Houghton Mifflin Company. All rights reserved.

2. 35% of the people had been promoted. 90% were much happier with the balance.

3. Women starting families, men wanting to spend more time with their children and wanting to get more involved in the community.

4. Men and women both work, men are no longer the only financial providers for their family.

5. Some people have trouble keeping home and work separate and work during their free time.

Vocabulary in Context, page 274

A. Jigsaw Sentences

1. c (before)   **2.** a (after)   **3.** e   **4.** b (after)   **5.** d (before)

B. Expressions

1. Everything that you have to give, commitment

2. Nontraditional benefits

3. Are seen as a person with personality traits

4. Things worked out well.

5. Relax and think of something else

6. Resolving conflicts and fixing situations

7. Fully and completely

Copyright © Houghton Mifflin Company. All rights reserved.

Text Credits

p. 7: "The Brady Bunch No More: Families Grow Less Traditional," by Kate Stone Lombardi, *New York Times,* October 5, 1997. Copyright © 1997 by The New York Times Co. Reprinted by permission.

p. 13: "Stolen Childhood," by Jeffrey Derevensky, *The Montreal Gazette,* April 16, 1996. Reprinted with permission from *The Montreal Gazette.*

p. 20: "When Fertility Drugs Work Too Well," *Newsweek,* December 1, 1997. Copyright © 1997 Newsweek, Inc. All rights reserved. Reprinted by permission.

p. 23: "Eight is Too Many," by Ezekiel J. Emanuel, *The New Republic,* January 25, 1999. Reprinted with permission from Ezekiel J. Emanuel, "Eight is Too Many," *The New Republic.*

p. 31. "A Small Crime," by Jerry Wexler. Reprinted by permission of Jerry Wexler.

p. 40: "Hitting a Century," from *Newsweek,* June 30, 1997. Copyright © 1997 Newsweek, Inc. All rights reserved. Reprinted by permission.

p. 42: Excerpts from "Alternative Healing: What Really Works," by Salley Shannon, *Reader's Digest,* August 2000. Reprinted by permission of Salley Shannon, the author.

p. 44: "How Acupuncture Works," from *U.S. News & World Report,* May 13, 1996. Copyright © May 13, 1996, **U.S. News & World Report.** Visit us at our Web site at www.usnews.com for additional information.

p. 46: "Medicine's Latest Miracle: The Surprising Power of Acupuncture," by Rick Weiss, *Health,* January/February 1995. Reprinted by permission of the author from Rick Weiss, "Medicine's Latest Miracle: The Surprising Power of Acupuncture," *Health.*

p. 63: "Journey to Better Fitness Starts with 10,000 Steps," by Nancy Heilmich, *USA Today,* June 29, 1999. Copyright © 1999 USA TODAY. Reprinted with permission.

p. 70: "Choosing Right to Make Healthiest and Tastiest One and the Same," by Jane E. Brody, *New York Times,* December 29, 1998. Copyright © 1998 by The New York Times Co. Reprinted by permission.

p.78: "Some Shape up by Surfing the Internet," by Marion Roach, *New York Times,* May 25, 1999. Reprinted by permission of Marion Roach, a writer living in upstate New York.

p. 86: Excerpt from *Becoming A Master Student,* by David Ellis, Canadian Edition, Second Edition, © 1997. Copyright © 1997 Houghton Mifflin Company. Reprinted with permission.

p. 88: "Memory Quiz," *Time Magazine,* June 12, 2000. Copyright © 2000 Time, Inc. Reprinted with permission.

p. 90: "Memory," by Geoffrey Cowley and Anne Underwood, *Newsweek,* June 15, 1998. Copyright © 1998 Newsweek, Inc. All rights reserved. Reprinted by permission.

p. 103: Excerpts from *Becoming a Master Student,* by David Ellis, Ninth Edition. Copyright © 2000 by Houghton Mifflin Company. Reprinted with permission.

p. 113: "Self-Fulfilling Stereotypes," by Mark Snyder, *Psychology Today,* July 1982. Reprinted with permission from *Psychology Today Magazine.* Copyright © 1982 Sussex Publishers, Inc.

p. 117: "The Man Who Vanished Into His Past," by Marcia Sherman, *New York Times,* July 3, 1999. Copyright © 1997 by The New York Times Co. Reprinted by permission.

p. 131: "The Flaws of Memory," by Tom Siegfrid, *Dallas Morning News,* September 4, 2000. From "Memories may be beautiful and yet they're often wrong," by Tom Siegfried, *Dallas Morning News,* September 4, 2000. Reprinted with permission of the Dallas Morning News.

Copyright © Houghton Mifflin Company. All rights reserved.

P. 141: "Wireless Nation," and "Wireless Countries," from *USA Today,* August 25, 1999. Copyright © 1999 USA TODAY. Reprinted with permission.

p. 145: "Where Cell Phones Get a Ringing Endorsement," by T.R. Reid, *Washington Post,* May 27, 1999. Copyright © 1999, The Washington Post. Reprinted with permission.

p. 150: "The Nuisance of Overheard Calls," by Joyce Wadler, from *New York Times,* October 25, 1998. Copyright © 1998 by The New York Times Co. Reprinted by permission.

p. 165: "Invasion of Privacy," by Joshua Quittner, *Time Magazine,* August 25, 1997. Copyright © 1997 Time, Inc. Reprinted with permission.

p. 180: "Nobody's Business," by William Safire, *New York Times,* January 8, 1998. Copyright © 1998 by The New York Times Co. Reprinted by permission.

p. 190: "Key to Creative Living: Reclaiming Our Passion," by Ned Herrmann, from *The Creative Brain,* © 1993. Reprinted with permission from Ned Herrmann. Copyright © 1993 Brain Books, Lake Line, NC.

p. 200: "Mental Breakout," By Tawn Nhan. Reprinted with permission from *the Charlotte Observer.* Copyright owned by the Charlotte Observer.

p. 209: "Humor Found to Aid Problem Solving," by Daniel Goleman, *New York Times,* August 4, 1997. Copyright © 1997 by The New York Times Co. Reprinted by permission.

p. 215: "Happily Ever Laughter," by Peter Doskoach, *Psychology Today,* July/August 1996. Reprinted with permission from *Psychology Today Magazine.* Copyright © 1996 Sussex Publishers, Inc.

p. 223: "Seeing Pessimism's Place in a Smiley-Faced World," by Erica Goode, *New York Times,* August 15, 2000. Copyright © 2000 by The New York Times Co. Reprinted by permission.

p. 233: "Knowing Goals Best Way to Build Career," by Fiona McNair, *Southam News,* May, 1999.

p. 237: "Why Good Workers Make Bad People," by Richard Sennett, *New Statesman,* October 9, 1998. Reprinted with permission from *New Statesman.*

p. 247: "To Shirkers, the Days of Whine and Roses," by Eve Tahmincioglu, *New York Times,* July 21, 2000. Copyright © 2000 by The New York Times Co. Reprinted by permission.

p. 254: "Employee Attitude on Work," by Robert Scally, *Discount Store News,* October 26, 1999. Reprinted by Permission from DSN Retailing Today. Copyright © Lebhar-Friedman, Inc. 425 Park Avenue, New York, NY 10022.

p. 255: "Research on Employee Retention," from *HR Focus* Employee Retention Survey. 2000 HR Focus Employee Retention Survey.

p. 257: "Loyalty has to be Earned," by Diane Sears Campbell, *Orlando Sentinel,* August 1999. Reprinted with permission of Knight Ridder/Tribune Information Services.

P. 262: "The Office as Utopia," by Joanne Chianello, *The Montreal Gazette,* March 7, 1998. Reprinted with permission from Joanne Chianello, "The Office as Utopia," from *The Ottawa Citizen,* January 19, 1998.

p. 267: "How Less Can Mean More," by Rex Huppke, Associated Press, February 1999. Reprinted with permission of The Associated Press.

p. 272: "Open letter to an Editor," by Joe Grimm, *Editor & Publisher,* April 24, 2000. Copyright © 2000 ASM Communications. Reprinted with permission.

Copyright © Houghton Mifflin Company. All rights reserved.